COMFORT ZONE

Nick Holmes

To my family for their unwavering support.
My wife Jenny and children Olivia, Savannah and Grandson Marley and
Sons-in-laws Ben and Rory.
A special mention to my daughter Savannah for typing seemingly endless notes
of hand written script. Thank you.

CONTENTS

*All the great people I had the honour of serving alongside
in the Armed Forces, Police Service and at Barrick Gold.
To those who supported and encouraged me to succeed, you know who you are.
You have my eternal gratitude.
A massive thank you to Sonia Harvey at Mandarin Creative Solutions Ltd
for the cover art and design.
Thank you to my publishing team at Kindle Book Publishing.*

PROLOGUE

It's April 2011, I'm in Africa, Tanzania to be precise and it's 40 degrees in the shade, I feel like I'm in a sauna but fully clothed, the humidity is almost overwhelming. I have been 'in country' for two days and haven't yet acclimatised from the unusually cold April back in England. Only two weeks ago I was a serving Police Officer a Chief Superintendent, bound by bureaucracy of every description, monitored, scrutinised, working in a world hamstrung by risk aversion and the new dawn of 'austerity', but more on that later.

It's Sunday morning and I am about to meet the head of the Tanzanian Secret Intelligence Service in a hotel lobby. We hadn't met previously but I had something for him, a brown bag containing $25,000 USD. I recalled being told, 'It's okay Nick, all you need to do is introduce yourself as the new guy, shake hands, hand him the 25k and leave.' I clicked the remote of my land cruiser, took a deep breath of Indian Ocean air and headed towards the Seacliff Hotel. Bag in hand I tried my utmost to look cool in my newly acquired duty-free Oakley Flak Jackets, when in truth, I was shitting myself. Handing $25k in a brown bag to an unknown African and me working on behalf of a US/UK regulated gold mining company, what could possibly go right?

My thoughts were flooded with the briefings I'd had on Anti-Bribery and Corruption legislation. And as I walked towards the Seacliff I wondered, 'This might be the shortest time anyone ever spent in a job, I could be sacked or worse in my first week here.'

As I entered the lobby I had already decided – things would have to change, this was really uncomfortable. But I had spent most of my adult life living outside of my comfort zone so it was a familiar feeling of nerves and excitement. Like the good soldier I once was, I arrived five minutes early and took a seat in the lobby. As my mind drifted I was brought sharply back to reality when a diminutive man with skin as black as coal wearing a business suit (on a Sunday) walked through the main hotel doors. He had a wise, intelligent face and carried a cell phone in each hand. He was flanked by two similarly dressed men but much younger and larger, these boys had clearly spent far too long in the gym. And then came that feeling I knew all too well, creeping up on me yet again, insecurity. Was I up to all this? Flashbacks of self-doubt played in my head, back to the day I collected my dismal 'O' level results at Rastrick Grammar School, the first time I got off of the train at Lympstone Commando training centre and the time I conducted a choir at Christchurch Cathedral at Oxford University in front of some of the world's leadership elite. I immediately placed all thoughts of insecurity to the back of my mind as I rose to greet them and offered my outstretched hand to the main man.

To my relief he took my hand in both of his and as he shook it, he smiled and said, 'Mr Nick, very pleased to meet you,' then with barely a pause, 'do you have something for me?'

This guy was confident and assured, no doubt a product of years working within the international intelligence community. He introduced himself as Mr Ngowi, said he looked forward to working with me and with that he turned and left escorted by the gym buddies.

The Tanzanian Secret Intelligence Service (SIS) worked initially with the Chinese during communism and latterly the Americans who entered Tanzania after their embassy was destroyed by Islamist terrorists in August 1998, killing 11. This attack occurred simultaneously with the US embassy in Nairobi, Kenya (213 victims) and was co-ordinated by Osama bin Laden and is when he first came to the attention of the US.

I was new in country and also to the role of Corporate Investigations Manager for Barrick Gold, the largest gold producer on the planet. The learning curve towards becoming the Director of Security would prove to be massive with lots of bumps on the way. But how did I end up here, miles from home, from family and friends, all that was safe and familiar? Well, the fates conspire in mysterious ways and this was certainly a million miles from Brighouse, West Yorkshire where I spent my youth but my experiences in the previous thirty-five years, achieving success against the odds no doubt helped me to survive and succeed.

CHAPTER ONE

Humble Beginnings

I was born in Huddersfield, West Yorkshire growing up in the small town of Brighouse only recognised outside of 'the North' by the Brighouse and Rastrick Brass Band who had a hit with charts with 'The Floral Dance' fronted by TV icon, Terry Wogan back in the day.

My dad worked as a draughtsman whilst Mum, as was the norm in the early sixties, stayed at home to look after the kids, me and my sister older by four years Sheridan. The pair of them smoked like chimneys and Dad liked a drink whilst mum was teetotal. I clearly inherited my dad's genetics. I can remember now how our semi-detached home always smelt of stale fags.

We moved around a lot with Dad's work and I changed schools frequently. I never seemed to settle in well at school but somehow managed to pass the 11 plus and went on to Rastrick Grammar School for Boys. It was Victorian in construction and in nature. Some of the teachers were fearsome, discipline strict and the corporal punishment was usually aimed in my direction. I became accomplished at dodging board rubbers and learning poems for reasons of survival. The English teacher Bill Howarth a Burma war veteran would take issue with anyone foolish enough not able to recite by heart whatever verse they had been given to learn. Retribution usually took the form of a running slap across the head which would often be forceful enough to lift the hapless victim from their chair and onto the solid parquet floor. How times have changed. But you might understand why my English homework was always on the money and I passed both 'O' levels. Looking back now I am certain old Bill suffered from PTSD.

The first life lesson I learned was – Prioritise. Risk against reward and/or punishment.

I was walking home one day after school with Dave 'Phleggie' Green when I got into a spot of bother. Now Dave was a bit of a 'whipping boy' at school and he was pencil thin and seven stone wet through but I liked him and he lived nearby. I wasn't a smoker but Phleggie offered me a drag and for some inexplicable reason I accepted. Just as I started to choke on the acrid smoke the schools Head Boy walked past. Without breaking stride he said, 'If I have fish for tea I won't report you to the Head Master, but if I don't you know what to expect'. It was the school trip to France the following day and I went home and explained what had happened to my parents. My mother dropped me at school with my suitcase and the coach was ready to depart for France imminently. However I was immediately accosted by the Head Boy who told me I had to see the Headmaster. He clearly didn't get his fish dinner. In the Head's office the Head Boy explained he had caught me smoking. The Headmaster explained I would not be going to France due to my behaviour. I pleaded with him and said it was a one off. He agreed I could go but would be punished with six of the best. I bent over the Head's desk and heard the swoosh of the cane as it flexed first backwards and then onto my arse. Jesus it hurt but I sucked in the air and gritted my teeth as he delivered another five strokes. I went to the coach and was made to sit at the front with the teachers whilst my mates all had a great time on the back seats.

I hate to think back to it but I was bullied unmercifully at school which has no doubt led me to take exception to bullies in whatever form they may take. Nothing makes me angrier or more determined to put a stop to it than seeing the defenceless being treated unfairly. Being bullied almost daily for the first three and a half years of secondary school was a major factor towards my poor academic performance and general happiness. I wasn't a stupid boy but always in the bottom three of the class. My behaviour was poor and I would play up constantly in lessons, well everyone but Bill Howarth's. I would be placed on report card routinely and would have to get a teachers signature for good behaviour at every lesson for a week. It resembled a bingo card but I rarely got a full house. Strangely, or with hindsight, perhaps unsurprisingly once my tormentor had left having been expelled I finished fourth in the class by the end of that year. However this was too little too late as 'O' levels loomed around the corner.

My fortunes had changed in every respect once I was liberated from the bullying and one event sticks out in my mind. My friend 'Phleggie' was being bullied by the school hard man, who I will refer to as 'L'. A boy set for the military and who revelled in a scrap. He and I had never previously crossed swords but it all came to a head when 'L' stabbed 'Phleggie' in the arse with a set of protractors (how very grammar school). Defending my friend who was by now was bleeding profusely from his rectum, I grabbed 'L' by the throat without thinking and immediately realised what I'd just done. 'L' looked me dead in the eyes and spoke through his teeth 'Round the bogs at dinner.' In modern parlance, this reads 'Me and you, outside the toilets at lunchtime, you're in for a shoeing'. Needless to say standing up for my mate had consequences that I never really thought through. I had no option but to appear at the appointed time, out of sight of the teachers but in full view of the rest of the school keen to get a good view of the action. In those days the toilets were open air with just a wall around them. To be fair I wasn't a small lad, I was six foot tall and fit as a lath and after watching Bruce Lee in enter the dragon had been training in karate for a couple of years. But 'L' was also a judoist and stocky too, it may not come as a surprise to learn that he was also no stranger to the art of scrapping at dinner times. That's lunchtime in the north.

We circled one another and went for it. Blows were exchanged and we ended up grappling on the floor. Little damage was inflicted or received by the time the fight was broken up by the head of PE Mr Kedge. Rather than us shaking hands and calling it a day, Mr Kedge said, 'So gloves on after school in the gym and we'll get this sorted.'

Christ, just when I thought I'd had a lucky escape. I was back in the shit and it would be toe to toe, once again with scrapper 'L'. It is clear now that Mr Kedge was backing me to sort 'L' out, as prior to the fight whilst fitting my gloves he gave me some words of advice. 'Cover your head with your gloves lad and let him belt you for a minute, he'll tire quickly and then go for him!' I suppose looking back John Kedge was one of those younger, 'trendy' teachers and 'down' with the kids and he was the first teacher to have any kind of faith in me.

The bout was three rounds of two minutes in the school gymnasium with our peers as an audience once again. They gathered outside and I could see numerous squashed faces against the glass windows. They were ready for the rematch to begin. The bell sounded and I followed my instructions to the letter. As predicted 'L' came at me like a train raining blows incessantly at the gloves protecting my head. After what felt like forever he paused, tired by his fruitless exertions. I looked up and saw his vulnerability, just as Mr Kedge had suggested I went in with a right cross catching him on the temple, following up with a straight left to his nose causing it to explode.

One more right hook and he was done for, knocked clean out. There are fewer more exhilarating feelings in life, believe me. Mr Kedge smiled at me and winked. How times have since changed and I don't believe for the better.

Unwittingly I had now been elevated to the position of school 'hard man' or 'cock' as it was back then and I can't say I was too unhappy with that. I'm still not sure being called a 'cock' is that flattering though. In truth I'm sure there were plenty of boys who would have been contenders for the title but I was making the most of my new found status. 'L' kept a wide berth after our gym bout and I suppose that's no real surprise as I have often found that bullies pray on the weak and vulnerable and I was now far from that. My self-esteem which had been non-existent was beginning to evolve and I became more confident around others and in particular the opposite sex.

My dad bought me a Garelli Tiger Cross motor bike when I was fifteen. It was second hand but he wanted me to learn how to look after and maintain it which was no problem as it was Italian and therefore broke down all the time. But I had started a love affair with motorcycles and the excitement they bring which continues to this day.

My final year of school passed uneventfully and I left age 16 with just a handful of meaningless 'O' levels. The teachers and I finally agreed on one thing, sixth form was definitely not for me.

CHAPTER TWO

What to do with my life?

My father had at this point become fairly successful. He was a director of a large window company and being a member of the masonic order was 'Connected'. He got me a job with a mate of his, Billy, who owned an electrical contractor business. I was set on as an apprentice electrician and for the first time had some money in my pocket. That was until I bought my first proper motorbike, a Yamaha RD250 which I loved and subsequently wrote off in a 70-mph side on with a Rover towing a caravan. I can clearly recall it was either hit the car or the caravan so I chose the car. I was shunted forward so hard that in the impact my testicles made two perfectly formed hemispheres in the petrol tank, I somersaulted from the bike and over the top of the car. I can still see the female passengers image in my mind a look of complete shock on her face. I landed on my head the helmet visor gouging out part of my face. I was temporarily stunned but got to my feet to inspect the damage. My bike rear wheel was lifted six inches from the ground and the front welded to the car passenger door. As I stood looking remorsefully at the mangled machine the rear tyre exploded causing the traumatised passenger to scream and nearly pass out. The Police arrived and I was reported for careless driving. I couldn't really argue with that one. The end result, six points on my licence and no bike.

This would be the first of many vehicle related dramas and led to a life time of personal disdain for caravaners. But 'every cloud' at least this gave my parents the incentive to pay for my driving lessons, just as long as I didn't get on another motorbike of course. The bike was fixed and sold on. Much to the amazement of my driving instructor and probably anyone else who'd seen me drive I passed my test first time after only seven lessons. Dad put me on his insurance. I was 17 and cruising about in a brand-new Rover V8, who needed a motorbike? Even though I had discovered beer and put a bit of weight on I didn't struggle too much filling the passenger seat with female company.

I stuck with being a 'spark' for 18 months but quickly realised it wasn't for me. I just couldn't accept that this was going to be it for the rest of my life. Sure we had a laugh at work and the money was okay, but all the older guys I worked with seemed miserable, almost as if they had subconsciously resigned themselves to a lifetime of banality. Some of the older guys were real arseholes one such individual Kevin would ride me all day, giving me shit. He was a gruff aggressive bloke about forty years old with massive mutton chop sideboards. He didn't appear to get on with anybody, in fact I'm pretty sure he could fall out with his own shadow.

We were working in a huge carpet factory and it was a ten-minute walk to the coffee machine and he would send me there five times a day. What he didn't know was that on my way back I would add my own personal touch to his brew. He never once caught on. Another guy must have had some form of Tourette's as he was constantly spitting and twisting his neck.

Horrible for him I'm sure but Christ, the look on the faces of people who didn't know of his affliction it was the highlight of what were usually very dull days.

I had no idea what to do with my life but I knew it wasn't being an electrician and frankly there weren't too many options open to me at that time. I had a daily, weekly routine. Work, lunch in the pub, a couple of pints to wash down pie and peas, home after work, shower and I would be waiting at the pub door for it to open at 7pm which is where I would stay till closing time. Fish and chips or a takeaway on the way home… Repeat.

Bored with my life and impulsive as ever, at eighteen I went to the recruitment office in Leeds to join the Navy as an artificer. I took the test and passed but on my way out I noticed a display with pictures of tough good looking young men wearing green berets and tackling assault courses and it caught my imagination. I thought to myself 'That looks awesome and the girls will love it'. I signed up on the spot with barely a thought for what might lie ahead but for the first time I thought I may just have found what I had been searching for.

My parents seemed okay with my decision, they were probably just happy that I had found some form of direction and hoped that the discipline might curb some of my bad behaviour. I wasn't a 'bad' lad and had only attracted the local police's attention with my motorbikes, but I was always out on the lash with my friends and to put it bluntly, I'm sure they were tired of me falling through the door in the early hours often accompanied by a young woman. When I look back now I was clearly searching for something, something that would give me purpose, clarity, structure and direction.

Something that would build my self-esteem. To those around me I appeared confident and self assured but it was all a front.

CHAPTER THREE

Life turned upside down

I remember it like it was yesterday, standing on the platform at Lympstone station with all of the other new recruits, we looked nervously at one another sizing each other up. Some looked hard as nails and ready for what was to come. Others, like myself, clearly had little idea of what we were in for. I ran about one and a half miles a day and balanced this new found fitness regime with eight pints of bitter and a takeaway every night, I was confident this would suffice. It won't come as a shock to you to learn that I was considerably overweight, unfit and immediately felt way out of my comfort zone.

Remember, there was no internet, no social media, no SAS who dares wins and I had no idea what was required of a marine recruit. However, it's safe to say I found out pretty quickly. I was in 131 Troop and the accommodation blocks housed four men to a room. We were met by our Training Staff (TS) and Troop Commander, who spoke very loudly and made it clear that we all looked like a sack of shit. This did wonders for my self-esteem which was further damaged by the fact that I was given a uniform that was made for person considerably thinner than me. When I queried the fitting the quarter master with a smile on his face made clear that I would shrink to fit the garb in no time. As I recall it went something like this. 'Listen lardy, once you've had a few beastings, it'll fit like a glove.'

'Beasting! what is that?' I innocently replied. I soon found out.

Initially whenever anyone put a foot out of line, failed to undertake any instruction or presented themselves other than perfectly, it would result in a beasting for all. This took the form of simple physical pain through exercise or mental anguish by attrition. This didn't bother me too much and I realised fairly early on that I could avoid pain and discomfort by getting my act together not showing out as either brilliant or shit and doing things well. There is safety in the middle ground. The TS favourite beasting was the 'mud run'. Each day as the tide withdrew back to the ocean a massive estuary of knee-deep mud remained behind and the TS would utilise this natural resource as an instrument of torture. They would march us out in our clean kit and rifles out into the mud and we would emerge exhausted and filthy. Then we would reform as a unit and be told we had five minutes to clean our weapons and change into out next set of clean uniform. We were inspected again and marched back into the mud. By the end of the punishment pretty much every item of uniform would be filthy and the next few hours would be spent washing and ironing. But I discovered to my surprise that I was determined and mentally resilient and I revelled in this new competitive environment. The physical training was extremely demanding but I managed to avoid injury whilst others less fortunate were back trooped meaning their training would be on hold whilst they recovered. I can recall finishing the Tarzan assault course somewhere near the front and puking as soon as I stopped. The TS saw puking at the end of physical exertion as a positive trait for a recruit as it demonstrated they had clearly pushed themselves harder than most.

As training progressed myself esteem grew significantly and even though I was one of the youngest recruits, the TS must have recognised that I had some leadership potential. After two months I was made section commander with responsibility for other recruits and leading them in the field. My fitness was exceptional and I managed every task successfully. I knew that finally I had found my purpose and would make my family proud of me, but this feeling of success would be short lived as I was hit with news that would change my life forever.

I had called home each Sunday from the payphone but had only spoken with my father. Ten weeks into training I made my regular call and again my father answered. I asked him how Mum was and he broke down in tears and told me that my mother had left him for someone else. He was devastated and so was I. I felt a responsibility to be with him to make sure he was all right. The stability of my home life was something I never questioned or considered to be at risk. My father was already ill but continued to run his business and this event had taken a terrible toll on him personally. I felt I needed to see him to reassure myself that he was going to be okay whilst I was away completing my training.

With that in mind, I approached the Troop Commander to request a weekend of compassionate leave. I explained the situation and his response was brief and callous, 'Your dad's a big boy and so are you, I'm sure he can deal with it himself. Request denied.'

I was furious, what difference would it have made? 48-hours! I was performing well and had settled into life at Lympstone but now I was more than a little disillusioned. I called my father to explain and he understood, but he also made clear that if I wanted to leave the marines at the four month 'opt out' point he would take me into his business which was by now very successful. I made the decision to leave, still fuming that they didn't have the compassion to let me have 48-hours to check on my dad. The TS called me into their office and tried to persuade me to stay but my mind was made up.

I left Lympstone on a Friday by train full of optimism and looking forward to learning my dad's business and making a few quid. The future looked really promising. My dad picked me up from Leeds station and we went to the pub for a few beers with my mates. I was so happy to be home yet full of regret for leaving the Marines. I have reflected many times on my decision to leave as it is by far my biggest regret in life not having completed commando training. But at that time I felt I had no choice.

It was clear my father wasn't well and two days after arriving home on the Monday morning he died from a heart attack driving to work. My father's death was really difficult to deal with and compounded by my mother's absence but I had a great bunch of friends and the landlady and her husband at my local pub were amazing even taking in my washing and ironing.

Truly good people and I needed them. My world had fallen apart.

I hadn't spoken to my mother since leaving home for Lympstone and didn't again for a couple of years. My grandfather told me that my dad had changed his will leaving two-thirds of the house and assets to me and one-third to my sister. But the will could not be found and my mother took everything. She sold our family home to take up with the other man who didn't have the proverbial pot in which to piss and suddenly I found myself jobless, homeless, parentless and skint. How quickly things can change.

Needless to say I was devastated, I tried to rejoin the Marines but was told it would be six months before I could return. At this time and in the position I found myself in, I decided against waiting. I am proud to say I have never been out of work and I got a job driving a delivery van. Not the best of prospects but it kept me solvent. I couldn't settle back in Brighouse and was desperate to get away, but where?

CHAPTER FOUR

Bob tries 'Smack'

My best mate from school was Ray McLaughlin. He was six feet two and a brilliant footballer with a great sense of humour. Ray was smart and had got a job as an engineer but he too was restless and in need of change. So we saved some money and Ray and I jumped on a Freddie Laker special to New York and from there to South Carolina to stay with a good friend from school, Bob Haigh. Bob had been at school with us and was a real character always in trouble with teachers and the authorities but with a wicked sense of humour. Everyone liked Bob he was just one of those people you wanted to be around. My plan was to get a job and stay in the US. We had an eventful four months, experimenting with recreational drugs and exploiting the effect our English accents had on young female South Carolinians. We clubbed together and for $700 bought a bright red 5.2 litre Pontiac Firebird, resplendent with a gold phoenix on the hood. We frequented a local bar 'The Office Lounge' which was a cool bar with a shuffle board, juke box and a waitress called Pammy. Pammy was a great girl probably only in her mid-twenties but had been around the block. I think we probably all had a crush on Pammy. She would bring our Bud's on one tray and a selection of narcotics on the other. It was here I was introduced to weed, blow, crystal meth and quaaludes. I settled into a daily regime of weed with quaaludes reserved for the weekend club nights.

Two of the first guys we met were Johnny Ray and Greg who both worked at the upmarket hairdressers with Bob. Greg's dad who was around fifty owned the shop and was minted, with a girlfriend half his age. Greg was engaged but still liked to 'party' and Johnny Ray was his sidekick. Johnny Ray was a seriously good-looking guy and always seemed to be surrounded by women. I was more than a little jealous of Johnny Ray who was so at ease with himself and exuded confidence, unlike me.

However the reality of the drug world came into sharp relief when one night having consumed a few beers and a 'lude, we set off in the car to a club followed by two of Bobs friends, Johnny Ray and Greg. We arrived at the club and waited to be joined by the boys. After twenty minutes we became worried and drove back on the route we'd just travelled. After five minutes, we saw blue and red flashing lights and grew even more concerned, we were directed to slow down by a traffic cop with an illuminated baton and as we passed we saw Greg's car on its roof in a ditch. All of the windows were smashed and we feared the worst. We went to the hospital to try and establish what had happened to Greg and Johnny Ray and were informed they were both in critical condition in intensive care. We returned the following day and discovered that Greg was paralysed from the neck down and Johnny Ray had a fractured jaw, cheek and femur.

Johnny Ray had been the lucky one. We visited the boys a couple of times a week and Greg had suddenly seen the light and turned to God in the hope of recovery. It was like speaking with a different person. Johnny Ray on the other hand was more philosophical, he was a good-looking man prior to the accident and his face had taken a battering but he would recover.

This accident really brought home the reality of drugs to me, and after this I didn't partake, however Bob took a very different path.

Bob was a charmer, had the gift of the gab and women gravitated towards him. He was a talented hairdresser earning good money and had an enviable lifestyle. But one evening soon after the accident, Bob said he was going to try 'smack'. I was mortified and pleaded with him not to. I guess he had an addictive personality and sure enough he drew up the heroin into a syringe, tied off at the elbow and injected himself.

It pains me to say it but he became addicted very quickly. Soon after, my visa expired and Ray and I, unable to get any meaningful work left the States to return home. A short while later I heard that Bob had been arrested and imprisoned for armed robbery. He had lost his job and needed money to feed his addiction. I was stunned. His life had literally turned upside down due to his drug habit. I am sure this is why I became so anti-drugs having seen first-hand the damage it can cause.

CHAPTER FIVE

The British Army

I was sad to leave the States and even sadder returning to Brighouse. Nothing had changed. To me it was dull and uneventful and I could see no future for me there. I needed an escape route but where to? With the door to the Marines closed for now, I decided to join the Army. I took the generic entrance exam at Sutton Coldfield. In those days depending on how well you did you were handed up to four sheets of A4 paper. Each had a list of roles and units available, the better option being handed four pages of potential opportunities. As I recall I think page one had the Pioneer Corp (manual labour) and Parachute Regiment (say no more) and with each additional sheet the opportunities became more interesting. To my surprise I was handed all four sheets and was asked to decide what I wanted to do.

Impetuous as ever I said I wanted to be a Mechanical Engineer, which I think was on page three. I just had it in my head that I needed a trade to ensure I would always have work outside of the Army when I chose to leave. I had no grand ambitions and I guess I was in survival mode. I was left on my own for a short while when I was approached by an Officer who asked me to follow him into a side room. I had no idea why but dutifully followed. Inside were two other officers, I sat in a chair opposite their desk.

The officer in the centre asked: 'Why do you want to be an engineer?' I told them my theory, explaining I thought given my domestic situation getting a trade whilst seeing a bit of the world seemed a pretty good idea. The Officer went on to explain that I had scored the highest mark in the assessment and I should set my sights a little higher. He suggested that I should consider the Intelligence Corp. I had no idea what they did but being young, naïve and foolish I decided against it and told them so. *What a plonker.* I was being given a golden opportunity but couldn't see it, and I let it drift on past perhaps to a more deserving and grateful recipient. Looking back I just wanted to stay within my comfort zone and was scared to step into the unknown.

So, I duly pitched up for twelve weeks of soldier training at Bordon in Hampshire. Bordon by name and Jesus it was even more boring by nature. After my time spent in the marines this was a relative breeze. I was already fit, had completed weapons training and had all the basic knowledge of soldering, I had the fitness, discipline and self-confidence to go with it and I had a relatively easy time of it all. I had a new girlfriend, a part-time glamour model who was a truly good person and I was the envy of all who saw her. I had good friends around me and life was starting to improve. I passed out and headed for trade training, all I can say of this nine months of my life is 'it was forgettable'. I couldn't wait to get out to a unit and start enjoying myself again. It was about this time I realised I had made a mistake choosing engineering but I was signed up for six years so that was that.

I was posted to Germany attached to 47 Field Regiment, Royal Artillery and from the day I arrived in Gutersloh I wanted out. Sure the guys were a decent bunch and socially we'd have a laugh, visiting houses of ill repute (window shopping) and drinking a lot more than I should. In my first week I met the boss, a Sergeant Major who asked me my intentions. I made clear all I wanted was to be given the opportunity to attend the all arms Commando Selection Course and to be attached to the Marines. This would mean I would go through training again and hopefully this time pass out wearing a green beret. He agreed to nominate me for selection. I was so excited until I found out twelve months later that the bastard had never even submitted the application, what an arsehole, he didn't even have the guts to tell me 'no'. There was now a new boss in place and this time he did put me forward for selection on both 'P' Company, Parachute Regiment and Commando courses.

We had a reasonable social life in Gutersloh with our own bar on the second storey of our building where we would get pre loaded prior to, as tradition dictated, jumping out of the open window, attempt to grab a tree branch six feet away and climb down the tree to the ground beneath. This rarely went to plan with intoxicated blokes launching themselves into thin air missing the tree completely and smashing themselves into the dirt below. It is here I met Dave Burgess who was a Corporal and one of the technical boffins in our group. Dave wasn't the archetypal computer geek as he was built like a tank and played rugby for the regiment. We became good friends.

Every year the Army ran skiing training in Bavaria for the lucky few chosen. I was one of the fortunate few skiing for two weeks, one week Langlauf (cross country) and another week of downhill skiing. I loved downhill and got to know the full-time instructors and the Captain in charge, Richard. Over a few beers I convinced him that I should stay full-time to look after the vehicles and they wouldn't need to send anyone else down there. He agreed, I couldn't believe it and I stayed for three months, skiing every day and never so much as changed a spark plug. I qualified as an instructor and became part of the team. It had been six months since my applications for both the Commando and Parachute Regiment course, and whilst in Bavaria I learned that I had been accepted for the latter and had three months to prepare.

My daily regime would be ski for about six hours. Followed by a nine-mile run after 'work'. I felt in the best shape of my life and by the time I returned to Gutersloh, I was running with a 40lb backpack.

Six weeks prior to departure for Aldershot I was talked into playing sevens rugby for the Regiment. I knew the risks of injury and thought I'd taken things easy. Then it happened, I jumped for a grubber kick and when I landed with the ball in hand, ruptured my Achilles tendon. There isn't a word to describe my anger and disappointment. I had to rest my foot completely in the hope it would repair in time for 'P' Company. I had just been issued new uniform and boots for the course and hadn't broken them in which would prove to be a major issue for me in the weeks ahead. I made a full recovery and set off for Aldershot. I was so convinced I would succeed and not return to Germany, that I sold my beloved BMW 3:20i, another mistake.

On arrival at Aldershot I was shown the accommodation which was by far worse than any place I had stayed before. Four cots to a room and a metal locker each, shared toilets and showers. This didn't bother me one bit, I was on a mission and felt excited to begin. I met a few of the other guys who all seemed as focussed as I was. It wasn't going to be a competitive process with each man pitted against the others. This was all about individual performance.

Day one began with a briefing which laid out the physical and mental challenges ahead. The physical would be okay, but I had heard that many who had gone previously had failed with the challenges above ground. 'P' Company had assault courses in the trees, imagine a zip line assault course at heights of 30–40 feet. Some required the candidate to climb and then jump across open spaces between platforms, with no safety net. Apparently many had bottled it and were withdrawn immediately. You were then required to jump from heights wearing a parachute. Initially jumps would be from a balloon basket at 500 feet and then a troop carrier airplane, but back to day one.

I had all of my new kit on and felt great. We had an easy six-mile cross country run with minimal weight to carry, this should be a breeze. Which it was until about three miles into the run when my feet started falling apart. The skin on both insteps were shredded by the rock-hard seams of the new unbroken boots. I finished the run hardly out of breath but my feet were another story. I returned to the room to inspect the damage. Shit, they were wrecked. Both insteps were bleeding and all the skin had gone. Desperate to stay on the course I bathed my feet in white spirit to try and dry out the wounds and toughen the skin. The pain could only be described as excruciating but it was nothing compared to the thought of failing the course. I tried to soften up the seams that had caused the issue. And with my feet taped up I started day two with the next run and assault course. The pain was ever present but I was pushed on by adrenalin and the fear of failure. I finished the week having completed all the challenges presented but then came the foot inspection by the course staff. I unwrapped my feet and the corporal took a deep breath when he saw the mess they were in.

They had started to weep puss due to infection, despite daily foot spas in white spirit. He shook his head and then came the words I could hardly bare to hear, but knew in myself they were coming. 'Sorry son, you can't continue on the course.'

I was told I could return anytime once my feet were sorted. I wept with frustration and bitter disappointment. My journey was over. Months and hundreds of miles of preparation all for nothing. Well, maybe not for nothing as with every personal failure we learn more about ourselves, and I knew that I had a well-developed determination to succeed and mental resilience, two of the key ingredients of success.

I went home for the weekend got drunk for three days straight and returned to Germany. God, I was deflated.

CHAPTER SIX

The wrong side of the law

On my return my mate Dave decided I needed cheering up and arranged a weekend trip to Cologne. We drove down in his BMW, parked up at midday and headed straight for the pub. Cologne is a beautiful historic city no doubt but we didn't intend visiting the Cathedral or immersing ourselves in the culture. Dave and I had other ideas, it was drink and female company we were after. We found plenty of the former and were so drunk we had little chance of securing the latter. We did nearly secure company but of the wrong persuasion as Dave headed into a gay bar but we didn't realise until our drinks were in hand and we looked around for the ladies. We quickly realised there were none. Far from being uncomfortable we had a laugh with the guys in there even stopping for a second drink. It was then agreed that before we were totally incapacitated we should have a look at the red-light district. Afterwards we took a taxi back into the centre Dave joked about doing a runner at least I thought it was a joke until the taxi stopped and when I looked at Dave all I could see were the soles of his trainers moving at speed from the taxi door. I had a split second to make the decision. Do I follow or pay the fare? Drunken decision made I legged it after Dave. I caught up with him and we headed to a McDonalds for some food. As we sat munching on a burger I looked over Dave's shoulder towards the door where I saw the taxi driver holding a metal bar, accompanied by a couple of his pals. I informed Dave of our situation and waited for the inevitable melee. The taxi drivers came straight for us and the pushing and shoving started. Thankfully, the police arrived and Dave and I were arrested. We denied everything and said it was a case of mistaken identity a story we stuck to when handed over to the Military Police later that night. We had a couple of hundred quid each in our wallets and claimed there was no sensible reason we would not pay for the taxi. Which is partly true, it wasn't sensible at all! We were released the following morning without charge but on bail and would to be re interviewed back at camp. Once again we stuck to our version of events and were not charged. We were lucky especially Dave as he had just secured an Officers Commission and was bound for Sandhurst. Dave left the Army with the rank of Major. Everyone knew we were guilty but couldn't prove it. It was the last time I did a runner from a taxi.

So what was I going to do next? Well, the decision was made for me and within four weeks I was on my way to Northern Ireland to support the Regiment with our time split between the Maze Prison and the Ardoyne in West Belfast. The Maze was infamous, and considered one of the most escape proof prisons in Europe. This maximum security prison housed Protestant and Catholic terrorists in accommodation blocks which viewed from above formed an 'H' and were therefore known as 'H' Blocks.

We arrived on the afternoon of 25 September 1983. Which unbelievably was the day 38 Irish Republican Army (IRA) prisoners decided to escape. They possessed two firearms which had been smuggled into the prison.

They overpowered the prison guards (one later died of a heart attack) and were driven in a delivery van through security cordons. The van was blocked from leaving the outer perimeter and the prisoners ran in different directions. One prisoner shot a prison officer and he in turn was shot by a soldier positioned in a watch tower. In all, 35 prisoners escaped and three were recaptured. When we arrived all order was restored but there was a massive search to locate the escapees. A somewhat eventful start to the tour and that was about as exciting as it got.

The day-to-day of the Maze was routine and pretty boring comprising three hour 'stags' in a watch tower with the occasional foot patrol. The boredom was sporadically interrupted by football matches between the Catholic and Protestant prisoners and I had a perfect view from my lofty perch. It was hilarious, two groups of men kicking lumps out of each other with the occasional brawl. I guess the Prison Governor thought it would give them a chance to let off some steam in a safe environment and reduce flash points in the prison. The Protestants usually won but of course the Catholics had 35 men fewer to pick from.

I got a call from the base in Germany which really picked me up. I had applied for a permanent posting to Northern Ireland and I had it, a two-year stint in Londonderry. I would return to Gutersloh pack my belongings have a couple of weeks leave and back to Londonderry.

I spent time in West Belfast, the Ardoyne to be precise. What a shithole, it was a Catholic stronghold and IRA central. We were hated by everyone there. As soon as the kids could walk and talk they'd be out on the streets telling us to 'fuck off home.' 'Is it a war you're wanting, you Brit bastards!' Charming.

The upside was that we always knew where we stood. Any opportunity to give them shit was seized upon. We had rules of engagement which in reality meant no engagement. Paddy would literally have to point a gun in your face before you could open fire. Which, given we knew every one of the key players and would see them on the streets daily, was frustrating.

Visible by day but sneaking about in the shadows taking pot shots or organising riots by night. Riots and petrol bombs were routine in 1983. You always knew when the schools had finished for the day, bricks and bottles would fly our way. The kids were brainwashed from conception to hate. In their situation no doubt we'd be the same. Our living conditions were abysmal, four bunk beds per room, a plastic covered mattress which made you sweat profusely. The bedding was grey horse type blankets which had the comfort and softness of sandpaper. We had to 'hot bed' that is one guy would get out of the cot to go on stag or patrol and the returning soldier would jump in the still warm and often moist bed. After four months on tour with no time off, it was time for some leave and a holiday.

CHAPTER SEVEN

The woman who 'saved' me

My good mate from home, Chris had joined the marines shortly after I had, but had stayed the course. We both had leave at the same time and decided to head for some Mediterranean sun. Chris went to a different school to me but lived nearby and once I left school we became good friends. Chris was a bit of a head case at times and unpredictable but we got along great.

My brother-in-law owned a travel agents so it made sense to seek his advice. He recommended the Greek Island of Mykonos. Which neither Chris nor I had heard of. It looked great and within a couple of days we were on our way to Heathrow Airport. It was at this point whilst looking for our check in desk we noticed something wasn't quite right. I approached an airport employee and asked him where the check in for Mykonos was. He gave me a strange knowing look, smiled and pointed in the direction of our check in. Once in the queue I realised that there was a disproportionate number of men in pairs that were clearly not visiting Mykonos for the ladies. I got chatting with a middle-aged couple and during the conversation she asked if Chris and I were a couple too. Christ, I was mortified! Did we really look like a gay couple? On reflection the answer was probably, 'yes'. Chris was already tanned, very good looking and I wasn't exactly a minger either. I did however have blonde streaks in my hair and an 80s' pornstar moustache. Yes, we looked like we might be that way inclined. Mykonos was the destination of choice of well to do gay men in the 80s. I made a mental note to punch my brother-in-law in the face when I got home.

But all good things must come to an end and the time had come to return home, me to Ireland and Chris to Arbroath. Jackie lived in Birmingham whilst Jenny lived in the nurses accommodation in Nottingham. As I travelled home in the coach reflecting on our fantastic holiday I realised I had just met the woman I'd been searching for. Jenny was perfect, as beautiful on the inside as the outside. She was incredibly naive and this made her all the more appealing, we nicknamed her Bambi. She only drank Coke, no alcohol and mostly ate chicken. Not very adventurous in those days.

I had built an emotional protective wall around myself and maybe as a consequence of previous events wouldn't really let anyone in to see the real me, the emotional, caring person I really was. I put a hard, devil-may-care front on but Jenny could see straight through it, maybe not so naive as I thought.

I was in Londonderry at this point and life wasn't too bad. I had a 650cc Kawasaki motorbike which was my pride and joy. I had my own self-contained room and a reasonable social life. My job was to maintain the fleet of 'Q' cars, (covert high-powered cars used by operatives in Ireland). Work was 8–5pm Monday to Friday and enjoyable. We were based in Ebrington Barracks at the edge of the River Foyle, an expansive stretch of water which dissects Derry, with the Protestant housing estates on the Water Side and Catholics the Bogside. They were connected by a large suspension bridge. The Bogside was out of bounds but even so several soldiers on and off duty had come a cropper over there. Some lured by an attractive female 'honey trap' and others like my boss's predecessor were shot and killed on duty. The poor guy was just sat in his car at traffic lights when an M60 machine gun in an upstairs window opposite opened up on him.

My boss was a Sergeant and if he hadn't worn a uniform you would never have thought he was in the military, he was quite laid back and un-regimented which was great and he mostly let me do my own thing. There was a Corporal, Dave; a Lance Corporal, Tim; then there was me, bottom of the food chain. Dave was from Bradford and had been in the Army for years, he was a moaner extraordinaire and his glass was always half empty. Tim was like 'Tigger' irrepressible with boundless energy. Tim was just one of those guys who gets shit done and we were good mates.

One conversation sticks in my mind from this time and it is one I have revisited countless times since as it was source of inspiration. I was having a beer in the camp bar with Dave the Corporal I worked with. We were talking about the future and what it might hold when he turned to me and said, 'you know Nick, me an' you just have to accept we're a couple of losers and you're going nowhere fast mate'. Ouch, that hurt and I am sure it was the catalyst that drove me to change my attitude and outlook.

I had little ambition up to this point as I had no real incentive, but that was about to change. Jenny and I wrote to one another most days or talked on the phone, and things started to get serious. Whenever possible I would see her in Nottingham, usually staying with her in the Nurses accommodation at the City Hospital. I knew if I wanted to make a real go of our relationship and for us to have a future together, which I wanted more than anything then I would have to get my act together. I had already decided that I would never get married whilst in the Army, I had seen too many broken marriages as a result of the demands of the Forces. I couldn't imagine leaving Jenny in married quarters whilst I was away for six or nine months. So I needed a job with real prospects. Easier said than done I had few qualifications and I really didn't fancy being a mechanic the rest of my working life.

It was Christmas 1984 and I was placed on 'Rear Party' which is not as much fun as it sounds. The reality is about 80% of the Army went home for Christmas and New Year but I had to stay in Northern Ireland with the other unfortunates in case anything kicked off. My mate from my time in Germany, Andy 'Paddy' Lennox was on leave and home in Coleraine which was about 35 minutes drive away. He invited me up for New Year to meet his family and friends. Andy was a small guy and wore round rimmed specs he wouldn't have looked out of place selling PC's in Curry's, but he had a brilliant sense of humour.

I arrived at the Lennox house about two in the afternoon on New Year's Eve. I shook his dad's hand and hugged his mum, they were lovely and so welcoming. She passed me a can of Harp larger and talked about all of the daft stuff Andy had been up to. About 4pm his dad announced he was off to the pub and we said we'd see him there soon. During the conversation that followed Andy explained that his next-door neighbour was Catholic and had been given the title Pope John by his dad and that he and his dad, a Protestant didn't see eye to eye. This was illustrated for all to see when we arrived at the pub. I opened the door to see Andy's old man rolling around on the floor with his neighbour. I couldn't believe it they were both in their 60's for Christ's sake. We split them up and sent his dad packing but stayed for a couple more beers to get ready for the big night. After a few pubs round town we ended up in a nightclub which was heaving with people, deafeningly loud and pitch black the dark only punctuated by the DJ's strobe lights. I had a great time, everyone was so friendly and out for a good time.

I was pretty drunk but as I reached into my pocket to pay for a round, I realised my wallet was missing, I sobered up immediately. My wallet containing £400 cash and my Army ID card was gone. Losing an Army ID card was a £400 fine and a month in prison. SHIT. What the hell do I do now? I was frantic and asked anyone who looked like an employee if a wallet had been handed in, just my luck. It hadn't.

As a last resort I approached the DJ booth. I asked if he'd had my wallet or ID handed in at which point and to my horror he turned off the music, turned up the house lights and announced through the PA: 'I've got a soldier here who's lost his wallet, has anybody seen it?' I wanted to disappear into thin air, that was until a voice in the crowd shouted. 'It's here, I've got it!' The guy came over and handed me my wallet all intact. The DJ dropped the lights and the music crashed back on. I shook my saviours hand bought him a drink and decided it was time to leave in case I had attracted unwanted attention. Andy and I made a swift exit, checking no one had followed. What a lucky escape that was, on two counts.

I thought the night was over prematurely but this was Ireland and as we walked down Andy's street there were numerous open house parties going on. We went from one to another and as midnight approached the lady of the house we were in let me use her phone to call Jenny. The following morning and nursing a blinding hangover I ventured downstairs in the Lennox house. Andy's mum had made us an Ulster fry, a full fry up accompanied not by a mug of Yorkshire tea but a can of Harp. I loved this place. I said my goodbyes as I had to be back at camp and thanked them for their hospitality.

Part of our role in Derry was to run and maintain The Water-ski Club, and its ski boat and equipment. In the school summer holidays instead of working on cars. The Lance Corporal, my mate Tim and I went waterskiing every day with the married squaddies kids. We would take them out on the water for a few hours put them back on the coach home and then ski on our own for a couple of hours. We joined a local ski club in Coleraine skiing on the River Bann and made new friends from all walks of life and religious persuasions. It was a breath of fresh air after Derry.

You would never have believed that in 1984 with all the sectarian hatred in places like Derry that only 29 miles away in Coleraine life was as normal as anywhere else in the UK mainland. We loved Coleraine and had many good nights out with our new mates, drinking to the wee small hours. It was a time before karaoke but that didn't stop me one night climbing on top of some poor families table and belting out a drunken rendition of Billy Idols 'White Wedding'. Great times.

In my spare time I decided to restore a knackered old mini for Jenny. She couldn't drive but I thought if I gave her a car she could learn. I borrowed some parts from the Army and spent hours, stripping, fixing, welding, filling and painting. By the time I'd finished reflooring and replacing metal so thin you could almost see through it, it weighed more than a tank. But I drove it back to Nottingham and presented Jenny with the keys. What a romantic, a changed man! I taxed it and put on four new tyres so Jen would be good to go. If she was going to learn to drive, the candy apple red mini which she called 'Roostie' was perfect. I left her with it and returned to Ireland to the usual routine. Work all week, Friday night disco at Strand Road Royal Ulster Constabulary (RUC) club, recover Saturday, back out at night, recover Sunday. Monday morning back at work – repeat.

Part of the extra duties I had was as duty driver for the Officers stationed in Derry. I would collect them from married quarters in a 'Q' car and drive them into work at Ebrington. Officers and enlisted men like me would never usually have a conversation and if we did it would be one directional. I.e. me being told what to do.

Perhaps inevitably though we would chat en route and I got to know them as human beings and most were ok. The Commanding Officer, a Colonel was a great guy and on the short list to be the UK's first Astronaut in space. He was a typical Army Officer, confident, well spoken and a product of the private educational system. He did however have his idiosyncrasies. One day he was a passenger in my 'Q' car a Lancia Delta, a lovely upmarket car of the time. He tried to re-tune the radio from Radio 1 to Radio 4, when after five minutes of expletive peppered frustration at not finding his favourite news channel he ripped the stereo from the dash, opened his window and tossed it into the road. It was hilarious but I always made sure I had a Radio 4 preset whenever I collected him in future.

CHAPTER EIGHT

In trouble again!

Relationships are key in our lives and I was beginning to understand and cultivate them with the officers I came into contact with. Some were arseholes of course, they're officers but most were just normal well educated and well-trained guys trying to get on in the world.

The exceptions were a real nuisance and I had a brand new out of the Sandhurst box subaltern (second lieutenant) on my first tour of NI. We had been in country six months and looking forward to going home. I had my hair cut and highlights put in (before Mykonos), after all it was the 80s and I thought I looked a bit like Simon Le Bon if I squinted in the mirror.

When he saw my hair he called me into his office. I couldn't fathom his overreaction. I was a good, hard working team player who caused no issues and got shit done. He had always been onside and I know he rated me. That seemed to count for very little as he ranted on at me. He opened up with, 'So, it is clear you are either queer or mentally unstable, which is it?' I couldn't believe what I was hearing, who was this guy? I didn't reply and gritted my teeth as I didn't want to say what I wanted to say as I valued my liberty. He threw me out of his office and never spoke to me again. Tosser. But as I say, he was the exception.

My second run in with authority came at Ebrington Barracks, it was a Saturday and I had been working on my bike and needed to road test it. Given that the parade square was the largest vacant piece of tarmac around I blasted across it turned around and wheelied all the way back.

I returned to the garage and put the bike away then back to my room. Then there was a knock on my door and when I opened it saw two Military Police officers in full uniform. I was duly arrested for my antics on the square and put in a jail cell in the barracks. I was told by the Sergeant that I would be kept in 'til Monday when I would face a disciplinary review. I sat and thought through my options as I really didn't fancy 48-hours in the nick. I asked for a phone call and rang the CO. He was brilliant. I explained what had happened and that it was an innocent mistake and he asked to speak with the Sergeant. I didn't hear what was said but it was clear Sarge' didn't like it. He put down the phone and glared at me. 'You fuckers think you're better than everyone else, don't you?' he said. I didn't reply, thinking it would be better not to wind him up any more.

'You're released,' he said, 'and don't let me catch you anywhere near that fucking square again, understand me?'

'Yes, Sergeant,' I dutifully replied. I had literally, just got out of jail free.

I knew that I would never meet anyone as amazing as Jenny and decided I would ask her to marry me but there was a slight issue. She was from a good, fairly well-off family who were old fashioned Scots folk. I was really worried that they would see me as a loser with few prospects outside the military, not that I had that many inside and incapable of providing for their daughter.

I agonised for weeks and decided I needed to leave the Army and get a job with real opportunities, but what on earth was I going to do? I ran through the limited number of jobs available that would provide stability and an opportunity for progression. To be perfectly honest with my qualifications my options were limited. I thought of the Fire Service, but that wasn't well paid and I didn't think it would give me the variety of challenges that I craved. It was time to stop messing around and get serious if I was going to get somewhere in life and provide a future for Jenny and me.

I kept coming back to the same option – Police Officer. Now it has to be said that I hadn't always enjoyed the best of relationships with the boys in blue... which stemmed back to age fifteen when I got my first moped. My local 'beat bobby' PC Albert Humphries seemed incapable of turning a corner without stopping me and giving me shit. To be fair to Albert he never reported me just gave me numerous bollockings.

Then there was Windermere, just after my dad died the lads decided it was time for a Bank Holiday weekend in Bowness, Windemere. This was a regular destination for us and people from all parts of the north of England would descend upon this beautiful quiet lakeside town for a few nights of revelry.

On this occasion I was looking forward to meeting up with a girl, Theresa from Skelmersdale, we had met there previously and I was hoping to move things on romantically. I was 19 and she was 23 and far more mature than I was at the time.

So after a long day drinking a few of the boys decided it was a good idea to take a motorboat out on the lake. Why the boat keeper let eight teenagers, some clearly worse for wear, out on the water is beyond me with hindsight but off we cruised into the middle of Lake Windemere. It was a beautiful sunny afternoon and the lake was full of holidaymakers, but what came next was comedy gold.

It's fair to say that we were a mixed ability group when it came to swimming and so when Andrew 'Shez' Shirlow who was a headcase stood up in the middle of the boat and started rocking it from port to starboard there were one or two horror-stricken faces. Shez could then be heard shouting 'women and children first' as the boat capsized bang in the centre of the lake.

If you haven't been to Windemere the lake is enormous and it was a half mile swim to shore or forty meters to a small island. I helped my mate Dave who was not the most buoyant of lads to the nearby shore and then saw the Police motor launch in the distance heading our way. Shit, I wasn't hanging around to get nicked and put in a jail cell dripping wet through. So three of us, me, Mykonos Chris and Irslan another good mate decided we'd swim for it. It's amazing what the human body can endure. An afternoon in the pub followed by a half a mile swim. There were some very confused faces on the shoreline beach as we trudged fully clothed from the water. The other five lads were all on a free boat trip to the local nick, but I was sure we would see them later in the pub. We ran to my car which was parked in town to head back to the B&B for a change of clothes. When we got to the car I insisted they take their wet gear off before getting in the car. Chris stripped off and got in the passenger seat, I jumped in to drive and Irslan stripped, threw his clothes in the boot just as I accelerated away, leaving him bollock naked in the car park. He chased the car through the busy Windemere streets and having had a laugh at his expense I slowed down at a traffic light and he dived into the boot. All I could hear was muffled obscenities from the rear of the car. We had all had a lucky escape.

After a shower and change we headed back to the pub where I saw Theresa. We had a good chat and things seemed to be going really well. But having paid a visit to the gent's when I returned she was being chatted up by another guy. I wasn't best pleased in truth and I approached him to make my feelings clear. He didn't take the hint so we got into an argument and then a bit of a scuffle in which he didn't fair too well. The police were on scene and I was arrested. I was clearly out of order and perhaps more immature than I thought but to be honest this was out of character for me. Maybe it was just a bad time in my life and I wasn't dealing with it too well.

I was taken in a police van to the nearest station about 15 miles away, when we arrived one of the PC's gave me a shoeing in the cells. I think that was the first time my nose was broken. The following day I was charged with being drunk and disorderly in a public place and summonsed to court where later I was fined the maximum £50 fine. That was two weeks wages back then.

After my performance Theresa didn't really want to know and I can't blame her. The lads all got released without charge and we returned home. My immaturity could have cost me my future with hindsight. Fate conspiring with me on this occasion.

So, back in NI, I decided to apply for the Police. I had applied for my home force, West Yorkshire and I returned home on the Friday and was due at Bishopgarth Wakefield, the Headquarters of West Yorkshire Police on the Monday. There was an assessment and interview process over a three-day period so I collected the keys for 'Roostie' the mini and drove to Wakefield. I parked in the Police car park and started a series of psychometric and written tests before the final interviews. At coffee break on the first day one prospective recruit walked into the room and said, 'You won't believe this, someone's parked in the Police HQ car park with no road tax and four bald tyres!' I got this sudden sinking feeling. No, she couldn't have, could she? I casually enquired, 'Jesus, you're kidding what kind of motor is it?' to which he replied, 'A red mini.'

Incredible, Jenny had sent me off to the biggest interview of my life at a Force HQ in a car with no tax and bald tyres. You couldn't make it up! So, at lunch time I got the car and moved it from the car park and hid it off street around the corner.

Disaster averted I cracked on and eased my way through selection. The Chief Inspector who ran recruitment made time to chat with me and I felt assured that all was good and I was on my way to being PC Holmes.

However, life is never straightforward it seems. The final 'formality' of the recruitment process was the 'Home Visit' which was where a Police Sergeant would come to your home to check that you didn't live in a brothel or that your dad wasn't a drug dealer and then after a cup of tea and a slice of cake, you were in.

My home visit was slightly different as I was in NI and had no home or parents to make tea and cake. A couple of Sergeants from the Royal Ulster Constabulary (RUC) came to Ebrington and met me in the office. We had a very pleasant chat and all went well until the closing question which went like this. 'So, Nick, we have to ask this and tick the box. Just to clarify, you have no previous convictions?' My heart stopped momentarily. Was this going to be a problem? Was my stupidity from back in Bowness going to ruin my future? I replied, 'Well yes I have a conviction for drunk and disorderly, is that a problem?' The lead Sergeant snapped shut his folder containing the interview form and said, 'Sorry son, we can't accept applicants with a previous conviction.' He got to his feet as did his mate and they left. I was shell shocked, then I recall my conversation with the Chief Inspector from Wakefield and decided in desperation to give him a call. I had nothing to lose.

I got straight through to Chief Inspector Challenor and told him what had happened. He must have detected the obvious desperation in my voice and reassured me. 'Don't worry son, we all make mistakes, drunk and disorderly is no big deal. I've got lads through selection with wounding convictions.' Really? I thought, but the relief ebbed through me like a wave. I was in and now had prospects of a bright future to offer Jenny.

CHAPTER NINE

Leaving Northern Ireland

The first time I proposed to Jenny she turned me down. Her way of making me fight for her favour and not making it look like she was besotted with me, which clearly she was! Having accepted my proposal at the second time of asking I needed to come up with the cash for an engagement ring.

But first I had to ask her father, Harry for his permission and he agreed. I got on great with my prospective in-laws and Jenny's three sisters, Jac who I met in Mykonos with Jen, Sue and Maggie.

All was good, now for the ring. My pride and joy and pretty much the only thing of value that I owned at the time was my Kawasaki Z650. I loved that bike, but not enough to tax and insure it. In Ireland if I ever got stopped by the RUC I would show my ID card and that would be that, and to be fair I only took it out on the road a couple of times. But she had to go and with the proceeds Jenny and I went to Fattorini's Jewellers in Bradford, who famously made the original FA cup, which no doubt added about 15% to their prices. Jenny selected a gorgeous engagement ring which looked very similar to that of Princess Diana's only far, far, less expensive and I'm pretty sure Charles didn't need to sell his Aston Martin to pay for it.

I returned to Ireland and having had my Police application approved and given a start date, handed in my request to leave the Army prematurely. I had signed for six years but had served five so it was at the discretion of the CO (Colonel Radio 4), if he would approve it. I had talked with him about my intentions several times on our shared journeys and when I submitted my formal request he called me in to his office, shook my hand and said: 'Mr Holmes, you are leaving one honourable profession for another, so go with my blessing and gratitude for your service!' What a great bloke. I was given a leaving date, three months hence 8 September to coincide with starting Police training on 11 September 1985.

In the days that remained I worked hard on my fitness and kept my head down and out of trouble, almost. On a trip to Belfast in a Q car riding solo I passed through a village called Toome Bridge which sits just off the A6 Belfast – Derry Road. I had a dodgy wheel and a slow puncture so decided to pull off the A6. I pulled into the roadside near a graveyard. No issues there I thought but then saw a large number of headstones bearing the engraved heading of 'Volunteer' and 'IRA' with some very recent dates attached. This I discovered later was an IRA stronghold. I was armed with a 9mm Browning and could see the RUC fortification at the bottom of the road about 500 metres away and considered making my way there rather than being exposed as I was, but then my mind was made up for me. Four curious locals crossed the road to see what I was up to and asked me as much. I put on my best Belfast accent acquired and honed over years of conversations with RUC and friends in the water-ski club. They chatted away as I made a quicker wheel change than Lewis Hamilton's pit crew, I said my farewells and sped off into the distance.

Soon it was time to leave NI. I had enjoyed my time there but at times reflected on where I was going in life and what I would amount to if I stayed doing the same things on repeat. Policing, of which I actually knew very little, would prove to be the best decision of my life and provide me with some amazing opportunities.

I left NI on the Friday but was buggered about by the Army until the last minute. I needed a number of departmental signatures on a discharge card to be released. Some were great and wished me well, one guy was a complete prick from start to finish, he was the quartermaster and every time I presented myself to hand in my kit he said he was too busy. My ferry was at 6pm from Belfast and it was close on a two-hour drive. Quartermaster prick finally signed me out at 4pm. His behaviour epitomised everything I disliked about the army. It could be so petty and blinkered to reality where rank overruled common sense. As I drove out of the gates to Ebrington Barracks I felt completely liberated. Free to find myself and my place in the world, I couldn't wait for Monday and a new life with Jenny beckoned.

CHAPTER TEN

Police Constable Holmes – Brighouse

Monday came and I found myself at Dishforth Police training centre in North Yorkshire, it was a former RAF base adapted for Police training and Forces from all over England and Wales would send around 150 recruits to be trained in law and the practicalities of policing and to meet the physical requirements of the role. It was still quite regimented back in 1985 with a drill square and a requirement for all recruits to march from point A to point B.

Each class of around 20 people had a Right Marker who was ex-military and took charge of the drill elements of training and marching around camp. There were two of us who were ex-Forces but I was made Class Leader. This was a relief as I hated drill. Was this to be a sign for the future? Maybe I wasn't such a loser. My role was to represent the class and their welfare, I would raise any concerns to the Training Staff (TS) on their behalf and also make sure they did as they were told and were where they were supposed to be when they were supposed to be. The day-to-day training consisted of classroom law and procedure with weekly Monday morning exams which had to be passed in order to continue on the course. Each day we would do physical in the gym or cross country runs of five or six miles. Again the course success criteria was to pass all tests including the physical. Some recruits were way off the physical requirement even after ten weeks of training but somehow managed to pass out.

In truth I found the classwork enjoyable I was learning something that was not only new but interesting and relevant to the job I would be doing. At school I found studying hard and could not retain information well at all, I don't know if it was subconscious resistance but that's how it was. My father would despair at my inability to understand relatively simple maths. Police law and procedure I found easy, I was like a sponge absorbing knowledge. I was really interested in the subject and I wanted to learn. I performed well in the weekly exam despite a lack of weekend study as I was usually in Nottingham with Jenny. If I struggled with an answer my mate Geoff an ex-professional footballer with Notts County would show me his paper. It always really pissed him off that somehow I always managed to get a higher mark than him. But *quid pro quo*, I did iron his uniform and bull his boots.

I really enjoyed the physical and found it relatively easy. There's nothing hard about getting paid to learn new skills and keep fit. I was surprised how well I had adapted to my new profession but as in any training and development regime some people really struggled. It took me back to Marines training. Some of the recruits were seasoned Navy lads who opted to move across to the Marines. They found the discipline, domestic chores and general personal management easy whilst I and others struggled to begin with. It was a similar scenario now and we would finish work and dinner by 5:30pm and then it was time to sort out our personal admin. This took me a full 45-minutes to sort lockers, beds, washing, ironing and all the kit cleaning. Some guys hadn't finished at lights out. I quickly exploited the situation making a few quid to supplement my beer money by ironing kit and bulling boots.

In the evening it was quite relaxed and we could go to the camp bar for a pint which I did most evenings. On one occasion the Training Staff came in, they were all Sergeants hungry for promotion which was the only reason any respectable cop would end up teaching at training school. I got on great with my two class TS Sergeants, John Scott and John Wall. John Scott ended up as Chief Constable of Northumbria

Police, I guess training school worked for him. John Wall who was a Detective Sergeant back in South Yorkshire happened to mention that one of the female instructors Doreen had a 'crush' on me. Christ, that's all I needed, I was trying to be the good soldier, 'volunteer for nothing and keep my head down'. I did not need this distraction and it could be a risk to my future. Fraternising with the TS was a no, no. God knows what she saw in me, I had my hair in a skinhead and looked like I'd just left prison rather than joined the Police.

In any event and after a few drinks in the bar one evening, Doreen also from Northumbria made a bee line for me. I had little choice but to humour her. She was a well-built woman full of confidence and seemingly unconcerned how her behaviour might be perceived. She was more tactile than a masseuse and I made some excuse about needing to study and left.

Doreen was a persistent woman and over the following weeks took every opportunity to spend time with me and my mates.

The last Thursday of every month was the payday disco. Doreen must have pre loaded in her room and was a little worse for wear and I saw her head towards me on the dance floor, she pushed my mate Geoff to one side and grabbed me. I'm pretty sure the soundtrack playing was a bit more upbeat but Doreen must have thought it was the last dance and drew in ever closer taking a firm hold of me. After the dance concluded I made a sharp exit.

This was getting awkward and now everyone knew. From that point I avoided Sgt Doreen whenever possible.

Jenny and I were making plans for the wedding and also looking for a house, which occupied most weekends at home. The ten weeks of training flew by and I excelled which really buoyed my confidence. There were some smart people on the course and I was competing with them, more than holding my own. I made some good friends, but of course I wasn't popular with everyone due to being class leader. I wanted us to do well and could be a little harsh and judgemental on some of my less experienced classmates and I was impatient. I like to think this motivated them to succeed and develop but I was 25 and still learning how to be a leader myself. Where had this new-found drive and ambition come from? I am pretty sure that for the very first time I had goals to aim for and achieve and not only that I had fortuitously found a job which I was really enjoying with endless possibilities and opportunities ahead of me. In addition I was amongst a peer group of people against which to gauge my abilities and I drew confidence from being amongst the front runners.

As the end of the course drew closer we were asked for our posting preferences, where we would like to work as newly qualified beat cops. West Yorkshire is one of the largest Police Forces in the UK and I was desperate to avoid my home town of Brighouse. I knew I would end up dealing with people I had grown up with and it was a rough town. I dreaded the thought, so I put on my form 'anywhere but Brighouse'. So when the postings were duly announced everyone seemed pleased with their new stations. Mine read: 'PC 1904 Holmes – Brighouse'. I was gutted, what a start to my career. Some better news came in, I was nominated for best recruit at Dishforth. Something I had never really considered an option, clearly someone thought I had potential.

At the end of training there was a passing out ceremony where the good and the great are invited to a pass out dinner. It was a black-tie affair in full dinner suit. During the proceedings the award of best recruit would be presented, I had been informed that I was runner up which was fine by me and I looked forward to the dinner, a few drinks with my mates and seeing Jenny at the pass out parade the following day. Geoff and I got suited and booted and with great excitement entered the mess hall, we got a drink and chatted about the future as Geoff would be on his way back to Nottingham. I then saw Doreen approaching at full speed. It was clear from the moment she spoke that she was already well on her way and it was only 7pm. She dismissed Geoff out of hand, looked him in the eye and said, 'run away little boy'. He looked at me with a smirk and left us to it. I was feeling very uncomfortable as she wasted no time making clear her intentions for the night and I was even more terrified. Thankfully we were called for dinner and I was off the hook. It turned out Doreen was there with her Chief Inspector husband... was she mad? I thought my career would be over before it even began. I avoided her for the rest of the evening, staying relatively sober excited for the final day and starting the job for real.

In truth the pass out was comparable with any in the military. Immaculate uniforms, bulled boots, medals (for those that had them), a brass band, dignitaries, all the pomp and ceremony you could wish for. Sadly this is now a thing of the distant past as it seems that as a country we have an aversion for celebrating success and seemingly find competition distasteful. Only someone who has never tasted success could subscribe to that concept.

Jenny and I drove home in a car that was taxed and insured with tyres that were legal and we celebrated my passing out with her family.

CHAPTER ELEVEN

Back where it all began

So, Monday came and I presented myself for duty at Brighouse Police Station. I was still full of trepidation as the last time I walked through those doors was to produce my licence and insurance for PC Humphries. I met my inspector Stuart Brooke who was a really nice guy and he could hardly contain his amusement when he introduced me to my Tutor Constable Dave Watson. Yep, that's right, Holmes and Watson. I wondered if PC Humphries my teen years nemesis might still be in the job and I didn't have to wait long to find out as I bumped into him on day one. He was a great bloke and shook my hand, wishing me well.

My tutor Dave was a great cop, the best street cop I ever worked with. He had a second sight instinct for crime and criminality. His arrest/conviction rate was four times that of any other PC. We hit if off right away and I learned as much as I could from Dave. We were together for ten weeks and then if he and the Inspector thought I was up to it, I was let off the chain to work on my own. Dave was a climber and very focussed. He had little time for those who weren't as committed as he was which in reality meant everyone else. He was a serious guy and we didn't have too many laughs but he was a great thief taker.

I took to policing immediately and loved every second, apart from that is waiting for the inevitable pub fights to start at the weekends. Once they kicked off its all systems go and the adrenaline gets you through but the anticipation of crossing swords with someone I grew up with would always make my stomach churn.

Dave and I were prolific and soon I would hear colleagues with more experience and much lighter workloads call me 'lucky' and 'cocky'. I could live with that. I was becoming ever more confident in my ability and if that was perceived as arrogance then that was fine with me. As for lucky, one thing I have learned in my life is that luck is usually self generated. World class footballers like Ronaldo aren't lucky. They work hard to hone their considerable skills through personal determination and drive, fuelled by ambition. This is what makes them the best. A lack of ambition, drive or work ethic doesn't make you unlucky, it makes you lazy.

As was required in those days I worked my way through all the traffic offences and minor crimes such as criminal damage and burglary and soon I had an example prosecution file for them all. After 10 weeks I was let off the leash and for the first time patrolled unaccompanied. It was a weird feeling patrolling in a uniform and big hat. You are conspicuous and I felt incredibly self-conscious but I soon got used to the attention both positive and negative. Brighouse had a busy town centre with 34 pubs and a couple of night clubs, it was encircled by housing estates some more prosperous than others. Population 38,000.

In hindsight it was a good place to start my career as I gained hands on experience very quickly. My probationary period was two years during which time my service could easily be terminated if I messed up or wasn't able to make the grade. After a year I received a huge compliment, I was to be posted to Elland which was semi rural with a small town centre. There were only two cops per shift so each officer had to be trusted to work largely unsupervised. I went on my Police driving course for three weeks, passed and moved to Elland.

On the long, dark and frequently wet nights on foot patrol in Brighouse, I would often jump into one of the patrol cars to warm up and have a chat. This was obviously not lost on my Inspector who I overheard comment: 'He was bound to pass his driving test, his arse is never out of the bloody car!' Harsh, but true and anyway foot patrol is boring, rarely did I catch the bad guys whilst out on foot. It had its upside though. I had made a number of contacts in the retail sector of the town centre and one of these was Donna an attractive hairdresser with her own shop. Donna cut my hair, for free of course and gave me a door key so when I was on nights I could use the shop, make a brew and have twenty minutes on her sun bed. The good old days.

My very first shift in Elland was 10pm–6am nights. I was transporting my gear, cuffs, baton etc in a panda car from Brighouse to Elland in time for the 10pm start. Driving through the town centre a young man flagged me down. I asked what was up and he replied nervously, pointing towards the Council Offices and said, 'Two men have just broken in to that building.' He had a friend with him and a car so I told him to get in and wait whilst I went to investigate. As I made my way toward the scene I realised I had no cuffs or baton but I did have my police radio. I told control what was happening and suggested they send some back up.

It was then I saw two men exit the building through a window. They walked towards me and I challenged them. 'Just stop there lads, where have you just come from?'

The taller of the two a skinhead with earrings and facial tattoos replied most discourteously, 'Fucks it got to do with you?'

It was clear from their demeanour both men had been drinking and that this was going to go down 'the hard way'. Fortunately, for me anyway, I was at my physical peak, training each day and into body building at the time. I told Skinhead he was under arrest and took hold of him by his jacket. On hearing this his side kick seemed more than a little perturbed. He was smaller than Skinhead, five feet 10 and skinny wearing a Levi jacket. These days he would be considered feral. So rat boy shouts: 'Do him Kev!' and I know it's about to kick off.

I looked to my star witness for help and he was sat with his mate in his car shitting himself, clearly there was a limit to his public spirit. No help from him then! I took in my surroundings and the streets are almost deserted.

Kev the skinhead made his move and threw a punch which I managed to avoid and it made contact with my shoulder. I countered with a straight right into his face. He stepped back and to my right I saw rat boy taking a run towards me, he leaped into the air like a bad impression of Bruce Lee, missed me completely and as he landed I caught him with a beauty on the beak. His nose erupted and he turned, running away followed by big Kev. I ran after them and after about a hundred yards, saw the skinhead taken to the floor by a member of the public. He's was shouting and swearing but a massive bloke had him pinned to the floor. I thanked him but big Kev just won't shut up threatening to do all sorts of vile things to the helpful member of the community. The big guy asked me if he could have two minutes alone with him before I nick him... Of course I said no but then found myself distracted by something going on in the opposite direction. I heard a couple of dull thuds and the guy tells Kev his name, this clearly resonates with him as he immediately apologised for any offence he may have caused.

Assistance arrived and Kev was taken to the cells on suspicion of burglary and Police assault. I spoke to the member of the public and he informed me he had recently been released from prison on licence for manslaughter. Well, I suppose everyone deserves a second chance. I thanked him and wished him well. Now I understand why Kev had a change of heart...

On speaking to my star witness I established he was cruising the council square toilets (cottages) looking for company and was reluctant to get involved. Fortunately I wouldn't need his evidence to convict.

Back at the station I worked with the Criminal Investigation

Department (CID) to identify rat boy. A quick look through the intelligence reports on our prisoner Kevin Oldfield reveals his usual side kick to be one Bernard Holten. I pulled his photo and bingo, just like an episode of *The Bill*, it's that easy. Accompanied by two Detectives we arrive at Holten's flat on Field Lane, council estate. I knocked on the door and bearing in mind it's 1am at this point, a fully dressed woman in her early twenties answers the door.

'What do you want?' she asks nervously.

'Is he in?' I ask.

She clearly knows why we're there. 'No, he hasn't come home tonight.'

As we're talking I look over her shoulder and see a faded Levi jacket hung on a coat rack covered in blood. It's late and I've had enough messing about. I shouted towards the top of the stairs, 'Bernard, get your skinny arse down here.'

A sheepish looking Bernard pops his head around the wall at the top of the stairs: 'How d'ya know I was here?'

I point over his girlfriends shoulder, 'Your jackets covered in blood you pillock, now get down here.'

He comes down the stairs and doesn't look too good. 'You broke my fucking nose!' pointing at his bright red appendage now facing in a slightly different direction to when I first saw him. I arrested him and took him to the station where for the first time I worked alongside a seasoned Detective interviewing and processing the prisoners.

So my first shift at Elland was eventful and the arrest of two high profile burglars did my reputation no harm at all. It later went to court as they pleaded not guilty and they even had the audacity to accuse me of assault. They were found guilty and that was that. Elland was the kind of place where as a cop you could do either very little or be as productive as you liked. Having had a taste of detective work, I was keen for more.

CHAPTER TWELVE

Standing out from the crowd

Jenny and I had just bought our first house together in the local area. Jenny was still living and working in Nottingham whilst we sorted the house ready for habitation. We were skint, I was using an old Honda CX500 to get to work come rain or shine and it always seemed to be raining and my waterproofs clearly breached trade descriptions as I usually arrived at work looking like I'd pissed my pants. We had no carpets or furniture but we had each other and a honeymoon planned in the Seychelles. Then came a problem, our boiler packed in, in the middle of winter, obviously, because boilers never seem to break in the summer time! A new boiler would be over £1,000 and we didn't have it. I got talking with work colleagues and they suggested a call to 'Pete the plumber'. Pete was most helpful and helped us to claim on our house insurance as the boiler was damaged. The relief was huge as we thought our honeymoon would have to be cancelled.

Back at work I was as busy as ever and discovered a series of house burglaries in our area. I decided to try and find out who was responsible. The crimes occurred in the early hours of the morning between 5am and 7am, the suspect was described as a white male five feet 10 inches tall, wearing a baseball cap and grey overalls. Usually 'he' would force the latch from a window, enter the occupied home and steal small items of value such as jewellery and cash. I surmised that the offender chose the time as it would be shift changeover for the Police and would minimise their chances of discovery. I spent a few early mornings in plain clothes walking the streets and the only person I saw was a woman in her late 30s but she didn't exactly fit the description. The burglaries continued unabated as did my annoying series of early shifts. It was then whilst on foot again I saw the same woman. She hadn't seen me but was acting suspiciously. She took a baseball cap from her jacket, put it on and walked down an alleyway running between two rows of houses. I followed out of curiosity and saw her disappear through a side gate. She may have just been going home after a nice walk but something told me that probably wasn't the case.

I opened the gate as slowly and quietly as possible and as I entered the back garden saw the soles of a pair of trainers vanish out of sight through an open window. I called for back-up, which was the early shift coming on duty, no doubt sat around the briefing table slurping a brew and scoffing warm toast. I hid out of sight near to the window and waited for her to come back out. Our burglar however had other plans, she had unlocked the back door and walked out into the garden this time carrying a bag. I emerged from my hiding place and crept up behind her and said, 'A bit early for a shopping trip love, isn't it?' She turned to face me and replied as calm as you like: 'No, just on my way to work what are you doing in my garden?' I laughed but before I could reply she bolted for the gate. It was shut and I caught her round the scruff of the neck and pulled her backwards restraining her. I told her to drop the bag and cuffed her. I told her she was nicked for burglary and waited for transport. The occupants of the house hadn't even stirred. My colleague had to wake them up and give them the good news.

There are not many female house burglars, in fact this was the only one I ever came across in my 26 years of service. I teamed up with the CID again to interview her and she admitted having burgled numerous houses and was charged. I was beginning to build my reputation with the CID with my ambitions to make detective well on track.

I would arrest and charge at least seven criminals per working week, way more than most of my colleagues but I liked to be busy. Then the Chief Inspector asked for volunteers to work on a cross border crime initiative, Operation Cross Flow, between Lancashire and West Yorkshire Police. I jumped at the chance mainly to have a change of scene from the routine of patrol work. We worked 10pm to 6am night shifts, two officers per car and our brief was to observe cross border traffic for any suspicious vehicles or occupants. We had intelligence reports that identified potential targets. It was exciting and I was buzzing. So all briefed up, in plain clothes and an unmarked police car, Operation Crossflow commenced. The first night we saw little activity, stopped some scallywags but found nothing to keep them for even though it was clear they weren't taking the slow road from Manchester for a Monday night out in Halifax. Nothing against Halifax but even on a Friday night most people from Halifax have found somewhere else they'd rather be.

Tuesday night started quietly and then I spotted one of our target vehicles. Two men occupied the front seats of an old saloon car which was nondescript. I was driving and started to follow. We were about ten miles from Halifax, it was pitch dark and we followed at a discreet distance for about three miles when the driver must have clocked us. In any event he floored his car and I responded. Knowing we had been sussed and for public safety reasons I had to activate the covert blue lights hidden behind the radiator grille and red stop sign on the dash and rear window.

Fortunately the roads were dead and we closed in on the residential outskirts of Halifax quickly. About a mile out his engine must have blown and my windscreen got covered in engine oil from his exhaust. The wipers struggled to clear the screen but we kept going. He pulled into a housing estate and he and his passenger bailed out with the car still moving, it hit a fence and came to a halt. I saw the driver climb a six-foot garden fence and gave chase, telling PC Parkin my colleague to get after the other one. He tried to get out of the car but still had his seat belt on. I promised myself I wouldn't tell anyone but never could keep a secret. I gave chase, scaled the fence and felt the warm flow of adrenaline flowing through me like a drug. I followed him over three back garden fences and caught up with him as he climbed the next. I grabbed his jacket but it just came away in my hands and he was gone again. I wasn't going to let him get away from me so over the fence I went. It was pitch black and I could see very little, then I heard a splash. I figured he must have found someone's Koi Carp collection and smiled inwardly, I loved the thrill of the chase. I found him soaked to the skin, in four feet of water. It was cold and I assumed he would come quietly relishing the thought of a nice cup of tea in the cells. I assumed wrong and he climbed out of the pond and took a swing at me. We exchanged blows and I wrestled him to the ground putting him face down on the slabs and shoving his arm between his shoulder blades just enough to make him know he was stuffed. As I put the cuffs on, the owner of the water feature opened the bedroom window to enquire 'what the fuck's going on' in his back garden. I identified myself and asked him to put the outside lights on so I could avoid getting my feet wet. I called control and they sent PC Parkin to pick us up. Parkin had lost his man.

We lodged the prisoner at Halifax, had a brew and returned to search the car. In the boot we found a burglars tool kit and loads of documentation to identify the two suspects. Their homes were raided by Greater Manchester Police and property from burglaries recovered. I was asked to stay on and work with the CID to interview the suspect I had arrested. I didn't hesitate and worked through the following day.

Our suspects fingerprints were matched to numerous burglaries of people's homes and he was sentenced to six years as he was a prolific offender.

Surely my detective spot wasn't too far away now I thought… if only that had been true.

Whilst still in my probationary period and with Jenny and I set for a future together in Yorkshire or so I thought she had asked if I would transfer to her home town of Nottingham. This was massive, and would mean losing all the career progress I had made, leaving my friends and an area I loved behind. But I applied only to be rejected out of hand. Their loss I thought and of course I had at least tried, for Jenny's sake. It was clear though she wasn't completely happy in Yorkshire.

I cracked on at work and finished my probation. I had a new Inspector recently promoted from the CID to uniform. Lynn was in her early forties, quite attractive and in good shape. I seemed to see more of Lynn than any previous Inspector as I had been trusted to work unsupervised in Elland. We chatted and got to know one another better and she asked me to show her the local area. She drove as she had her Inspectors Police vehicle. After about an hour of the night shift she pulled up in a remote location. Lynn was a forthright woman there was no small talk and she made it clear she wanted an intimate relationship. I could feel my core temperature rise and didn't know what to say. It was awkward but Lynn was either oblivious or didn't care. She reached across and tried to kiss me. I stopped her and blurted out something about us being potentially compromised and the rank differential which made her pause for thought. She knew I was married and that clearly wasn't an issue for her but she may have reflected upon her position of power and my relative vulnerability. She drove back to the station and she talked as though nothing had happened and that was that.

We saw one another at various social gatherings and after a few drinks she would always make an approach but I steered clear and gave her the cold shoulder. I discovered later I wasn't the only focal point of her attention and she had more success elsewhere.

Then one night Inspector Lynn came over to Elland to visit the night shift. It was about 11:30pm and she parked her car on Main Street outside the one and only Chinese takeaway which unsurprisingly was full of drunken blokes fresh off the last bus from Halifax. Lynn had gone walkabout to see one of the other cops on shift but it was getting rowdy. I watched the crowd of about twenty from a distance with my partner for the night a Special Constable and then it all kicked off, they surrounded the police car and began rocking it side to side. I feared the worst, this thing was going on its roof and soon. I radioed Lynn to return and move her car. She obviously didn't quite grasp the gravity of the situation and replied saying she'd be there in ten minutes. We didn't have ten minutes and I told her as much but there was no reply. I called for back-up knowing it would be about ten minutes response time which would likely be too long. I told the Special to accompany me. My plan was to approach the crowd and try to calm the situation, cops never run into potential trouble primarily because you lose perspective on the situation before you and taking it steady allows time to take in the scene and plan. I obviously didn't convey my intention well enough to my Special because inexplicably for no reason whatsoever he ran the 20 metres into the crowd, baton drawn and started pushing people away from the car. I had no choice but to follow. The crowd smelled blood, two cops and clearly no back up, we were easy pickings for a drunken mob.

Punches rained in on me so I drew my baton, whacked a couple of people as hard as I could and they backed off a little. I took one guy down on the pavement but had no chance of cuffing him so just pinned him down, time ticked by in slow motion, two or three men started walking back towards me and I gave it my last shot of bravado. I held my truncheon out pointing it at them and said, 'first one to get here is wearing this.' I thought this would stall them even make them think twice but it didn't and they kept coming, I told the guy on the pavement to 'stay down' and got to my feet and waited for a battering, but only after I pegged one first. And then as if it were some unrealistic episode of *The Bill*, a Transit van turned the corner full of hairy arsed coppers angry to have missed out on the fun. They made up for it quickly though and meted out some summary justice whilst others saw the inside of a police transit van which in those days was not somewhere you wanted to be. I had only suffered a couple of bruises but was happy that the balance of pain inflicted was in my favour that night. My Special was lucky he just had a bloody nose but I couldn't fault his bravery and told him so.

Another dull night in the sleepy backwater was over but only after Inspector Lynn arriving after the action had ceased, apologised for ignoring the warnings.

CHAPTER THIRTEEN

The green shoots of success

I finished my two-year probationary period and was confirmed in the office of Constable. The Divisional Chief Superintendent Mr Davey AKA Lord God Almighty summoned me to his office so I drove to Halifax to meet him. His PA showed me to his office and I was greeted by a big man who was warm and friendly. He told me I had been identified as an 'Officer of potential', whatever that meant and asked me, 'What do you think your colleagues say about you?'

Difficult one that but I replied, 'Some will say I'm a good cop and others will say I'm over confident which if I'm honest doesn't really bother me sir.'

He smiled and said, 'They used to say I was a cocky bastard son, and look where I'm sat. You keep on doing what you're doing and fuck 'em.'

And so that's what I did, for the next 24 years.

Soon after I got a call from the Detective Inspector, he asked me to join the CID team for a pint after a 2–10pm shift. I got to the pub and it was clear the detectives had been there a while. Back in the 80s and 90s CID would always go for a pint on duty. 'Intelligence gathering' I think they called it, looking for criminals in the pub. In all my service I never heard of anyone from CID nicking someone from the 2–10 pub visit.

I had a brief conversation with the DI, who at that stage of my career was next to god in status. I was seriously flattered as he asked if I wanted the next aide to CID position. Did I want it? I would have walked over burning coals for it. It was going to be a few months before it could be arranged but I was ecstatic. Back then for someone so young in service to make the CID was a real achievement.

Then came the bombshell. Jenny and I had moved into our second home only months previously when an official looking letter arrived addressed to me. I opened it reading and then re reading its contents and was immediately faced with a real dilemma.

The letter was from Nottinghamshire Police asking if I was still interested in transferring. I knew if I said yes they would take me in a heartbeat, but I really wanted to stay in Yorkshire. My mates were all there and my career was going really well. We had a lovely new home and I was really settled.

I knew if I transferred I would be back at square one with new surroundings, no friends or contacts in a Force I knew nothing about. I considered the idea of just binning the letter (I still wonder whether I should have), Jenny would never know but I knew how much she wanted to be back in Nottingham, close to her family. At the time even I didn't realise quite how much impact this decision would have. Jenny was thrilled, and asked if I would re apply and if they didn't want me this time she would happily settle in Yorkshire and never mention moving back to Nottingham again. So I replied to Nottinghamshire in the affirmative and waited to hear back. Sergeant Boot the recruitment officer called me down for an interview which went well considering I didn't really want to be there.

They said they'd be in touch and kept banging on about Notts being the top performing Force in the country. 'How did they know this' I thought? How did anyone know who was good, bad, or otherwise? I would hear this complete bollocks repeatedly in the following months and years. They really were in a state of delusion and everyone there believed it but in the not-too-distant future everyone in the country would know the reality. I didn't realise at the time but West Yorkshire really was a top performing force and I understood this clearly once I had something to measure it against.

I waited several weeks for a response but nothing. Jenny had been offered a job in a Nottinghamshire Hospital but needed to confirm with them urgently and she also had to give four weeks' notice to her current employer. I was in limbo and only weeks away from joining the CID. I rang Sgt Boot out of frustration mentioning that my wife had to give notice to leave her job and to confirm her new appointment, oh and there was the small matter of a house to sell before we could find somewhere to live in Nottingham.

And his response! 'I'm not permitted to give you a yes or no at this point but tell your wife not to give up her job.' I took this as a clear indication that I had been knocked back and I told Jenny. She agreed and I was delighted. Better look for a new suit I thought full of joy.

Two days later a letter dropped on the doormat, and of course it was from Notts Police. It read, 'Dear PC Holmes, we are delighted to offer you the position of Police Constable with Nottinghamshire Police.'

I was gutted. Sgt Boot, what an absolute tosser. Jenny was happy of course and we put the house up for sale immediately. We gave our respective employers the news and letters of resignation and counted down the days. It felt like a bereavement. We sold the house almost immediately and made a substantial profit, which we could use to up-scale in Notts. We wanted to live in the affluent area of Ravenshead by Newstead Abbey but simply couldn't afford to. So, we bought a new build in nearby Hucknall.

I was told I would be posted to a market town called Arnold so Jenny and I paid the area a visit, it had a smart new Police Station and a prosperous town centre. Not too bad I thought, I might actually enjoy it here. I had a big leaving do in a local pub in Brighouse and said my goodbyes to friends and colleagues in Yorkshire and we moved into Jenny's parent's house in Ravenshead whilst our new build was being completed.

On my first day at work I drove to Arnold, Police HQ and met my Inspector. Lew Davies was a gruff local man, very experienced but a bit rough around the edges. That said he was a really good guy, straight talking and would prove to be very supportive in the challenging months ahead.

I told him I was very much looking forward to working in Arnold to which he replied: 'Arnold lad. No, you're going to Bestwood.' Bestwood? I'd never heard of the place! However everyone else clearly had, it was infamous. I met a few of the staff and went with the Inspector to Bestwood Station. It was a small prefab in the heart of the estate with an open plan car park. What a dump. Lew introduced me to my Shift, Rota 2. I got the immediate feeling that I was as welcome as a Crown Court summons. The shift were an eclectic bunch comprised mostly of work-shy loafers but there were a couple of good lads and I latched onto them for guidance and support. I knew it would be challenging moving forces but it was way harder than I ever imagined. I was right out of my comfort zone, like a fish out of water, everything was different. From the brand of police radios that operated differently to West Yorkshire to the 10-code system (a short code system to quickly communicate your status with up to 20 different codes).

Back in Yorkshire, 10/13 meant an officer needs assistance whereas in Notts, it meant you're going for a meal break. I felt like I was starting almost from scratch, even the paperwork was different. In those days there were 43 Forces operating 43 different ways. Madness. One thing hadn't changed though I was still a thief taker and in Bestwood. I could nick as many bad guys as I could handle. The way I always looked at my less productive colleagues was that if they weren't nicking baddies then there were more out there for me. My intention was to be as prolific as possible and get noticed by the CID and hopefully within a year get to where I had been before leaving Yorkshire.

I soon got the hang of the new systems and processes and settled in to a routine. Bestwood was an absolute shithole. There were of course some good honest people trapped in council housing amongst some truly vile individuals and extended families. Most gardens didn't have water features or rockeries but more knackered old cars with no wheels and on bricks and a sofa or mattress to complete the look. There were several organised crime families all vying for ascendency, money and power by any means necessary. Fear and intimidation were their currency.

On my very first night shift I came face to face with two brothers from one such group. It was the week before Christmas and I was called to a report of a several serious assaults at a house party. When I got there I saw a number of men with blood pouring from various injuries, it was mayhem. I established that three men had been ejected from the party. They had left but returned a short time later to attack anyone they could find with baseball bats, covered in Christmas wrapping paper. Very creative, I thought. I got the suspects names, gathered the troops and nicked them. On this occasion they got sent down for Section 18 Wounding with Intent as 17 and 20 year olds. In the years to come they would terrorise the estate, running every criminal enterprise possible, maiming and killing several people along the way. This wouldn't be the last time we would find ourselves across an interview table from one another.

CHAPTER FOURTEEN

The new sheriff in town

I continued to work hard and after only a few months Lew did the annual round robin and asked who was taking their Sergeant's exams. I said I was even though I hadn't even considered it. It wasn't on my radar I was focussed on getting my aide to the CID. But it was a free day off work, four hours of exams then to the pub for the rest of the day. I didn't intend on doing much revision if any. However two weeks later I had the rug pulled from under.

Lew, in the mistaken belief that I was studying hard for the exam and without telling me, appointed me Acting Sergeant for the shift. Some of my less productive colleagues were most unhappy about this and made their feelings known. How could I be made A/Sgt when I wasn't qualified? Good question I thought but Lew had the answers: 'No one else is qualified so I can pick who I like, Nick's doing the exam no one else is and he'll pass so needs the experience.'

Jesus Christ, now not only did I have to study, I had to pass or these loafers would have a field day. One such tosser, not qualified or even taking the exam went to the Police Federation (union) to complain. The Divisional Commander, Chief Superintendent Burrows got wind of this and unbeknown to me called the tosser in to question his rationale. I understood on good authority (Lew) that it was a brief conversation with tosser given the option to 'Shut the fuck up' or he would be posted to Grindley-on-the- Hill (the station placed furthest from his home address). He left the office tearful and no doubt considering the error of his ways. He was mute on the issue from that point and left in no uncertain terms on who had the bosses backing.

However I was still the 'new boy' an outsider and there was clear hostility which I found strange. Why did it bother them so much? And what possible impact would it have on them? But I believed in myself and these people would prove insignificant in the long term. Plus I knew if I waited long enough I would get an opportunity to repay the tosser for his vindictive stupidity.

I kept my head down, worked hard and managed the section as Acting Sergeant. I studied every available hour and actually enjoyed the learning, probably because it was mostly relevant to my day job and the job I sought as a Detective.

The time was fast approaching when the Detective Inspector would select the next aide to CID. I put my name forward and hoped for the best. My Acting stint ended with the arrival of a new boss, Sgt H. He was experienced and had a Detective background and I was optimistic of a fruitful relationship. That notion was soon quashed as tosser and the loafer squad got to him first. He pinned his colours to the mast on our first week of night shifts together.

Our general routine would be to parade on duty at 10pm then a 20-minute briefing which included identifying targets for arrest, curfew or bail checks to see if the criminal suspect was adhering to the terms and conditions set by the courts. We were assigned geographical areas to patrol with individual call signs and meal times. At 1pm most of the shift would come in for refreshments and the obligatory game of cards. I came in 45 mins later and Sgt H was sat playing cards with tosser and the other loafers. It was pretty much the first conversation we had had and casually in front of everyone he says: 'So you're the blue-eyed boy then?'

A little surprised I replied, 'What?'

'I said, you've been shown undeserved favouritism by getting Acting Sergeant and I know why.'

Again I replied, 'Oh, really Sarge enlighten me. Why?'

'You're dad's a Mason and we all know you lodge boys stick together, so strings were pulled,' he said.

I could feel the anger boiling up inside of me but I remained calm. This guy was a joke – Detective? He hadn't even established the basic facts to support his very public accusation. 'Well that's interesting Sarge as my dad's from Yorkshire like me and he's dead. So I guess he must be sending messages from the grave.' I gave everyone around the table a look that could kill and left them in no doubt what contempt I held them in including Sgt H. I couldn't stand to be in the same building as these idiots so I went back out on patrol, seething. It was moments like these that just strengthened my resolve and I was determined to pass the exam.

On reflection, after the exchange he must have realised that he had successfully made himself look a complete knob. Even if he didn't, I let him know a few years later when I became his Inspector. What goes around comes around. You just need to be patient, they never hear the gunshot that kills their career.

I studied for at least 30 hours plus a week and it was hard going. There are three volumes of police law and procedure, each the thickness of a house brick. There's a lot to learn and the problem is, you need to know as much of this as possible because you have no idea what's coming up in the exam. Within a few weeks I had sat the exam which took four hours and comprised three papers. Traffic, Crime and General Police duties. I was fairly optimistic that I had done well, I had studied incredibly hard but there is so much to learn and you need to know it all.

Exam out of the way I focussed on arresting as many high-profile criminals as possible to impress the Detective Inspector. One of these was during another set of nightshifts. I was doubled up with Mark Naylor, a Constable like me, a decent lad and not a bad cop. Everyone else on shift was in for their meal break but I wanted to patrol the area of Rise Park where there had been dozens of dwelling house burglaries over a few months and CID didn't have a clue who was responsible. It was then I got a radio message from the control room that a resident on Rugby Close, Rise Park heard a noise next door but knew the occupant was away with work. My adrenaline started to flow and I was excited but I exercised caution. I didn't want anyone to hear the police cars noisy diesel engine so parked a couple of hundred yards away. I told Mark to go to the rear of the house which as it turned out had a six-foot fence at the top of a steep banking. I ran to the front holding my baton and handcuffs to stop them rattling. The house appeared secure and in darkness. I made my way down the path at the left-hand side of the house finding it was reasonably well lit by the street lights. I approached the rear cautiously and peeped around the corner. I could see that the patio door had been lifted from the base runner and had been moved to one side leant against the other window. I could hear muffled sounds of movement from within, my excitement built and I knew this was going to be confrontation time but I didn't know how many intruders might be in the house. I stepped back and told control to send back up, I didn't wait for a reply. I later found out the Control Room staff had left the room unmanned, a complete 'No, No,' and so didn't send anyone, Great! Mark heard the call and knew there was a burglar in the premises but he was sliding up and down the banking at the back fence and couldn't get over. I heard sounds of movement and went back to the rear corner of the house. I saw a dark figure backing out of the patio doorway holding a large object in both arms in front of him. I wasn't quite sure what to do next but crept up behind him, tapped him on the shoulder and said, 'What's all this then?' Shocked and clearly surprised he threw his arms in the air the home owners prized stereo crashing on the patio. He was in survival mode and turned quickly and in a panic threw a fist in my direction he missed and I struck him to the side of his head but not hard enough as he was still standing. I pulled my truncheon and he turned and bolted straight into the six-foot fence, I hit him in the kidneys and grabbed him around the neck pulling him to the ground. He fought back and I shouted: 'Where the fuck are you Mark?'

'I can't get over the fence!' he shouts.

'Come round the front NOW!' I replied. I turned the burglar onto his front and managed to cuff him. Mark arrived looking sheepish. 'Where's back up?' I asked. He looked as bemused as me. I called control to update them. 'One, three five (arrest) on scene for burglary, where's our back up?'

Silence. Then a couple of long seconds later, 'We didn't hear the call...' One eventually replied. *Wankers*, I thought.

A car was dispatched and took the prisoner to the custody suite and then Sgt H makes an appearance. 'Good collar that.' I didn't even reply, like I gave a toss what he thought. However Inspector Lew did tell me soon after that Sgt H had submitted a recommendation for a Chief Constables Commendation, probably at Lew's instruction. I never heard anything further on that issue, for a while.

When I searched the prisoner I found a Commando dagger tucked in the waistband of his jeans and wondered briefly what might have happened if he had pulled that during the melee. I searched the house and saw some framed photographs of a man in uniform. I smiled to myself the home owner is a Marine, hence the dagger. I later spoke with the Marines mother and she told me her son is in the SBS (Special Boat Service). Lucky for the burglar he wasn't at home I thought.

I worked through the night and with the CID the following day researching all the burglaries the suspect may have committed. I interviewed him and he seemed to respect me for arresting him and dealing with him like a human being. During the tape-recorded interviews the suspect admitted to over seventy house burglaries. We matched forensic evidence including fingerprints to a number of them. Given the weight of evidence and having been caught red handed he made a full confession and was remanded in custody.

It was time to choose the next Aide to CID and a few weeks later the DI, Ash Parfrement asked to see me. Ash admitted that he knew nothing about me and I knew then I needed to fill in some blanks. It felt to me like he was going through the motions but I gave him my West Yorkshire story and told him that I had been accepted as the CID Aide back there which seemed to prick his interest. 'But what have you done down here son?' he asked me.

'Sir, I'll get my workbook so you can see for yourself.' I took him through the dozens of crime related prisoners, he looked impressed and then he paused his attention drawn by one particular name on the ledger.

'That one there, that's the Rise Park burglar,' he said.

'Yes, Boss, I nicked him on premises and interviewed him with CID.'

'He coughed (admitted) over seventy break ins?'

'Yes, Sir,' I reply.

'Son, I have to tell you your Sergeant has recommended one of your colleagues Mick L for the CID Aide.' Now, Mick was a good cop and had helped me to settle in at Bestwood but I couldn't help myself, I laughed out loud and told the DI the story on Sgt H.

My Sgt was really beginning to piss me off, back stabbing bastard. He had even told the DI not to waste his time on me as I wasn't up to it. However the DI seemed a very fair and reasonable man and we would get to know each other much better over the years ahead. He said he was impressed, apologised for not knowing me better before we met and that he would let me know the outcome. I knew then that he would ask around and do his homework before making his decision and so I asked Lew to put a word in. I needed all the help I could get to even things up.

Its exam results day and after countless hours of tireless study, it was finally crunch time. I needed to pass all three papers to qualify for the rank of Sergeant. I found the results envelope in my personal pigeon hole for correspondence at work took a deep breath and opened the envelope. As I read the results I got that warm rush of adrenaline and buzzed with happiness. I had passed all three.

With 49% required for a pass, in Traffic my most hated subject I scored 76%. I was elated, the feeling of success and achievement felt fantastic and something I hadn't felt too often previously. My career ambition was to make Detective Sergeant and I now felt confident that I would achieve that goal. That evening Jenny and I celebrated with her family. As it transpired I had scored so well when compared nationally that Inspector Lew and the Divisional Commander recommended me for the external National Accelerated Promotion Selection.

Being accepted on this scheme would mean fast tracked promotion to the rank of Superintendent. I didn't expect to be successful as it was almost exclusively university graduates that were accepted but nevertheless being recommended for immediate promotion meant I had a golden ticket at the next Sergeant boards. Things were going my way that's for sure and I then heard that I'd been accepted for immediate placement on the CID. I couldn't quite believe how quickly things were moving.

'Fuck you Sgt H,' I thought, I'd done it and my career had lift off. I had the bug for success and it was addictive. Inspector Lew was delighted for me and we had a good chat about the future. He was convinced that I would go far and told me so. I had his support and that of the Divisional Commander the Chief Superintendent. My self-esteem was growing but I knew I needed to keep a level head as I was still the new boy and had ruffled even more feathers by being accepted on to the CID.

Despite being told it was impossible for her to conceive by a consultant gynaecologist we found out Jenny was pregnant. We had been trying for the best part of four years so it was great news. We hadn't planned for this however and thinking it would be just the two of us going forward had taken on a 100% mortgage, bought two new cars on finance and I even had a sports bike. The mortgage interest rate was going up like a temperature gauge on a summers day, finally resting at 15.5%. We were beyond our financial limit despite both working full time, the interest on our £65k mortgage was £839 a month and we had a repayment mortgage so had even more to pay back. Jenny's salary just covered the mortgage but we had two cars to pay for and all the other usual household expenses. Yes, we were skint with a baby on the way but we were very, very happy. The building society gave us a repayment holiday of six months so we only had to pay 50% of the mortgage which really helped in the short term.

I would occasionally go to the football with a few of my work mates to watch Nottingham Forest play. I got a ticket for the 1989 FA Cup Semi Final against Liverpool at Hillsborough which was played on my birthday 15 April. There were five of us and we made a day of it having a few pints beforehand in the pubs by the ground. It was a beautiful spring day and everyone's spirits were high. There was no animosity between the rival supporters as we mixed heading for the ground. Around 53,000 tickets had been sold for the match which was also shown on television. As we entered one end of the ground it became immediately apparent that the opposite end of the ground appeared very congested whilst we had a considerable amount of space. This pre dates all seated stadia, which followed soon after in large part as a result of what followed that fateful day.

The game kicked off and after only a few minutes of play people from the Liverpool supporters end spilled onto the pitch. In truth I had no idea what was going on and many people around me thought that it was a pitch invasion. It was however clear from the chaotic scenes that unfolded that something serious was unfolding before our eyes. I saw members of the public and Police Officers carrying the injured to safety whilst several bodies lay still on the ground. The scenes were horrific but I hadn't realised the full gravity of the disaster until I returned home to my worried family. This predates mobile phones and I never thought to call them but they had seen the disaster on TV in far more detail than I had and were concerned that I might somehow be involved.

The Police made mistakes that day and as a consequence the management of major sporting events was completely over hauled and professionalised. I would later become qualified as a senior officer and routinely manage major public and sporting events.

CHAPTER FIFTEEN

Promotion time

The only downside of starting on the CID is having to buy new suits, shirts and ties and proper men's shoes. Jenny wouldn't have any of the two suits for £100 stuff, so it was Pierre Cardin and Armani despite the fact we were broke. I'm still not sure what the CID office thought when I appeared on day one looking like I'd fallen out of a shop window, all brand new and raring to go.

The work was steady compared to uniform and the quality much better, I wasn't dealing with scumbags all the time – only half of it.

I loved the CID from the off and I knew I had found my vocation. Plenty of overtime, more personal respect within the job and from the public; it was win, win. I only worked days and afters so no more night shifts. I worked hard and ploughed through work. I got a couple of Commendations for high profile criminal prosecutions and then found out on the grapevine that Sgt H had binned the one for the Rise Park burglar. Such a nice man.

I had a search warrant for a house in Bestwood where a well known 'handler' lived. These are the people who take stolen goods from the original thief and trade them onwards. I had Force Support with me to help gain entry and search the premises. I also had a young probationary PC with me so he could experience the execution of a warrant. We arrived at the address at 7am I knocked politely on the door but there was no reply.

Force support had brought their latest toy a hydraulic ram which when placed between the door frame would open outwards pushing the frame apart and the door would just pop open. The ram was produced, all shiny and new and attached to the battery. The ram in place the officer pressed the power button and... nothing, the battery was dead. Plan 'B' was to force the door open with a universal key, a small battering ram but the Sergeant in charge decided to take charge kicking the door with all his might. Now the door had a glass pane and wooden surround and his foot slipped off the wood and went through the glass and when his foot dropped onto the glass it severed his Achilles tendon. Not a great start to my warrant and the young cop with me nearly passed out there was so much blood. The door was rammed open and we got on with the search. The occupants were upstairs and clearly knew we were there but decided against letting us in.

Warrant shown, we looked for the stolen property. The young PC got the short straw and had to search the loft which was chock full of so much rubbish you couldn't see the floor. Which was a problem because the young cop fell straight through the ceiling and down the stairs. It was like pulling the plug on a sink full of water, all the crap in the attic followed our poor PC down the stairs. This was turning into a keystone cops disaster made worse when we didn't find any stolen property. In typical police humour the young cop was given a new nickname, 'Lofty'.

At this time I was also going through selection for HPD (High Potential Development). I was hugely outside my comfort zone but tried to understand the selection process criteria and prepare as best as I could. I passed the first two phases out of three which certainly exceeded my expectations. Made up of psychometric and numerical, problem solving exercises I seemed to do all right. All the other candidates I met were graduates and the process was academically skewed towards them. I can recall one of the questions asking which country was Machu Picchu in? As a 27-year-old I had never heard of it. Of course with age comes wisdom and I've heard about and seen it numerous times since and every time I see yet another travelogue of

Peru I think back to HPD selection and wince at my ignorance. I fell at the final hurdle, the three-day selection. During the one-on-one interview with Lady Mayhew she may as well have been speaking in Greek. I had no clue what she was really asking, it was bizarre and completely alien to me. We talked about cats, the feline kind for ten minutes and to this day I have no idea why. Maybe that's something they learn at University.

The Deputy Chief Constable (DCC), John Culley called me in to break the news. He was genuinely disappointed for me and I think he wanted me to break the mould if I'm honest. Kindly, he assured me of promotion at the earliest opportunity. I was grateful for his support and thanked him.

Promotion boards were run a couple of times per year and candidates were paper sifted out on the strength of their application. The next step was for the candidate to give a presentation on a given subject followed by a structured interview. The boards came quickly but I was ready and well prepared. As I waited nervously outside the interview room the secretary to the DCC walked by and gave me a smile as she opened the interview room door to inform them I had arrived and was ready for interview. I heard a voice say, 'keep him waiting five minutes. I want to see him sweat' This made me laugh to myself and strangely made me much more relaxed. I went into that room thinking, 'I'm the one everyone else has to beat.' I have always approached competitive processes this way. I prepare meticulously and when I step in for selection don't even consider my opposition, I focus on me and the task at hand.

A week later on a Friday afternoon (it was always a Friday afternoon so that no calls or appeals could be made as it was the weekend) I took a call from the Head of Personnel informing me I had scored highest in the selection boards, meaning I would be promoted almost immediately. This was a potential problem, so asked to be deferred to allow me to complete my CID course. I hadn't had a date for the Detective Training Course but thankfully and to the annoyance of some I was moved up the list of Trainee Detectives waiting for a course and would be going within a couple of weeks. At least now I could focus on completing my CID course before I got promoted otherwise I would end up in uniform for the rest of my service. In the eighties you were usually either uniform or CID all of your service. I intended to break that pattern as I saw a more beneficial path working between and across the two disciplines.

A couple of weeks after the Promotion Board my daughter Olivia arrived. Jenny had been in labour for over thirty hours and it seemed she would never make an appearance. She was born at City Hospital, Nottingham on 12 May 1990. From the day she was born until this day she has been the perfect child. We enjoy a very close relationship and are the best of friends. She is my harshest critic and greatest supporter and I know I can always depend on her. I feel for those who do not have a close relationship with their children and I know how fortunate I am.

CHAPTER SIXTEEN

Watching the Detectives

The CID course was ten weeks duration based at 'Tally Ho' in Birmingham, the Police Training school for West Midlands Police. It is close to the Edgbaston Cricket ground and only five minutes from the city centre. I had to leave Jenny and Olivia who at this point was only a few months old but it had to be done. I had a career plan and it was in motion. Despite our financial difficulties, we had been putting something away each month for Olivia in a savings account. It wasn't a decision I'm particularly proud of to raid my daughters savings to fund my social activities in Birmingham but I told myself and Jenny that we should look on it as an investment as when I got promoted and back on the CID as a Detective Sergeant we would be much better off financially. I didn't really believe what I was saying but it actually turned out to be true.

We arrived at Tally Ho all suited up. 40 expectant and excited students from twelve Forces. I felt pretty relaxed, I had recently passed my exams with flying colours and knew most of what we were about to be taught. Some Police Forces insisted that to remain in the CID their candidate had to pass the course final exam. This wasn't the case for me so I was looking forward to meeting new people, learning a bit and generally having a good time.

The first day we settled into our rooms, one per candidate with a single bed, dressing table, shower and toilet cubicle and a wardrobe. I unpacked all my personal stuff including photos from home and sound system, as I can't survive without music and arranged my suits, shirts and ties in the wardrobe with military precision. I suppose the forces taught me to be organised and well presented and personal appearance was important to me in making the right impression. So all squared away I headed for our welcome meeting.

We congregated in the lecture theatre and the Training Staff appeared on stage introducing themselves in turn to the expectant audience. The Course Director, a Detective Chief Inspector, asked the audience for a show of hands from candidates required to pass the final exam to remain on the CID. I was surprised how many there were. Poor sods, I thought. He then announced, 'The good news for you lot is you will all pass. Now relax and enjoy the course you're here to learn but also build lifelong relationships and have some fun.' The relief was palpable. He also said one other thing which was, 'you only get one CID course, you can always get another wife'. It made me laugh at the time but how true it turned out to be. From my knowledge there were at least three divorces as a direct result of that course.

The course was really enjoyable and I loved every minute of it. It was hard being away from Jenny and Olivia but I made the most of it and I returned home each weekend which kept me in touch with reality. Every night in Birmingham was a trip out somewhere and the local Detectives on the course were instructed to show us a good time. So we went to every back street pub in Birmingham with most having an after-hours 'lock in'. They would shut the doors at closing time and we would carry on drinking.

Whilst I drank far too much I was still very fitness minded and worked out every day, even at Tally Ho. I would do aerobics at lunchtime skipping the meal and then hit the weights at night before dinner. Somehow I still managed to put on half a stone of blubber, but I really did hammer the booze and Birmingham's world-famous Balti curry. I met some great people on the course and it seemed like we were always laughing about something and somewhere in the middle I may have even managed to learn something.

The first week of the course we ran through 'Stop and Search' practical scenarios. Where and under which circumstances someone could be stopped and legally searched. We had to video each interaction with a member of the public. Back in the theatre the videos were replayed and debriefed. Everything went by the numbers until a video was played featuring my new mate Dave Heggarty. Dave was from the City of London Police and a real West Ham boy. Six feet five and a professional cockney. As the drama unfolded he is seen wearing a policeman's helmet which didn't really go with his suit but he was role playing. The scenario was that a jewellers shop had been robbed nearby and the member of the public to be stopped fitted the robbers description. Could he be lawfully searched or not? Fairly straightforward you would think. Dave can be seen casually sauntering along the street the member of the public approaching from the opposite direction.

Dave puts out the palm of his hand and politely asked the man to stop and asks, 'Can I have a word please sir?'

The member of the public is compliant and Dave asks him where he has been, explains why he has stopped him and that he fits the description of a suspect. The man gives a plausible explanation which Dave appears to accept. But just before Dave allows him on his way he asks the man if he recognises a car in the distance behind him. As the man turns to look over his shoulder Dave does no more than drop the watch he's taken off his own wrist into the breast pocket of the man's suit. This goes unnoticed by the man who, as he is walking away, is accosted by Dave who reaches into the man's pocket and produces the watch whilst at the same time telling him, 'you're nicked son'.

Unbelievable, but hilarious. The Training Staff are speechless seeing one of their students fitting someone up on a training exercise.

One evening it had been decided we should have a night out at the beer Keller which is actually a converted cornmill next to a lovely river. On the coach en route we are told that each week a local woman nicknamed KY Julie attends the event and chooses one lucky individual who she takes outside at the end of the evening to engage in something more intimate. It's always a member of the emergency services and usually a Fireman. However on this occasion all the Firemen must have been rescuing cats from trees as there weren't any there, so KY Julie selected a member of our party and was last seen heading for the river bank.

This isn't unusual, at Wakefield the home of West Yorkshire Police training school a woman was found to have stolen the Police warrant cards from several officers with whom she had a relationship. Some women clearly do have a fixation for men in uniform.

As the course drew to a close I was asked to deliver the end of dinner speech on the last night. I was flattered and rather than study for the final exam, set about preparing my speech. Fortunately, during the final week I received a call to go to the Course Directors office. You have to remember this predates the proliferation of mobile phones. I had no clue what I had done wrong but with trepidation knocked on the door. On hearing, 'enter' I walked in. The DCI held out the landline phone in his hand. 'Someone back at Force wants a word, mate.'

I took the phone, 'Hello, DC Holmes speaking.'

It was the Superintendent, Head of Personnel, 'Hello, Nick, I have some good news for you. You need to come back to Force to see the Chief, you'll be promoted to Sergeant this Thursday.' I was delighted of course but also conflicted. Thursday was exam day, no drama missing that but it was also our end of course do and I had my speech to deliver. I asked what time they needed me at HQ and it was 10am. I could be in and out pop to see Jenny and Olivia and back in time for the dinner, sorted.

When I got back to class people were genuinely delighted for me and of course the drinks that night were on Sgt Holmes courtesy of Olivia's savings. I wasn't the only one guilty of stealing their family silver. I was stood at the bar one night when one of my colleagues paid for a round with a travellers cheque. Unbeknown to his wife and kids he had blown all their holiday spending money.

I went home on the Wednesday evening to see Jenny and Olivia. It was a great time to be alive. Husband, father, a new home, Detective and now Sergeant. I thought of the conversation with Corporal Dave in that bar in Derry which changed me forever and smiled to myself. What he said had haunted me but I thought, 'I might not be such a 'loser' after all.' I was beginning to understand who I was and my potential for achievement and success. I was growing as a leader and more importantly as a person and if what my senior managers and colleagues were saying had any substance, then the sky was the limit, and I was hungry for more.

I returned to Tally Ho leaving it as late as possible to try and avoid the exam. I arrived at 4pm but my bubble burst when the course Director saw me and made clear I had to sit the 90 min exam paper. As I sat alone in the exam room he passed me a can of lager and the paper.

'I won't be long,' I said, annoyed that I hadn't come back sooner. I blitzed through the paper in 40 minutes and handed it in. I didn't bother to get my mark as I had a dinner to dress for and I didn't want to miss the party.

I met up with my classmates and we had a drink and a laugh whilst getting ready. All the guys wore black tie and dinner suits and the ladies evening dress. I had picked up a pair of Sergeant stripes back at Force for my uniform but fixed double-sided tape to them for later that evening. I had my speech rehearsed and off we went for pre dinner drinks and canapés. It was a truly joyous occasion. I had made so many new friends in those ten weeks when we had lived in each other's pockets. It was a surreal experience, devoid of any real responsibility almost a parallel life to the one I had worked so hard to build. Jenny took care of everything, child care, house work and a full-time job whilst I studied (a bit), drank (a lot) and generally had a good time. I would need to make up for it when I got home but promotion helped a lot and unbeknown to me, Jenny was already house hunting in Ravenshead. I wasn't the only one in the marriage with ambition.

After dinner it was speech time and I had decided not to single any one out but generally take the piss in the nicest possible way, out of every staff member and course student. As I rose to my feet I stuck the chevrons on my arms and everyone cheered. Good friends. It took a while, maybe too long but everyone had a laugh at one another's expense and it went down well.

We partied until the early hours and then retired for the night. Home time tomorrow.

CHAPTER SEVENTEEN

The big, bad city

It's true that after ten weeks away from the reality of home and work it took a little time to re adjust but I was promoted and given a new role.

Uniformed Sergeant at the City of Nottingham. This was my first real man management position and I had a section of 12 officers. The norm in most stations would be one sergeant to five or six Constables and I had 12 to manage, so twice the workload. I also found out I had been given two problem children but they weren't young cops they were long in service old hands who had fallen foul of the discipline code. When I arrived at Central I met with the Superintendent, Head of Operational Policing, Jim Smith. He was a Scot, down to earth but clearly switched on. We spoke in his office for about thirty minutes. I can't recall the gist of the conversation but I can remember as I got up to leave he said, 'Good luck son, you'll do well, you came in here like a fucking whirlwind and we need some of that around here.'

I wasn't conscious of this. I was enthusiastic yes and keen to get on with the new challenge but I suppose he was just used to apathy as being the norm. Looking back I am sure I was given my two problem children as a test but also whoever made the decision must have believed I could manage the situation. It was probably Jim Smith.

Nottingham City covers the busy city centre with some thirty thousand students, a thriving retail sector and an expansive night time pub and club scene attracting people from all over the UK. At this time the urban myth which people took as gospel was that the women in Nottingham outnumbered the men seven to one. No surprise then it was the number one destination for stag parties.

I got to know my shift individually looking at their work records to see what they focussed on and how busy they actually were. I was told numerous times by them that they were swamped with work and had no time for patrolling the streets. So I did a bit of analysis myself. In uniform at Bestwood I was comfortably managing 12–16 cases at any given time as well as being on response car and the occasional foot patrol. The average case load I discovered at central was five! I made clear where I wanted them to focus and my work load expectations. As time passed they upped their game and I supported them by managing workloads equally and being visible with them out on the streets.

The first of the problem children was Danny Watts but he was a great bloke, very experienced and had been moved from the Drug Squad back into uniform. He had some difficulty surrounding the evidence chain of some drugs he had seized and they were not where they should have been when Complaints and Discipline came calling. I'm certain it was nothing criminal or even deliberate it was just Danny was the world's most disorganised person. When we met he was enthusiastic and keen to do his best. He would need support as he had been out of uniform for years and his paperwork was a disaster. But Danny was always supportive and keen to help and his sense of humour was infectious. I learned that Danny had a part time job as a comedian and magician which didn't surprise me at all.

His Police collar number was one hundred. Yes, 100 Watts. They love a little joke in the Police.

My other problem was Graham another old lag who had been moved from a cushy semi-rural posting for poor discipline and insubordination. He clearly didn't know when he was on to a good thing or when to keep his mouth closed. It was clear that it would be a battle to get Graham back on message and to being more of an asset than a hindrance. He was the typical barrack room lawyer always taking a cynical view of the world and in particular, Policing.

The key to motivating Graham was in identifying his strengths and playing to his ego, making him feel valued for his experience. He would never be a star but he did add value to the shift and became much less of a pain in my arse.

I had developed a career game plan to get me to Superintendent. It was my plan and I would need lots of pieces of the puzzle to fit together at the right time for it to work. But I knew that I needed to have a plan and a structure to keep me focussed. I knew what development I needed and courses required to fill personal and professional deficits. The first challenge was making Detective Sergeant, my career goal from the beginning. I would need to do my time (as little as humanly possible) in uniform and then apply for the first vacant DS position.

I worked hard and my shift were the most productive bar non which caught the attention of the Senior Management Team (SMT). The City was different to the other five divisions as it didn't have a real residential population, it was more transient. It had a reputation as a violent place and I expected pub fights a plenty and regular disorder. The truth and reality was very different. Even on a weekend it wasn't that bad and unlike my rural experiences when if it did kick off you were probably on your own, the City had loads of cops there to assist you almost immediately, it felt comparatively safe to me. That being said, it did have its moments.

On a regular day shift I was walking from the police station to Market Square to check on the troops and get a break from the computer and paperwork. As I passed through Exchange Walk a narrow Victorian street with small shops either side I heard a commotion, it was coming from a jeweller's shop.

It was clear something was wrong, as I looked through the

window I first made eye contact with the shopkeeper who was extremely animated and then a large figure at the other side of the counter. I went to the door which was on an electronic lock release which the shopkeeper pressed and I entered. The large fella was even bigger close up. He was six feet five tall and built like a wrestler. Before I could ask what the problem might be the jeweller said, 'We're being robbed.'

'Great,' I thought and pressed my emergency call button on my radio. This opened the microphone allowing the control room to hear anything said. I called for assistance as the big guy turned towards the door to make his escape. I was in his way and not planning on moving so we grappled and he was so powerful that we fell out of the shop through the doorway and into the alleyway. He was strong and determined and threw me onto my back. Instantly I knew I was hurt but I wasn't letting go. He kicked out at me to break free but I held onto him long enough for assistance to arrive which came quickly, thank God and we got him cuffed. When I got to my feet I felt a sharp pain across my lower back. 'I think I'm in trouble,' I thought to myself.

One good thing about being in uniform is that when you turn up at A&E you get fast tracked. I got checked out at the hospital and they established I had slipped a disc in my back.

I had a couple of weeks off work at the convalescent home for Police in Harrogate. It was a grand former manor house built from Yorkshire stone with a doctor, physiotherapists, a pool and a gym. There were beautiful grounds to walk in and all food was provided, it was a five-star rehabilitation hotel. After two weeks of being physically pulled in different directions waking to the pub every night to keep the circulation going and even learning Pilates, I was fit to return to duty.

I got the nod that CID were looking for a Detective Sergeant but I had only completed eighteen months in uniform. But 'penance' served I hoped I could blag my way through selection. I prepared thoroughly for the interview which of course I knew would be biased in someone's favour. It was always a carve up in CID, mates of mates, the old school network, or who you played rugby, football or the coppers favourite pastime – golf with. I didn't do any of the above but the interview went well and there was an independent HR Manager on the panel of three, so just maybe it would be more of a level playing field. I guess it must have been as I got the job.

I know it sounds awful and elitist but even though there were many aspects of frontline uniform work I enjoyed, much of it was mundane and there were always personal dramas to deal with. Cops moaned a lot but I never took my personal shit to work and it seemed like I was definitely the exception. I always found it astonishing that some cops would put more effort into ducking work than it would have taken to have actually done it. Anyway, now that was in the past and I was a Detective Sergeant in the City. My career plan was on course and I couldn't wait to get started. My first shift was 8am–4pm on a Saturday which I soon learned would mean picking up prisoners that had been locked up the by the previous night shift. There were always lots of serious assaults and allegations of rape to pick up. The assaults were usually straightforward, either witnessed by other cops, doormen or CCTV which made the investigation much easier.

Invariably drunks fighting over a woman or someone who jumped the kebab queue getting filled in. It would mean taking witness statements, preparing CCTV footage as evidence, managing the exhibits such as blood-stained clothing and weapons and finally liaising with the defence solicitor and providing disclosure. This meant providing them with the basis of the prosecution case to allow them to advise their client whether or not to speak to the interviewing officer. If they were guilty the brief would invariably advise them to go 'no comment' which was 95% of the time, rarely did a prisoner talk to the interviewing officer so it was down to them to prove their case to pass the Crown Prosecution Service 'threshold test'. What this really meant was proving beyond doubt they were guilty or CPS invariably wouldn't run it.

The sexual offence allegations were always difficult. Given the media focus on this important issue we all know that allegations of rape should be taken seriously and the default position must be to believe the 'victim'. But sometimes experience teaches us to be more circumspect. I lost count of the number of cases that were retracted due to false reporting and of course at the opposite end of the spectrum there were truly awful cases where the offender would be brought to justice and receive their just desserts. That said, and if I am being totally honest, I investigated numerous rape allegations that were false or malicious. I can only draw on my personal experiences but on more than one occasion I investigated complaints of rape by women who were in a stable long-term relationship but had gone out for the evening with friends and when intoxicated had sex with someone other than their partner. The woman would be wracked by guilt or perhaps showing visible signs that would betray to her partner her activities and in a moment of panic would make a false report to the Police. They would not intend for the police to catch the alleged offender for obvious reasons but would have a plausible explanation to their partner on returning home. I am certain that at the time of making these reports they never imagined the level of investigation required, including intimate forensic samples from them, seizure of clothing, detailed statements taken by trained experts in the field, CCTV to be viewed to trace their steps and those of the alleged offender, sexual offence counselling and more. It is one thing to claim an event happened in a specific location with a description of the offender but once the investigation snowball starts rolling and the evidence is pieced together the clarity around the event improves significantly.

One female actually flagged down a passing motorist and when he stopped told him she had been raped, just so he would feel sorry for her and give her a lift to the pub. But as they always do, things snowball, the driver called the Police and stayed with her in the pub even giving her £20 for a drink until they arrived. When spoken to by the police she had to either admit what she had done or continue with the lie. On this occasion the story was perpetuated for 72-hours until proven to be a fabrication. The time of two detectives for three days wasted.

Rape is so impactive on genuine victims it should never be used as a weapon for revenge. False allegations create an environment where it is much harder for genuine victims to report a crime as they fear they will not be believed. The truth is genuine victims of serious violent crime receive excellent care and support from the Police and their partner agencies and those that claim falsely to have been raped risk trivialising the issue.

On my first weekend as a DS, I investigated three rapes. One of these was a woman who claimed to have been having an on/off relationship with the man who attacked her. She reported that she was at home in her living room accompanied by a friend when the accused 'H' arrived. She went to the bedroom with him leaving her friend downstairs and with her five-year-old son asleep in the bedroom next to hers. At this point she alleges that the 'H' forced her to have sex against her will. She said that she couldn't call for help as her son would have woken up and come into the room which would have been deeply distressing. She had some bruising which supported her account of resisting the attack. When I interviewed her friend she corroborated the story and said the victim told her of the assault immediately after the man had left the property. In cases of sexual assault this is known as an 'early complaint' and is admissible in evidence.

Fairly clear cut, you might think! My Detective Constable partner Trev and I located and arrested the suspect 'H' a 28-year-old man who we establish has three children to three different women. During the interview with him he made it clear that he only had casual relationships with women except for the one with whom he lives, a 19-year-old and the mother of his infant son. During questioning he maintained his innocence throughout claiming it was a 'booty call' – just casual sex and that it was a regular thing between them and was entirely consensual. Evidentially it was more difficult to prove rape as both parties stated that sex had taken place. Therefore forensic evidence was unhelpful. What was required to be established is the issue of 'consent'. The victim claimed she was raped against her will, which she maintained was made clear to the suspect. The suspect claimed sex was consensual. How then do we establish the truth?

Trev and I gathered all the available evidence which we presented to the Crown Prosecution Service (CPS) Their position given the statements from the victim and the early complaint witness statement was that they would support a charge and remand him in Prison custody where he would be remanded until his trial. The suspect was facing a probable seven years in prison. However, Trev and I believed he was telling the truth but even after several conversations with the victim she was adamant that she had been raped and that she wanted her attacker in jail.

Now here's the tricky bit. I instructed Trev to re interview the witness who was in the lounge at the time of the alleged rape. To be fair Trev was trying his best to be helpful to her by making clear that if she was to lie in the Court the maximum sentence for perjury is seven years and that he believed that she is lying. After some introspection she decided enough was enough and that she isn't that close a friend to our victim to warrant going to prison for her. She revised her account which clarified the events of the evening in question. The suspect had arrived at the house as expected as her friend 'the victim' had already told her that he was coming round and that she would be having sex with him that evening so to listen out for her son in case he woke up. The witness then went on to say that the suspect came downstairs said goodbye to her and left. Her friend came down soon after in tears as she was furious with the suspect.

The 'victim' then told the witness that after sex she had said she wanted to see more of him and have a proper relationship and not just casual sex. He had replied telling her she was just a 'booty call' and that he had a partner and child of his own and he didn't need another one. She said he had spoken to her like she was a whore and he had made her feel used and worthless. She told her friend she would make him pay for the way he treated her and it is at this point she decided to concoct the story that she had been forcibly raped. She had injured herself so make it appear that she had been forcibly raped. She asked her friend to support her story and she had agreed, not understanding the gravity of the consequences. Trev recorded a formal retraction statement from the witness and came back to brief me.

I informed the CPS and the suspect what had happened and released him without charge. 'H' knew he had had a lucky escape. After all he was only a few hours from a windowless bus ride to Lincoln Prison. I hoped that this might be some kind of lesson in morality for him but I doubted he would learn from it. I reinterviewed the 'victim' who admitted everything but showed no remorse whatsoever. She said she would have been happy for him to spend the next seven years in jail. I charged her with wasting Police time which went... absolutely no where as it was dropped by the Crown Prosecution Service later on.

Rape is a very serious matter for both, a bona fide victim and wrongly accused suspect. Rape is easy to allege and incredibly difficult to disprove. The initial assumption should always be to believe and support the victim.

Sadly though probably because it was a city centre my colleagues and I investigated numerous false allegations.

CHAPTER EIGHTEEN

Opportunity knocks

After about nine months of working hard as a DS, busy establishing my credibility amongst the hierarchy when another opportunity arose. The City had been suffering an increasing number of street robberies, often violent, always terrifying for the victim. At this time the City was home in term-time to over 30,000 students studying across the two University campuses'.

They were young, often naive and ambivalent to crime prevention advice. They may as well have had 'victim' stamped on their foreheads to make it even easier for criminals to target them. The indigenous street robbers from St Ann's, The Meadows and Radford had a field day, stealing cash, credit cards, cell phones and pretty much anything else they could use or sell on. The problem was out of control and becoming politically untenable for both the University Vice Chancellors and Chief Constable. Nottingham was starting to hit the national headlines for the wrong reasons and student applications were diminishing at an alarming rate. Hardly surprising, what parent would want to send their pride and joy to a crime ridden City?

I had just completed my intermediate CID course in Wakefield where I learned far more about complex, serious and series investigation methods such as DNA and psychological profiling, the use of cell phone data to gather evidence of conversations and to geographically map cell phones (and their owners) to certain locations.

So to mitigate the risk facing the City of Nottingham a Robbery Squad was established with one Detective Sergeant and eight Detective Constables and I was chosen to lead it. This was a great opportunity not only to resolve a cancerous problem in the city but to build on my CV and gain invaluable experience in leadership and serious and series crime investigation. But such opportunities are not without risk and I had to succeed or my reputation and status would be in jeopardy and I might fall by the career wayside. Once again I was pushed outside my comfort zone but I was becoming used to living in that space and actually relished it. This was a new team and there were some who would have been happy to see it and me fail. Teams are often perceived as elitist probably because they attract talented and ambitious individuals who are prepared to work hard to be successful. Often those not motivated to succeed or step outside their comfort zone don't like to see others do well.

It was 1994, I was 34 years old and as a late joiner at 25, I had some catching up to do. I had been guaranteed my Sergeant's position through the support of my managers and partial success on the National Accelerated Promotion Scheme. But now it was solely down to me to make success happen. Fortuitously the force introduced an internal scheme similar in design to the National APS and having recently passed my Inspectors exams applied immediately.

The boys on the Robbery Team were great, self motivated, bright and what they may have lacked in experience they made up for with enthusiasm. You always had to be on your toes as the boys were always up to something, anything for a laugh. I enjoyed working 'hands on' with the team, and we established our credibility quickly. One day Andy one of my team members and I were out looking for robbery suspects that we had identified when we came across a man wanted for failing to appear at Court on robbery charges. He walked into a relatively quiet street in Radford and we parked the car and followed on foot. We approached him and told him he was under arrest. He immediately kicked off and as I tried to handcuff him he started lashing out. We all fell on the ground and I wrestled with him to get the cuffs on, managing to secure one wrist. Then it erupted, from nowhere a large number of locals appeared, shouting abuse and egging the suspect on to resist. I called for assistance leaving the channel open so the control room could hear and record what was going on. I got a second handcuff on but as I tried to stand up Andy and I were attacked by the mob who were kicking at us repeatedly. This was getting out of hand and I hoped the back-up would arrive as soon as. The van had gone to the wrong street and then realised their mistake but eventually turned up and arrested a number of the mob. Andy and I had our man but I don't mind admitting I was beginning to think we were in for a real hiding. When the matter got to Crown Court Andy and I thought it would be a quick guilty plea and job done but our man had pleaded not guilty to the assaults on us and produced seven witnesses to corroborate his account, which was that we attacked and assaulted him. After the sixth witness gave similar testimony I was worried, even I was beginning to believe them and I knew it was bollocks. If I was doubtful, then the judge might actually believe them as it all sounded quite plausible. When the final witness took to the stand the Judge turned to her and warned her of the sentence for perjury. It did the trick and she said that the accused had attacked us and that the crowd, some of whom were witnesses in court had also attacked us. It was a massive relief. The accused was sentenced for the initial robbery to five years and an additional twelve months for Police assault.

Back in the office I devised a basic intelligence system to collate all robbery suspects details including photographs, mobile phone numbers and clothing as many wore the same expensive trainers, jackets and caps over and over. Once we had their photograph we built albums of suspects which allowed victims to identify their assailants. This predated any meaningful intelligence system which simply didn't exist at this time. We arrested and charged dozens of offenders and started to work on the Courts and decision makers such as the Crown Prosecutors, Magistrates and Judges. I made presentations to highlight the impact on robbery victims many of which were traumatised, some even dropping out of University and also the damage caused to the reputation of Nottingham City as a place to work, live, study and visit. It did the trick and we had some significant sentences passed for violent knifepoint robberies, seven years became the norm.

This sent shockwaves through the criminal fraternity who until the formation of the team had little chance of being caught let alone convicted. Robberies reduced significantly, I felt proud of my team but also successful in my own right. This was my team and success or otherwise was down to my leadership. I had minimal supervision and had a free rein as long as we were successful. Having an opportunity to create and build a successful enterprise was exciting, interesting and challenging and I thrived on it. I understood myself more and more I had found my forte not just as a Police Officer and investigator but enjoyed building new systems, processes and developing people and teams. I also knew that once the team had achieved success and was working effectively I would seek out the next challenge.

As I said before, once you've had the taste of success it's like a drug and once the job became routine or I felt I was coasting I immediately craved for more.

CHAPTER NINETEEN

Abbie Humphries

Then, on 1 July 1994 I was thrust into the largest investigation Nottingham had ever seen, before or since and for the next 17 days it dominated the lives of every person involved.

I took a phone call in the robbery office, 'There's a briefing at West Bridgford incident room in thirty minutes. Be there' and that's all I knew. I was at work in the City so drove the three miles to Bridgford and when I pulled into the street leading to the Station saw dozens of cars lining the footpaths and the station car park was rammed. Something big was happening, and I headed for the briefing room excited by what might lie ahead as I saw numerous colleagues from every corner of the Force in attendance. There must have been sixty detectives of various ranks present. I took a seat and then in walked the Senior Investigating Officer (SIO).

Detective Superintendent Harry Sheppard. I didn't know him personally but knew he had a fearful reputation. Supposedly he was aggressive and dictatorial and thought nothing of publicly humiliating anyone that displeased him. He was old school.

But in walked a reinvented Harry, he was smiling at those he knew but also appeared a little worried as he greeted everyone and I felt a positive vibe in the room.

He got straight to it. A new born baby girl, Abbie Humphries had been taken from her parents in the Maternity Ward of Nottingham's Queen's Medical Centre (QMC). The QMC is a huge facility the size of a small town. A woman posing as a paediatric nurse had approached the child's father, Roger whilst the mother Karen had gone to the bathroom. Roger in complete innocence handed his baby daughter Abbie over to the woman believing she was going for a routine examination. Neither he, nor Karen saw her again. Now it was up to us to find her and as any trained SIO knows in child abduction cases time is of the essence if the child is to be found alive. Harry made clear that this was 'THE' only priority for the force and every resource would be made available. As it turned out we would need them.

I pretty much lived at work for the following three weeks. But what took everyone by surprise was the scale of the international media's appetite for this story. Once it hit the UK headlines the worlds press seemed to descend upon the affluent suburb of West Bridgford. The local church hall was commandeered to house them for media briefings and it was standing room only.

Harry informed the team that he expected a collaborative approach where everyone had a voice and an opportunity to express their opinion. And so it was for the initial 48-hours but once the pressure came on top he gradually reverted to type and shut down anyone with an opinion that differed from his own. This stifled creativity and debate and no one dared challenge the decisions made.

I was a mere Detective Sergeant and my role was within the HOLMES Room (Home Office Large Major Enquiry System) named after the fictional character and super sleuth Sherlock Holmes and not sadly yours truly. The HOLMES computer system revolutionised major investigation of series and complex cases and if it had existed at the time of the Yorkshire Ripper he would have been brought to justice far sooner than he was and lives would have been saved. It wasn't but it was here now and would be the repository for thousands of information reports, witness statements, documents and actions. HOLMES was capable of facilitating searches on key words, people, vehicles, addresses etc and could link all of these disparate pieces of information together. If John Smith appeared as a person of interest the system could draw together a profile from information input to the system. So if you entered his name you would see, vehicles, addresses, associates, mobile phones, previous intelligence reports, photographs and criminal history.

I had been fully trained in all management aspects of the system. On this occasion my role was Action Allocator. I utilised the system to manage 'Actions' (tasks) that I prioritised and assigned to those working on the investigation. This meant I had to continually review the actions in the queue. This felt like quite a burden, if I missed something that could lead to Abbie's recovery or prevent harm to her I would be devastated. So every morning at 7am I would review all the pending actions and reprioritise where necessary, allocating HP (High Priority) tasks at the daily briefing and explaining their relevance. Officers would then complete the task and update the outcome of the action on HOLMES. Any intelligence such as Vehicles, Nominals (names) etc would be linked on HOLMES.

After a couple of days we were in full swing with dozens of staff working from the incident room. It was then we met Abbie's parents, Roger and Karen and her brother Charlie. They had asked Harry to meet the team charged with finding their beloved daughter. They were just a normal couple who were devastated by the loss of their child. They expressed their faith in Harry and the team and everyone in the room was touched by their grief. If motivation was needed by anyone, they just got it in spades.

I spoke to Roger and Karen explaining my role and they asked me if I had any children of my own. I told them of Olivia who was four years old and tried to reassure them that we would do everything possible to find Abbie and return her to them safely. I hoped I was right.

We were also joined by a documentary team from ITV, Central Television. They had been given permission by the Chief to have access to the investigation and they would watch and record pretty much everything.

That first evening they were there I got chatting to the producer who made their position clear, 'It'll either be a good news story for the family and Notts Police, or a disaster story, I don't see any middle ground.'

'Bloody hell,' I thought. This seriously needs a happy ending and I have my own small but important part to play and it will be recorded for all to see.

As the days passed there was no end in sight. Due to the TV coverage and some ill-judged information releases by senior officers we were swamped with calls and letters from the public and other Forces. Psychics and mediums came out en mass to tell us where we could find Abbie. All complete bollocks of course, but it still had to be read and processed wasting valuable time.

One key line of enquiry was to track down all expectant mothers due around the birth date of Abbie the theory being that one may have lost a child and have taken Abbie to fill the emotional void. We had a behavioural criminal psychologist Paul Britton attached to the team but he only spoke with Harry and in my opinion had far too much influence on the direction of the investigation. He would later face severe criticism for his role in the arrest and wrongful conviction of Colin Stagg in 1992 who was acquitted some years later for the Rachel Nickel Murder.

About six days in to the enquiry we had a call from a national newspaper. They had a letter from a woman claiming to have abducted Abbie. He motivation was purely financial and she wanted the newspaper to pay for her story. She gave details of a wig she had worn and the newspaper editor seemed convinced it was worth following up. He had a phone number and a first name. This was by far the most promising lead we had and Harry assigned me to conduct a background check and to locate the woman.

Harry also tasked Paul Britton and Sue Gregory to work with me and to start work on a suspect profile, Sue was a Senior Social Worker assigned to the outside investigation team. It was about 6pm and most of the enquiry team had left for the day. Since I was given the job as Action Allocator and wasn't even a part of the outside investigation team and I wondered why Harry had chosen me to locate and recover Abbie.

I found the address through a phone subscriber check with the telecoms company and with this information Sue, Paul and I headed for the social services office that covered the area of Eastwood where she lived. It was about midnight when we read her social services files and Paul was convinced that this woman met the profile of our abductor. She was mid thirties with several children of her own but had mental health issues and had been violent towards her previous partner in the recent past. The address was a mid-terrace and I had a floor plan of the internal layout with all entrances and exits. There were no dogs in the house so no nasty surprises hopefully. I had a team of Force Support officers ready to go as these men and women were trained in effecting entry to premises and controlling any threat faced.

It was about 1.30am when I briefed the team leader telling him what to expect when we got there and what items other than Abbie of course we were looking for. My spirits were high and the adrenaline pushed back any fatigue I might have felt as there was a strong possibility that we would soon have Abbie safe in our custody. We approached the house quietly and Force Support did what they do best. They tried the door but it was locked so reverted to the 'universal key' a large 40 kg cylinder with handles either side, a mini battering ram which split the door frame with ease allowing us to enter. The team secured each room and I entered the living room. The house was in a terrible state, thread bare carpets, a tatty three-piece suite, wallpaper peeling off the mouldy walls and sat on the tatty sofa was our suspect. A diminutive woman in her 30s but she looked much older. She'd had a hard life. We found five children in the house living in squalor. Three to one bed which was a mattress on the floor and ages ranging from 5 to 16 years old.

I looked at the team leader for some positive confirmation that he had found Abbie but he looked back at me ashen faced and shook his head. No sign of Abbie. We searched the house and found press cuttings of the abduction hidden under the carpet and a receipt for a brunette-coloured wig, this wasn't looking good. I updated Harry and continued the search. At that point it looked like she was our abductor and with no sign of the baby, we were all extremely worried. I cautioned the suspect and when I spoke to her it was clear she had some significant psychological issues and that it was pointless trying to get anything meaningful from her at that time. The suspect was arrested to be taken to West Bridgford for interview and her children were taken to a place of safety by Sue. The house was locked down as a crime scene to be examined later that day. I was deflated fearing the worst as I drove back to the incident room arriving back at 4am. I met Harry on my return and filled him in on the details, we were gutted. It was late and I was emotionally drained. There was nothing else I could do here and now so I drove the 45 minutes home. It had been another long day a 22-hour shift. I fell asleep thinking about Roger and Karen and what they must be going through. My own daughter, Olivia just four years old and so precious, I couldn't imagine life without her. Roger and Karen were completely powerless and totally dependent upon us, the Police to find their new born daughter. That responsibility weighed heavy, believe me.

I returned to work at midday after a fitful sleep rerunning the previous day's events and the priority action list in my dreams. We debriefed the events of the previous night with the entire enquiry team present and two senior Detectives were tasked with interviewing our suspect. We tried to carry on as normal but still feared for Abbie's safety. Soon it became clear to the interviewing officers that our suspect was a fantasist with significant mental health issues who had created an elaborate hoax in an attempt to extort money from the media. Even though it was disappointing that we hadn't caught the abductor it was a huge relief to know Abbie was probably still out there, alive and well. In truth, statistically, we were told that if an abducted child is not found safe and well in the first 72-hours then it is highly probable that they have been killed. That said, these statistics related to older children not infants so we were optimistic that we would find her alive.

Every SIO (Senior Investigating Officer) conducting a serious crime investigation begins with a hypothesis which is predicated upon the facts surrounding the case. Those things that are known. The differing theories relating to Abbie's abduction were all reasonable and the key hypotheses were:

Abbie was taken from her parents by a white female in her 20s. Her motive may have been either:

1. To replace a child recently deceased post or ante natal.

2. To care for the child as her own.

3. Taken on behalf of a third party.

It was clear that whoever the abductor was they had Abbie with them in public for some time on the day of the abduction and someone would most likely have seen both baby and abductor. It was also highly likely that the suspect lived locally in the Nottingham area. Harry's intention was to gather as much information as possible on women who fit the above criteria and to visit them. This included, all recently bereaved mothers of infants or stillborn, recently delivered mothers and any women who were reported to have a newly acquired baby.

For the officers tasked with visiting these women they were given clear instructions chief amongst which were:

4. See the female in person.

5. See the infant in person.

6. Check and verify the birth record book (the red book given to all mothers of a new born). Simple you might think, I did, yet not everyone seemed to interpret the instruction as literally as intended

105

and it would prove costly.

During the following days we received an overwhelming amount of information but I kept on top of the actions ensuring that the target 'Mothers' group were all seen and the instructions undertaken. Once completed I would update the HOLMES system and close down that line of enquiry unless of course there were any outstanding issues.

One such 'Mother' action was to visit a house on Brendon Drive, Wollaton – quite close to the Queen's Medical Centre. The officer was tasked to see the mother Julie Kelly and the baby and cross check details in the red book.

The action was returned as completed and filed by me as such.

Harry became increasingly irritable and seemed to overly rely even more on the opinions of Paul Britton, that may not have been the case but it seemed that way to the rest of the team. At the same time there were rumours circulating that Harry was to be replaced with a fresh pair of eyes, a new SIO as Command thought the investigation lacked focus and was getting side tracked. Probably they were just getting a ton of shit because Abbie hadn't been found and it was eating a large portion of the Forces annual budget. It is true that initially on Britton's advice, Harry took a softly, softly approach, initially appealing to the abductors conscience which clearly didn't work and in my experience criminals seem to have had the 'conscience' strand deleted from their DNA. Following that, he appealed on national TV to friends and family of the abductor to help. This produced huge amounts of information and hoaxers which side tracked the investigation for days. Gary from Gloucester was the main hoaxer claiming to know the whereabouts of Abbie and sucking in valuable investigative resources even resulting in TV appeals and the eventual realisation that Gary was a hoaxer. Gary was charged with wasting Police time and remanded to prison for his own protection.

I was seventeen days into the investigation and at 8pm on the Friday and after another 13-hour shift my work was done. I decided to have a quick pint in the station bar before heading home for the night. The station bar was full of cops and their families and it was like walking into a parallel universe. I had practically lived and breathed the investigation and had no social life at all whilst everyone else was just living their normal life. At the bar I was met by the Central TV producer who bought me a much-needed pint of Stella. We chatted and I asked him what his plans were now we were heading quickly towards our fourth week of filming. We had got to know one another quite well after seeing each other every day and he was relaxed but candid. 'Well, Nick, we're pulling out on Monday and it rather looks like it will be a bad news story for the family and of course Notts Police.' *Shit*, I thought but then what else could they do? We must have missed something somewhere along the line or we would have found the abductor by now surely? And then literally within sixty seconds of this conversation one of the incident room staff appeared and approached me, he could hardly contain his excitement, 'Nick, you need to come back into the room, I think we've found her,' he said in a hurry. I didn't even get chance to finish my pint and dashed back to the office.

All thoughts of going home disappeared and I was feeling positive for the first time in a while. In the incident room a small group of people who were still working had gathered. Harry opened proceedings. 'We think we've found the abductor. The midwife for one Julie Kelly has just returned after 14-days holiday in America and has only just seen the news. She states Julie can't have had a baby as she is only three months pregnant.'

'We had previously left a message for the midwife to confirm the birth of a girl to a Julie Kelly of a house on Brendan Drive but she had only just got it.'

The name rang a bell so I checked HOLMES and said, 'Boss, Force Support have been to this address and signed off the action as completed. So they must have checked it all out.' I reported. Harry wasn't convinced, 'Get hold of the officer who signed off the action,

I want to speak to him.'

So Harry sketched out a plan, surveillance was placed on the front and rear of the house and all movement would be filmed and logged. As far as we knew, the occupants, Julie Kelly her partner Leigh Gilbert and his mother were all home. Central TV would film everything. I was tasked once again with gaining entry to the house and locating, identifying and retrieving Abbie.

Accompanied by an entry team of Force Support we headed to a holding point. Harry had spoken to the Force Support officer who had visited previously and he had admitted to not seeing either Julie or the red book. They did however speak to Leigh Gilbert who in the Officers words acted like any proud new father but said his wife was in bed poorly so they decided not to disturb her. The Officer saw congratulatory cards from family and well wishers openly on display so all appeared perfectly normal. I can only imagine the conversation Harry had with him. A very painful lesson to learn for the individual concerned.

The house on Brendon Drive was a smart semi-detached on a typical lower middle class suburban street and just before 1am we got the word to execute. Force Support knocked politely and were greeted by a stunned Leigh Gilbert faced with a small army of Police Officers. I informed Gilbert why we were there and moved past him to go upstairs. Force Support secured the downstairs rooms. I headed straight for a bedroom which I somehow instinctively knew was where Abbie was and opened the door.

Julie Kelly was awake and got up from the bed, I saw an infant in a cot at the bedside. I told her why I was there and asked Force Support to secure her downstairs. She did not say a thing which gave me real hope that we had found Abbie but doubts raced through my mind. What if it wasn't her? What if I got the identification wrong or wasn't 100% sure? Totally irrational I know but I had to know I was right. The weight of responsibility felt incredible. Abbie had a birthmark that we had not made public as well as a shock of blonde hair that she was born with. I picked the child up from the cot and confirmed her gender – check, blonde hair – check, and then finally her birthmark – check. She looked so vulnerable but she was clean and looked cared for, no doubt completely oblivious to all of the fuss and commotion around her. This was Abbie Humphries and she was in my arms and I wasn't letting her go until I saw Karen and Roger.

I let everyone know the confirmation over my radio, wrapped her in a birthing blanket given to me by Karen and carried Abbie down the stairs and out into the cold night air. I was emotional, and felt an immediate perhaps irrational connection with Abbie. Maybe I just felt protective of her in the absence of her parents. I had got to know Karen and Roger over the past 17 days meeting and speaking with them regularly. This had become far more than just a job for all of us. I walked along Brendon Drive holding Abbie, followed by the camera crew and when I was asked how I felt I found it difficult to answer and said, maybe, just maybe with a slight tear in my eye, 'I'm a little bit choked if I'm honest.' In the following weeks and months I got ripped unmercifully for that. But sometimes it's good to show that cops actually have emotions too.

We headed to the Queen's Medical Centre where Abbie was given a clean bill of health by a paediatrician and then the door opened and in walked Karen and Roger weeping uncontrollably. We all hugged as I handed Abbie to Karen. It was incredibly moving just seeing the relief and unbridled joy in their faces. They needed time together as a family so I said my goodbyes and headed back to Bridgford. After a debrief with Harry and the team I called my wife Jenny and she was at work on an early shift at the hospital. She said she knew something must be happening when I hadn't come home from work the night before. Living at work and having little outside contact, not even watching the news I hadn't realised quite how Abbie's story had gripped the wider public. When Jenny passed on the news of Abbie's recovery to her colleagues I heard a huge cheer and spontaneous round of applause. Special moments that we will cherish forever.

You might wonder as did I how Julie Kelly managed to convince her partner and family that Abbie was her baby. She had planned the whole deception for some time. Nine months previously her boyfriend Leigh had told her he was leaving her, she panicked and her response was to tell him he couldn't leave as she was pregnant with his child. He agreed to stay and from that point she feigned pregnancy. She put on weight and ensured that everyone even Leigh only saw her fully clothed. He fully believed that he was an expectant father. As the months passed and the due date loomed ever closer Julie Kelly decided to steal another mother's baby. She bought a wig to hide her own hair and dressed as a hospital worker. It was then she decided to take a newborn baby from her parents.

Security in 1994 was not what it is today and Kelly was able to walk straight onto the maternity ward pretend to be a nurse taking the baby for weighing and take Abbie from her father's arms. She left the unit without being noticed or challenged and went straight home. Her parents and partner believed she had given birth unexpectedly and the celebrations began. It's a little wonder that when Force Support checked the address they were taken in by what they found, it wasn't exactly a stolen child being hidden from the outside world. But if they had done as the action instructed they would have established it was in fact Abbie at that address.

At the end of another 24-plus hour shift I went home cuddled Olivia and watched the news. Olivia may have been only four years old but I know she understood her daddy had done something important and was amazed to see him on the television. That night there was to be a 'Abbie Humphries two hour special' on ITV and I set my video recorder. On the Saturday I took the family for dinner in Nottingham and was immediately recognised by strangers who had followed the story on TV. I had people thanking me, shaking my hand and it felt good. Most of a policeman's life is spent dealing with negativity and bad people and rarely do you get positive feedback. So

I made the most of this time as I knew it would soon end and I would be back to reality.

The TV documentary aired and in the end it was a good news story for Nottinghamshire Police. I appeared on *Crime Stalker* a TV show followed by an interview by Anna Soubry, a Barrister, TV presenter and these days Politician. My headline in one Sunday paper was 'The Safest Arms in Britain' which was my introduction on the show. I enjoyed all of the media attention and gained confidence from it. Central TV hosted a 'wrap' party for the enquiry team and we drank the place dry. The producer made a big fuss and presented me with a framed photograph of baby Abbie in my arms as I left Brendon Drive.

It had been an incredible three weeks or so and one that left me elated and brimming with confidence and ambition. I never did find out why it was that Harry selected me to recover baby Abbie when I wasn't even a part of the outside investigation team. I have a theory that he was thinking ahead to all the media attention and probably thought I would present a positive image for policing and would be able to handle the attention.

A month or so after Abbie's safe return Jenny, Olivia and I were invited to attend Abbie's christening. It was a lovely sunny day and it was great to see the family united and happy again. They had sold their story to a national newspaper for a six-figure sum, so out of huge adversity came some good and they would be set up for life. Soon after they emigrated to New Zealand where they still live today.

CHAPTER TWENTY

By hook or by crook

The Inspector Boards were not too far away and that would be my next goal. Jenny and I were skint, as usual and hadn't planned a summer holiday but the overtime I had earned on Abbie's case gave us enough to book a cheap Disney holiday in Florida. We had a great time despite staying in the worlds crappiest motel but the weather turned after a few days so we left Kissimee and headed for Clearwater where we stayed at the Hilton on the beach which wasn't crappy at all. Olivia learned to swim and we soaked up some much-needed rays and relaxation.

On our return it was back to the Robbery Team and planning for the Inspector Boards. The Detective Inspector, Ken called a meeting of the eight Detective Sergeants and once again in true old school Detective fashion selected his favourites to put forward for any Acting Inspector opportunities. Of course as expected I didn't get a mention and knew I would have to seek opportunities elsewhere. At this time cronyism was rife in Nottinghamshire Police. Every selection process appeared to be a carve up and if you didn't know you had the job when you walked into the interview then you invariably didn't get it.

As a Sergeant I had applied for two positions one on Force Support and the other Detective Sergeant on the Drugs Squad. Force Support was a closed shop. If you hadn't done time on there as a Constable then you had zero chance getting on as a Sergeant. A friend of mine was interviewed for the same position as me and had been on Force

Support previously and because of that was in the loop. He knew he wasn't in the running because his best mate had told him the job was his but he had made the effort to show willing and position himself for the next vacancy. His mate got the job as predicted and he got the next vacancy. I decided that maybe Force Support wasn't for me. I had more chance of being the next man in space.

The Drug Squad interview could not have gone better I had prepared meticulously and stormed it. I didn't get the job. I did find out a few years later when sharing a car journey with a member of the interview panel, that I had come top on the interview process but it was pre-ordained that another guy, Bill, who played rugby with the Drug Squad DI would get it. I would work with Bill later when we had both left the Police and he confirmed this.

So Ken the DI considering who would get the acting Inspector opportunities said to me, 'Sergeant, you haven't got enough wool on your back so it won't be happening this time.'

I smiled at him. *Fuck that*, I thought, *I've got a different plan.*

So I went to see the Divisional Superintendent Jim Smith who I knew rated me and had previously been very supportive. I told him of the CID situation and asked him to keep me in mind should any uniformed Acting Inspector opportunities arise. He seemed impressed that I was willing to go back into uniform from the CID to gain the experience. I kept my head down and after a few short weeks got the call. I was Acting Inspector at Central. I don't know if it was complacency or apathy but none of my CID colleagues who were intent on promotion had even approached the Superintendent for acting opportunities.

One thing I know is you have to seek out opportunities, they will very rarely land on your lap. You need to push outside your comfort zone as it is there that you find the real learning, opportunity and recognition. You need to stand out from the herd if you want to get noticed. I was a rank outsider for promotion but the worst-case scenario would be gaining experience and more evidence of performing well in the rank and importantly experience of the selection process. I was given an Acting Inspector position in the City and set about building my evidence portfolio of accomplishment in the rank. In any fair job selection process the strongest candidate is usually the one who has proven ability in the position applied for and policing is no different. All I needed was a level playing field on which to compete.

The Inspector Boards were a few months away and the news from Human Resources came down the line. They were outsourcing promotion selection to an assessment centre at West Yorkshire Police. They must have finally had enough of the old boys' network influencing outcomes, I thought. Now it really was game on and I was in with the same chance of promotion as everyone else.

My acting stint completed I attended the assessment centre run by my old Force, West Yorkshire Police at Wakefield. The assessment took a full day and the format comprised a series of police related operational scenarios with actors playing various roles.

I was the Inspector on duty in my office when the scenario would unfold. I had a background information sheet with some scenario detail and various facts as to resources, geography, demographic, finance and personnel issues etc. I had a Police radio to communicate with other parties if required. Then an actor walked in who dropped the first line known as a 'hook'. Such as, 'Boss, I've just witnessed one of my colleagues racially abuse a staff member.'

I then had to manage and resolve the situation. I was being filmed with two independent observers scoring my performance.

There were five or six scenarios. I planned and prepared for every likely scenario and using a guide of positive behavioural traits worked out the elements that would attract positive scoring. The things I said or did.

Once again I was outside my comfort zone but the adrenaline was flowing and this was a great opportunity. I felt confident going into the process and always had that mindset that I was the one everyone else had to beat. I actually enjoyed the day as it felt almost real and my period of acting in the rank had helped enormously in building confidence and providing context. Once the scenario unfolded I forgot about the cameras and the observers and just got on with it. These things are always easier of course when you have cognitively prepared and rehearsed. Assessment over I returned to Central now back as a Detective Sergeant.

A few days later the results were announced and not one of the DI's favoured sons had passed, but I had. I had scored the highest mark which meant I would be promoted almost immediately. I had done well, so much so that the Deputy Chief Constable called me in to his office and told me I had been identified as having the potential to be fast tracked to the rank of Superintendent. It was explained to me that the privilege of being on the Internal Accelerated Promotion Scheme (APS) meant I could plan my career path and choose where and for how long I wanted to go to get experience. This sounded like Willy Wonka's golden ticket, a real game changer and I was determined to be selected and to get the most from it. I successfully passed the interview and was accepted on the APS. Gone were any doubts I may have had of my ability and potential.

My plan was simple. Where did I ultimately want to be? In my mind's eye I aspired to be a Chief Superintendent more specifically a Divisional Commander. In this role I could have responsibility for up to one thousand Police Officers and Staff. I wanted to be able control and influence at the strategic level and if I'm honest I wanted the kudos that went with it. But most importantly I wanted to provide my family with a better future and financial security.

In order to achieve my ambitions I needed the experience to secure evidence of proven ability in differing aspects of Policing. However I had seen first-hand 'external fast tracked' Senior Officers moving too quickly through the ranks in order to achieve their goals only to be found wanting when they got there. They simply didn't have the depth of knowledge and experience required to succeed. I wouldn't make that mistake. My plan took form and I was promoted as a uniform shift Inspector back to of all places – Bestwood, albeit in a brand-new state of the art police station. I planned to do up to a year there and then six-month attachments to Complaints and Discipline and Corporate Development and then back as a DI to the CID. I had identified some training courses that I would need to realise my ambitions. I was working to a timeline where I could make Chief Inspector in two to three years and Superintendent two to three years after that. So Superintendent in five to six years seemed a reasonable goal.

However, I hadn't accounted for people and politics. My plan was approved by the Deputy Chief and I settled back in at Bestwood. In truth I didn't massively enjoy my time back in uniform as the role involved voluminous amounts of paperwork, personnel issues (as ever) and custody authorisations. Within the custody suit environment authority from Inspector or Superintendent is required by law for everything from house searches, taking samples from a suspect, keeping a prisoner in custody over 24-hours etc, etc. To be honest, it was quite boring as an Inspector back in uniform. I also had to work morning, afternoon and night shifts which after the sociable hours of working CID was a pain. The only highlight was getting 'hands on' one afternoon. I was working through piles of paperwork as usual but when I looked up I saw a young PC hovering nervously by the office door.

'What's up mate?' I asked.

'Boss, sorry, but there's no one around and I think there's a burglary happening in Bestwood.'

It was clear that he was fresh out of the factory. I called Control on the radio and established no resources were available to attend and the young PC couldn't yet drive a police vehicle so I grabbed the

Inspectors car keys and my 'cuffs and baton and headed out of the door. En route the PC explained that some suspected stolen property VCR, TV etc, had been hidden at the rear of a house in Bestwood and a member of the public had been keeping watch from their bedroom window. Two young men had taken the property into to a nearby house. It appeared as though we just needed to contain the house and make entry. I called control for back up but everyone was still committed. For now it was down to me and the new boy. I parked away from the suspects address and told the young cop to go to the front door as I would be coming in through the rear. 'Don't let anyone out,' I told him.

I informed control of our location and movements. I opened the rear door and saw what was clearly stolen property piled on the kitchen table. As I moved into the lounge the two youths in their late teens saw me and ran for the front door just as the young cop opened it. They pushed past him and ran, followed by me. I chased one kid through gardens, over several fences and at least once through one, catching up with him as he scaled yet another and as is always the case I grabbed him by the collar and his jacket slipped off him. So I had a handful of jacket but no burglar. I went over the fence again and saw him disappear through the gap in another fence into some rough ground covered in gorse bushes. I could hear my heart pounding in my ears, I was fit but 35-years-old, and the youth was about 18 and running for his life. He dived under and into the bushes and I followed, I grabbed his ankle and pulled him back towards me but he kicked out striking my right cheek bone. I remember thinking to myself, 'Right you little bastard, no more messing around,' and went in after him. The thorny bushes tore at my face and I eventually emerged to see him climbing yet another fence. I followed and shouted breathlessly into my radio, instructing anyone listening to cut him off. I was about 10-yards behind him and closing as he ran into the street and straight into the welcoming arms of an intercepting cop. I was shattered but filled with adrenaline. I was disappointed I hadn't caught up with him to return the painful complement but at least we had our man. I went back to the house, made sure the property was recovered and called the CID to get involved. As the adrenaline subsided I went to the station bathroom and saw my face in the mirror. My cheekbone was swollen and I had numerous bleeding cuts on my hands and face. I looked a sorry state. I cleaned myself up and thought to myself, maybe I'm getting a bit old for this. I certainly felt a pang of vulnerability which was uncomfortable for an alpha male.

CID established that the recovered property came from three burglaries the pair committed that day, so all in all a job well done and I made sure that the young cop felt valued for his part. He'd certainly have a story to tell his mates in the pub. The rest of my time at Bestwood was a mixture of routine, boredom and internal petty political game playing with a couple of 'lifer' Inspectors, guys who were coming to the end of their service and happy in their rank. But I guess it is all part of the rite of passage and part of the learning experience. It was still boring though and lacked real challenge. And that for me epitomises life inside the comfort zone.

They say, 'karma's a bitch' and it's true. Sometimes what goes around comes around. Remember PC Tosser from my early Bestwood days? Well, I got a call from a Vice Squad Inspector asking whether I would recommend Tosser for a position he had applied for. I made my view on him and his character flaws crystal clear. I don't know if that influenced any decision making but I later learned he had been unsuccessful in his application. I didn't shed a tear.

CHAPTER TWENTY-ONE

A necessary evil

After a little over a year I started with my attachments, firstly on the rubber heel squad (Complaints and Discipline) and then Corporate Development. It was strange being away from the front line but nevertheless a valuable experience. Complaints was just unenjoyable, I can think of nothing worse than investigating complaints against fellow cops. In my six months there I probably dealt with two genuine complaints out of thirty or so I investigated. Some members of the British public I'm sad to say are just vexatious twats who seem to gain tremendous satisfaction from wasting Police resources in order to satisfy their need to score points or cause unnecessary grief to another human being. I was glad to leave.

Corporate Development was an alien world to me. The Department consisted of a handful of Police Officers and about thirty or so Police Staff. A mixed bag of Analysts, Statisticians, Planners and Administrative staff.

Their main role in life appeared to me to be compiling information from around the organisation and then producing lots of tables, graphs and charts to show people what they already knew. To be fair to them this kind of business planning was relatively new to Policing and it would be re shaped and improved massively in the years that followed.

So in essence this resource served only the Chief Officers because individual business Heads of Service tended to know what was going on in their area of command. Performance management was virtually non-existent at this time but it would become a major feature in the years ahead. I've over simplified their role perhaps as they also informed the budget planning process and setting the simplistic targets everyone permanently chased. There was lots of bean counting but rarely any quality evaluation.

For example they could provide a figure for say the number of detected house burglaries in Division 'A' but could not evaluate their efficacy. They only counted what was provided to them and there was zero quality validation.

I was frustrated and needed a purpose. It was clear Nottinghamshire when compared nationally suffered unfavourably from house burglaries. So I looked at different national initiatives aimed at reducing and detecting burglary. I visited the best performing Forces and took ideas from them, building a new strategy for Nottinghamshire. It was more than locks, alarms and targeted patrol, but involved numerous partner agencies looking at reducing reoffending rates and proactively targeting prolific offenders. It included housing and welfare and drug rehabilitation. The plan was to remove as many of the causation factors from the Burglary problem as possible. By doing this in a problem-solving way we could minimise the risk and harm.

I also visited the secret countryside location of the Security Services to explore any 'technical' solutions that they might be able to offer in reducing criminality. It was a brilliant day and I met with the boss in his office to discuss the issues at hand. He was just like a fictional character from a spy movie but the real deal, the genuine 'M' of the Secret Service. On his desk was a Bren light machine gun mounted on a tripod. Yes, it was a little daunting and as for the man himself he wore a checked tweed hunting suit and bright yellow braces holding up the pants. He was one of those larger-than-life characters and a hell of nice guy. He opened the doors to their secret 'Q' branch research facility where I secured a number of highly advanced technical solutions to facilitate the surveillance of our target criminals. With every avenue explored to reduce house burglary, Operation Safer Homes was implemented Force wide.

It was around this time that I embarked on a Degree programme, a BSc (Hons) in Policing and Criminology. I didn't really see this as assisting my career progression but wanted to prove to myself I wasn't a complete duffer having wasted my grammar school education. It was hard going but I was working regular days with weekends off and Olivia had started school so I had the time to commit to it for the next three years.

I was busy collating evidence for what I thought would be the next inevitable promotion then one day I was in the office busy counting paper clips when a flustered looking Chief Superintendent walked in and said I had to be at a meeting with the Chief in 30 minutes. *Intriguing*, I thought and hopefully something of real interest at last.

Be careful what you wish for!

The Chief Constable Steve Green and the Chief Superintendent entered the room containing a number of Detective Inspectors and myself. Steve was an affable man and top of his class at the Police Staff College where Chief Officers are grown in test tubes to be sent out into the world to lead the 43 Police Forces in England and Wales. Steve had initiated a total force restructure which was described by one senior officer as 'a text book change management implementation of the grand plan. If only the plan hadn't been fundamentally flawed!' Everyone, even I knew the restructure was a bad idea in almost every respect and so it would prove in the years ahead.

As part of a national crime audit the Home Office had sampled some crime reports (C1) and detected crime write off reports (C2) and had found anomalies at two of the four policing divisions. I was tasked with undertaking a crime audit at 'A' Division the area covering Mansfield and Ashfield. I was told by the Chief Constable that I would be fully supported by the Divisional Commander and their staff to enable and assist the audit process. I doubted that, especially if there was fire beneath the smoke. We worked out a template, work schedule, time scales and the reporting process. I was to reveal nothing I found to anyone other than the Chief. The following day I arrived at 'A' Division HQ at Mansfield Police Station and was treated like I had the plague.

I physically removed hundreds of hard copy handwritten crime reports for burglary and auto crime. The Divisional Commander 'AC' approached me on day one. He was a proud but arrogant man, old school and he lived and breathed Policing and it defined him. He would routinely boast of his divisional detection rates that were the highest in the Force. He also had a reputation for being outspoken and vindictive. Great news

He said I would find nothing, that his Detectives acted with honesty and integrity but if there were any anomalies I was to give him the heads up. I was immediately conflicted but knew I could only play this one way and that was with a straight bat. As I read through the reports it was evident there was a large-scale problem. The C1 crime report was a handwritten paper copy and contained the location, time, day, date of the offence and the detailed MO (Modus Operandi). How the offender made entry, what was stolen, any mess made and point of exit. The C2 report was submitted when the crime was detected and included the offenders details and any property recovered and also connected detected crimes. Where there were other offences admitted they could be Taken Into Consideration know as TIC's.

The courts would sentence an individual for their crime but also matters TIC which might attract additional sentencing but with consideration if the perpetrator had freely admitted their crimes and assisted the Police. This was a means for a prolific offender to 'clean their slate' so if later on down the line new evidence came to light linking them to a crime TIC they couldn't be re arrested and charged.

After 48 hours my colleagues and I reconvened with the Chief at Force HQ.

'Gentlemen an update on where we are please.'

We started with 'A', I informed him that I had found dozens of burglary reports that had been closed as detected but devoid of any evidence on the C2 to support that conclusion. The transcripts and tape recordings of interviews with the suspect contained either contradictory or no evidence that they committed the crime yet the C2 had been filed as detected.

'How many are we looking at?' he asked.

'Chief... it's in the hundreds.'

One of the other DI's reported anomalies at one of the other Divisions but not on the same scale. The other Divisions were clean.

I'm pretty sure the Chief suspected what was going on for a while but possibly not the scale. I returned to complete the audit but the Chief must have put AC on notice because he once again turned up at my door and in a voice loud enough for everybody in the outer offices to hear said, 'You need to get a real job investigating criminals, not wasting time on a witch hunt.'

I replied calmly, 'Just doing what the Chief asked me to do Sir, before the Home Office do it to us.'

I didn't realise at the time, only much later that AC would sabotage my career, twice over the next few years. He was vindictive with a capital 'V'. What was it I said about 'karma being a bitch?' The outcome of our investigation prompted the Chief to report our yearly crime figures to the Home Office as 'unreliable' which meant that when the Home Office published the National statistics for the 43 forces in England and Wales in the media there was an asterisk next to Nottingham and a footnote stating 'unreliable'.

Nottingham was starting to flag itself to the Home Office as a troublesome Force and the Chief Constable did himself very few favours as he seemed intent upon challenging them at every opportunity. Of course there was only ever going to be one winner in that shit fight and it wasn't Steve, and so it proved.

CHAPTER TWENTY-TWO

Life's full of surprises

So I cracked on and gained more experience preparing myself for the next rank. I was a year into my Degree and though it was hard going balancing child care, work and studying it was manageable. Then just as Olivia had appeared out of the blue, next it was Savannah's turn. Jenny and I had finally become financially stable after years of juggling credit cards bouncing from one 0% interest rate to another. Jen was working full-time in a private hospital as a nurse in Intensive Care and had the potential to progress much further. So life was good with Olivia now five years old and at school. Jenny certainly picked her moments although I accept I may have played a part. I was lying in the bath no doubt feeling self-satisfied with my lot when in walked Jenny who sat down on the toilet seat.

She wasted no time. 'I don't know how to tell you this,' she said.

I must have looked confused as she said, 'I'm pregnant.'

We thought Olivia was a miracle and she was, but another! I knew my reaction to this news would be really important to Jenny and I put a brave face on, laughed and said, 'That's great news! Olivia will be thrilled.' Inside I thought – *a new baby*! How will we cope juggling our jobs and my degree, but quickly brushed those thoughts aside.

Back at work I applied for the Chief Inspector promotion boards. I had prepared my evidence to support my claim meticulously and submitted my application with optimism. On this occasion all applications were shortlisted by a panel comprising a Chief Superintendent and Human Resources Manager and guess who the

Chief Superintendent was? Yes, the one whose Division had the unreliable crime detection figures! I didn't even get an interview. I was on an accelerated scheme and didn't even pass first base. I knew something was off and had my suspicions but kept my head down and didn't appeal against the decision as it was still early days. I decided to make use of the time as an Inspector by gaining more experience and I applied for and got a job as a Detective Inspector in a newly formed Intelligence Unit. I moved to Carlton Police Station and really enjoyed learning new skills. My job was titled 'Intelligence Manager' the key elements being to manage all intelligence assets both police and civilian. I had detectives trained to cultivate and handle human intelligence sources (informants) who I would evaluate and task to gain information into specific criminal activity. All police officers were expected to submit intelligence reports detailing information they gleaned during the course of their duty. If they saw a target criminal they would submit the sighting with the location, time and date, what clothing they wore and any associates with them. This would form a piece of the intelligence jigsaw in trying to understand who was committing crime. The real trick is turning that information into evidence or actionable intelligence. It's OK for it to be common knowledge that Joe Bloggs is a burglar but without specifics and a target profile it was just speculation. Our job in Intelligence was to bind that information together to make disparate items of information into something that could be acted upon. It was rewarding work creating something from nothing and taking criminals off the streets. Ironically when I first took the Army entrance exam I was pushed by the selection officer towards the Intelligence Corps. I suppose I got there in the end.

Nottingham was hitting the headlines again and for the wrong reasons. There were a number of fatal shootings in the city and surrounding conurbation and huge amounts of resources were needed to staff the murder teams. It was clear that there was a significant Intelligence vacuum around Organised and Serious Crime and I was given the role of managing the intelligence function across all the ongoing inquiries. In the following weeks my team of six detectives and I pieced together the details of each organised crime group and gang across the city. Once we understood the problem, the individuals and their hierarchy it became easier to target them to destabilise and disrupt their criminal activities. I put a plan forward to Command for resources to implement a large scale and ambitious undercover operation across the two key geographic problem areas of the city, St Ann's and The Meadows. The plan, operation Real Estate was approved and several undercover 'Test Purchase' cops were deployed days and evenings, seven days a week for four months. The way the evidence gathering process works is as follows. The undercover cop is briefed on the target area and provided with all available intelligence to enable them to identify potential drugs dealers. They immerse themselves into the drugs user community in that area and are introduced to those dealing drugs.

They focus on class 'A' drugs where possible, such as crack cocaine, heroin and crystal meth. They are provided cash by the briefing officer and all serial numbers are noted. They keep a log of all purchases of drugs made. Surveillance methods are used to provide corroborative evidence of the purchase. These operatives are the real deal and they look and smell like the dregs of society. In the following months the operation led to the arrest and successful prosecution of over seventy drug dealers. This destabilised the criminal fraternity and took out many of the gangs 'foot soldiers' who were involved in serious violent crime and firearms offences. We had a much richer intelligence picture from this point and could support the serious crime investigations that were on going by identifying persons of interest.

Savannah Gabrielle was born on 17 July 1996. It was a glorious summer day, sports day at Olivia's school and Jenny had been up most of the night. I mooched around in my joggers making a leisurely breakfast oblivious to the fact that Jenny was in the advanced stages of labour. The midwife arrived, took one look at me and said, 'You'd better get dressed or we'll be delivering the baby in your lounge.'

I took the not so subtle hint and then got Jenny in the car. She was going into labour en route and I was panicking but we got to Kings Mill Hospital within 15 minutes and the midwifery team took over. They didn't even have time to change Jenny's clothing, she was put straight on a bed and without pain relief gave birth 25 minutes later. Jenny went into shock but the team looking after her were great. They managed her pain and she finally got some rest. Olivia was still at school and I turned up to see her competing in the various sports day activities, I called her over and told her she had a baby sister. She was ecstatic and ran around excitedly waving her arms and telling her friends and teachers the good news. It was a really happy time and I knew how lucky I was to have such a wonderful family.

We certainly knew we had Savannah though, she just did not sleep. Olivia had been a model baby and we'd been spoiled, I just thought that was the way babies were and we were clearly fantastic parents. I was wrong, Savannah was up every night, several times. Jenny and I juggled full-time jobs and the kids and studying. I seriously contemplated quitting my degree. I was 18 months into the three years and just couldn't bring myself to give up on it. I got up at 5am to study and then took care of the kids if Jenny was working. Like most parents we managed… somehow. Sleep was a rare commodity at that time in our lives, but you have to make it work.

I pushed on at work, I had made Inspector in 1995, applied twice for promotion over the next four years and was blocked, with hindsight I should have challenged my nemesis, AC. But I didn't, trusting, probably foolishly, that it would all work out in the end. So having been given the golden ticket in '95 it may as well have been the ticket to career stasis. Eventually in the year 2000 I got another opportunity. My nemesis was out of the equation and we were back at the assessment centres, no doubt in response to the complaints of cronyism and nepotism that had been clear for all to see in the previous five years. I knew this was my shot and I planned, practiced and prepared. When I came out of the assessment centre I felt confident and was vindicated. Once again coming top of the field, I was immediately promoted to Chief Inspector and posted to South Nottinghamshire, still based in Carlton where I had been the Intelligence DI. If I'm honest the job of a Chief Inspector is a bit of an anomaly it is neither one thing nor another. It's a limbo rank and in my opinion completely unnecessary. The pay difference from Inspector is minimal and the gap to Superintendent significant. In terms of responsibilities it actually felt like a step backwards as I had very few staff to manage, just a handful of Inspectors. I did however have a major pain in my backside. Let's call him 'SS'. An Inspector who as part of his duties undertook work for the Police Federation (Union). He was never where he was supposed to be and rarely delivered work on schedule or of substance. He would always claim to be on Federation business. Working with the Federation I tried to establish exactly what his responsibilities were and his Federation work schedule. In light of this new information I allocated important tasks to him to deliver on. He failed to deliver time and again. He was simply incompetent but in the police service at that time managers were reluctant to tackle underperforming staff generally and more so minority staff for fear of being branded racist. Racism is an allegation that's easy to make and difficult to disprove and the stink is hard to shift. I knew that he might make that allegation against me but I had a job to do and I was not going to make exceptions for an easy life. So I stuck to my principles and recorded everything in my pocket book. All I wanted was for him to do the job the public were paying him to do. If he wasn't doing it then someone else was having to pick up the slack. After several months of frustration with him I could hardly believe it, he actually approached me to support his application for promotion. I made it clear to him that I thought he lacked both the managerial qualities and the evidence of proven performance required and therefore I could not support his application.

Then a week or so later I received an email from Complaints and Discipline. I should have known it was coming but it still came as a shock and when I read the allegations I felt sick. Three counts of racism were alleged against me by SS and as I read the email I was filled with self-doubt. I honestly held a mirror up to myself asking 'Is this true? Is there any substance to these allegations? Have I missed something?' It is a truly horrible feeling but I knew in my heart of hearts I had acted fairly and impartially and I was furious. Using the race card without justification is about as low as it gets. Potentially ruining someone's career for personal gain whilst hiding behind race is despicable, but unfortunately it happens.

I read the times and dates of these alleged racist actions and started preparing my defence. To be honest it wasn't that difficult. I met with the Force Solicitor, Malcolm T who was a bright and committed advocate.

Malcolm was a rarity, a lawyer who believed in defending the right and prosecuting the wrong, no matter what. I explained in detail the background to my relationship with SS. I had logged every interaction with him and also his failure to deliver and his ability to never be where he should have been or where he said he was and always incommunicado despite having a Police mobile phone. I often wondered if he had a second job as he was never at this one. I had witness statements from several female and black and ethnic minority officers and staff who I had mentored, supported and promoted over the years and they shared my anger. No hard-working professional likes to see race used to disguise incompetence and a lack of commitment. The main allegation hinged on my actions and an alleged statement made by me to SS on a particular day and date at West Bridgford Police station. This would have been difficult to refute as there were, in his words no other witnesses present but the problem for SS and his case against me was that on this particular date I was on annual leave on holiday with my family. He was so dim and unprofessional that even when making false allegations against me he hadn't been smart enough to check that I was actually at work at the time. I worked with Malcolm and we had more than enough evidence to refute all of his allegations.

A date had been set for an industrial tribunal which would be held in the employment courts in Nottingham. I had waited nearly a year to clear my name and wanted people to know of his humiliation in the witness box when my lawyer would expose his deceit. The head of Force Discipline the Deputy Chief Constable was fully in the loop and I asked him several times what would happen when it was proven that SS had made false allegations against a fellow officer in a legal court of law. He always ducked the issue playing the usual political game, avoiding committing to anything that may reflect badly on him as an individual. Always less risk brushing race related problems under the carpet.

The tribunal was due to commence on the Monday morning when at 2pm on the Friday before Malcolm T took a phone call from SS's Solicitor. It went something like, 'SS will drop his tribunal claim of racism if he is promoted with immediate effect.'

MT called me and informed me of the conversation. 'And what did you say, Malcolm?' I asked.

He laughed and said, 'He's dreaming, I'll see you in court Monday morning.'

I laughed. *Good old Malc*, I thought, he wanted his day in court with SS as much as I did. He was as invested in this as I was having seen first-hand the evidence and the lies. Then came another call from MT, 'Now he's asking to be guaranteed a seat at the next promotion boards without having to undertake selection.' Again I asked him his response, 'Same as last time, Nick, he's getting nothing.'

At 4:58pm on that Friday evening MT received a call from SS's Solicitor once again, this time informing him that SS would be withdrawing his complaint and that the tribunal was cancelled. I was pleased it was over with but fuming that SS could just walk away with complete impunity. On the following Monday I went to see the DCC. I asked him what he was going to do about SS. Who had clearly misrepresented the truth and placed me in an invidious position. Really serious stuff in most people's eyes I suspect. His reply, 'Better to just put this behind us and move on.' I told him I thought it was a joke and that SS's position was now untenable and that he would be a pariah in the Force and the rank and file would see this as a complete double standard, damaging to the cause for equality within the Force. I was wasting my time and in my opinion he simply didn't have the backbone to take this on. I secretly hoped that something similar would happen to him one day... soon.

CHAPTER TWENTY-THREE

Finally educated but not that smart

Having stepped out of my comfort zone and into the scary world of academia I sat my final degree exam after three years of course work, assignments and exams. Even though time for study was limited with work commitments and the children I had enjoyed the experience, even teaching myself algebra, logarithms etc., which I now found as easy as I found it difficult at school. I suppose my attitude to learning had changed. I graduated at the University of Portsmouth and felt a real sense of achievement. I wasn't sure if having a BSc (Hons) would help me get promoted, probably not but the discipline of learning and the knowledge gained would definitely make me a better police leader in the years to come. My degree was useful as I researched subject matter such as prostitution and drugs that has much wider social relevance and I examined differing approaches from around the world and how they managed the issues. With a degree comes an element of credibility. Senior people in most organisations can be incredibly precious and without a degree a candidate would not even be considered for a position regardless of ability. So scroll in hand I had ticked off another milestone on my journey towards success.

It wasn't all work and I had taken up Open Water Diving. I was taught to scuba dive to 30 metres by a friend and colleague of mine who was a Master Diver. We practiced at a well know Diving Centre in Staffordshire, Stoney Cove and I had to learn all the basics of diving, how to use air tanks and regulators and a BCD (Buoyancy Control Device) I had to be able to calculate depths and decompression times, that is the deeper you go the greater the compression on the body and blood supply requiring a controlled ascent back to the surface. Come up too quickly and excess Nitrogen is retained in the blood which can cause the Bends and could be fatal. Training went well in the gloomy freezing depths of the cove and it wasn't my intention once qualified to cold water dive in a dry suit, I wanted warm water diving in the Caribbean in board shorts. Which is just what I did for a couple of years until I was talked into diving in the North Sea at Lindisfarne. It was a boys weekend trip but the weather was atrocious with freezing temperatures and howling gales, only four out of the thirty or so dive boat skippers were prepared to brave the turmoil of the ocean one of which was ours. I hadn't dived the North Sea before and was more than a little apprehensive. It was Baltic out there and even though I wore a dry suit my head was freezing, drenched by the rain and enormous bow waves that gave us a good soaking every few seconds. This just wasn't pleasant and not my idea of fun diving. But we arrived at the island and geared up. I had borrowed a weight belt with my usual diving weight to assist my descent but as soon as I entered the water and released the air from my BCD realised there wasn't enough weight to take me down. I didn't know then that the North Sea has a high salt content and therefore increases buoyancy.

The boat had disappeared, everyone else had submerged and I had no option but to swim down until the water pressure increased and kept me under. Swimming against positive buoyancy is hard work and I was knackered, breathing heavily and sucking oxygen from my tank at an alarming rate. I planned on reaching the ocean floor at thirty-two metres and then I could pick up some rocks put them in my pouches and use them to keep me under and to enable a controlled ascent back to the surface. As I reached the bottom I was surrounded by dozens of seals as fast as torpedoes but curious to say hello to their new guests. I stared at the ocean floor… it was a smooth as a babies bum, not a rock in sight. 'This isn't good,' I thought and I had no idea what I was going to do next. I knew that whilst at this depth I would be pinned to the floor but as I ascended to decompress the air in my dry suit would expand and naturally want to rise to the surface like a balloon with no counter weight to keep it in check. After 15 minutes I had to move upwards to 25 metres and as I did the air in my suit and my natural buoyancy forced me upwards like a cork I tried to swim down against the force but was breathing heavily with the exertion and even though I was slowing my ascent slightly I knew I had to clear my lungs of air or they could explode with the pressure. I looked up and the surface seemed close by so I filled my lungs with air for one last time and pulled the regulator from my mouth. As I neared the surface I tried to control the release of air from my lungs to prevent expansion but under estimated how far I had to travel and how desperate I was to breath given the exertion. I just had to breathe and my brain took over from intuition and I started to gulp down sea water. Fortunately, it wasn't for long and I broke the surface of the water gasping for air and panicking not knowing if I would be hit by the bends. I needed pure oxygen to counter the build up of nitrogen in my blood but I looked around and because I had surfaced 10 minutes early the boat was nowhere to be seen. I saw another boat in the distance and waved at them to pick me up to no avail. Eventually our boat reappeared and I scrambled in and shouted above the noise of the wind and rain for the O2. The skipper picked up the bottle and it was empty, it turned out they had used it to help some poor guy who had his leg amputated by a boat propeller the week before. They called the nearest boat and I finally sucked down some much-needed O2. I waited for the cramps of the bends over the next few hours but they didn't come. I had been lucky, it was a close shave. I didn't dive in cold water again and I was nervous getting in the bath at home for a while.

I had only been a Chief Inspector for seven months when the Superintendent promotion boards were announced. I had a ton of evidence some from my time as a Chief Inspector but loads from my five years as an Inspector. It's fair to say it is a little unusual to apply for promotion so soon after a prior promotion but I was on the fast track, had undertaken a significant amount of developmental work and needed to get my career back on track. And I thought, 'Well it's an assessment centre, so what do I have to lose?

As ever I prepared thoroughly learning all the competencies and behavioural traits of the next rank and by now I knew the drill. I had cognitively rehearsed every available scenario. So I went for it and scored highest overall. To be honest I didn't know if I would pass but the next rank held no fears for me, I was ready for a senior leadership role.

I had regained the ground that I had lost, having been shafted twice by AC and was promoted from Inspector to Superintendent in just nine months.

This was the big one though, the jump to Superintendent was significant both in terms of pay, pension and responsibility. I felt like I could finally relax a little now and enjoy the ride. I thought back to my time in the military and realised that the rank of Superintendent is equal to that of Major they even share the same rank insignia, a crown. I wondered what my old boss in Germany and Corporal Dave would think if they knew what I had achieved. I'm pretty sure they wouldn't believe it and I understand why. I lacked focus and ambition but more importantly, a reason, the motivation.

Following a restructure of the Force by the Chief Steve, where seven Divisions became four I was posted almost immediately as the Operations Superintendent to South Nottinghamshire Division based once again at Carlton. My boss a Chief Superintendent, Les K was a good bloke, very experienced and about three years from retirement. Les was still very enthusiastic and a good leader. He made his expectations clear to all and held his people to account for delivery. Like me, he had high standards and a strong work ethic. Once he had made my role clear to me he let me get on with doing what I was paid for, which was running day-to-day operational policing for South

Nottinghamshire. We had a good senior team and made strong progress in crime reduction and detection, the key performance measures for any Division. I loved my job at this point and was confident in myself and my ability to deliver. I felt to me that I was now doing what I was always meant to do, it just felt... right. I knew my people and had a good knowledge of the Division and it's challenges. I was once again outside my comfort zone but confident that I would learn fast and soon be on top of my game.

I was content for the very first time and I can reflect back now and understand how hard I drove myself in pursuit of success. Why? During my five years in the military I had absolutely no ambition other than to complete Commando and Parachute Regiment selection. I didn't seek promotion or recognition yet I clearly had some latent potential for leadership. Looking back I believe that the years at school continually reinforced a belief that I was a failure who couldn't be redeemed. I certainly felt written off by most of the teachers and the bullying definitely didn't help. To put some context around this, I had a geography teacher who I liked and he seemed to take an interest in me. He clearly knew I had much more to give and challenged me to succeed. I was in the bottom three of the class but he used reverse physiology to motivate me telling me that I was wasting my intelligence, that he knew I could do well but didn't have a hope of achieving anything. I set out to prove him wrong finishing fourth overall in the year. He was more delighted than I was and geography was one of the few 'O' levels I passed. Of course, it was always inside me but had been beaten into a dark corner waiting to be nurtured. And there it pretty much hid until I joined the Police. In the Forces I had shown to myself that I had the discipline, drive and determination but that isn't enough on its own, I needed someone to believe in me and that person was Lew Davies my first Inspector at Bestwood. My wife Jenny has and continues to be a huge positive influence on me bolstering my self-belief when self-doubt starts to take a foothold.

But as ever nothing ever goes according to plan and six months into my tenure at South Notts, the Force felt the full weight of Government intervention in the form of the Home Office (HO).

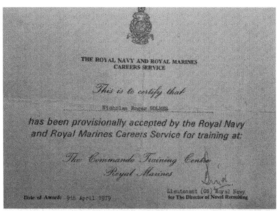

1. Acceptance to the Royal Marines, April 1979.
The biggest regret by far in my life was leaving.

2. Commando Training Centre Lympstone 131 Troop.
Me, back row third from the right.

3. Eighteen year old me posing with an Light Machine Gun in basic training.

4. Trying to look cool next to our newly acquired Pontiac Firebird in South Carolina, (1979).

5. Me and my best mate Ray with a local Greenville drug dealer (note the bag of weed in his hand).

6. My Class of '85 at Police Training school Dishforth. Me at back row far left with my Training Sergeant John Scott with the 'tash front row. John went on to be Chief Constable of Northumbria.

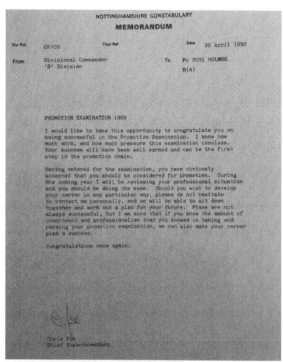

7. Letter confirming passing my Sergeants Promotion exam. I was promoted soon after.

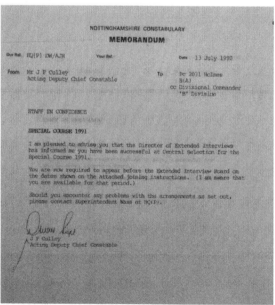

8. Feedback from my Special Course journey. I passed stage 2 but fell at the final hurdle.

9. *Promotion exam pass Certificates for Sergeant and Inspector.*

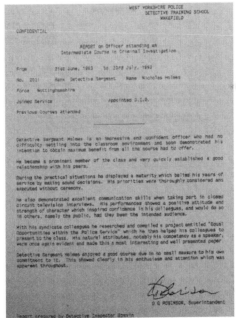

10. *My Intermediate CID Corse report which considering the amount I drank every night is amazing.*

11. *My course mates on the Junior CID course at Tally Ho. Dave Heggarty who starred in the stop search fit up is on my right behind the course director in the blue suit.*

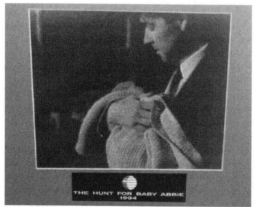

12. *The framed photograph presented to me by Central Television at the conclusion of the Abbey Humphries case. The photo is a still taken from the filmed documentary as I leave the house on Brendan Drive.*

13. *The Investigation Team with Abbies parents Roger and Karen and son Charlie with me holding baby Abbie. Harry Shappard the SIO is second in from the right.*

*14. My first super bike the iconic Honda Fireblade.
Not sure slippers are allowed on track these days.*

CHAPTER TWENTY-FOUR

Under scrutiny

In 2002 performance monitoring by the Home Office was in full swing. Each of the 43 forces were required to send monthly statistical returns to them for scrutiny. The key issues of focus being crimes recorded and detected within the range of criminal offences. Some carried far more significance than others, the stuff that made headlines at this point in history were the burglary of people's homes, car theft which was at epidemic levels as car manufacturers thought it was good idea to make them easy to steal and crimes of violence.

There were two main problems. Because of the crime recording anomalies found in the audit that I was part of, Notts were now recording absolutely everything whilst other forces were not. The second issue was that Notts had a very high burglary, auto crime and violent crime rate. Put that alongside a comparatively poor crime detection rate and the Home Office spotlight inevitably fell up Nottinghamshire Police and its Chief Constable Steve.

Once you are under the Home Office spotlight, everything changes. You go from being completely focussed upon your role and managing your business to achieve the key targets, to being completely distracted by numerous HO 'experts'. The reality was that these 'experts' were all police officers on attachment to the Home Office. You might ask yourself, why would someone with a career in their home force decide to move away from their parent force, family and friends? The answer is simple. For promotion. They were given a higher rank on a temporary basis and if they did an okay job over the

144

two years they were there they were usually allowed to keep it when they returned to force. So inevitably that part of the Home Office, Her Majesty's Inspectorate of Constabulary (HMIC) was staffed by a number of people who couldn't compete successfully for promotion in their home force and had little operational experience or credibility. So, as an experienced operational leader, being told how to do your job by people such as these was a bitter pill to swallow.

At South Notts our performance was relatively good but admittedly burglary and auto crime were a problem. I had researched and written the Force policy on burglary having travelled the country looking at best practice. This had been implemented drawing together Investigation, Intelligence, Offender Management, and state of the art Forensics.

Numerous partners worked together including Housing Departments, Social Services, the Courts and Crown Prosecutors and Drugs rehabilitation. Then HMIC arrived in the form of a temporary Chief Inspector to advise on how we might improve our performance. It was immensely frustrating to have an inexperienced officer reading at me from a manual on how things should be done when I had written the bloody manual. Every meeting was like groundhog day and we gained little benefit from the interdiction by the HO.

The only consolation is that HO cash was made available to fund proactive targeting of recidivist offenders. So the self-fulfilling prophecy of improving performance by throwing additional resources at a problem comes to pass, which was a surprise to no one. The Home Office take credit for improving Nottinghamshire's performance but in reality all that happens is additional resources are made available in the short term. Then it's back to business as usual as it cannot be mainstreamed and sustained. Clearly there were some lessons learned and subsequent improvements but the end definitely did not justify the means.

The major problem for Chief Steve was Nottingham City. In his Force reorganisation Steve had put all inner-city estates as well as the city centre in one basket as a Policing Division. This became the largest policing area by population in the UK and had all the problems to go with it. Burglary, drugs, violent crime, gun crime were all spiralling out of control and the new team put in to lead were not delivering. Another key factor that cannot be overstated was the decision by Steve to disband the Drugs Squad. After nine months at South Notts, Les and I were called to see the Chief. We were told of the crisis and it was clear that the pressure was on. Steve's job was clearly on the line and I'm pretty sure he didn't want to go down in history as the first Chief Constable to be sacked. The Force's reputation had been hammered and I reflected on the conversations I had been privy to when I transferred from West Yorkshire and the claims by colleagues that Nottinghamshire were the best Force in the country. I knew they were deluded back then as I could compare both Forces and West Yorkshire were miles ahead in every aspect of Policing from the advances in technology through to officer discipline and performance.

We had the weekend to prepare to move from South Notts' to the City. I was excited, flattered to have been chosen and nervous about what lay ahead. The expectation and responsibility to deliver was huge and I knew I would be living at work for the foreseeable future and once again working completely outside my comfort zone.

I knew as everyone did that the City was a monolithic beast and Organised Crime and Homicide were a huge problem with twenty-four ongoing murder inquiries. The Force had hit the national headlines with the title 'Shottingham' due to the number of gang related shootings. It was a massive task but Les and I figured it couldn't get any worse, so the only way was up. But I never imagined quite how challenging this would be.

CHAPTER TWENTY-FIVE

Loyalty and betrayal

With the old Chief Superintendent and Superintendent moved sideways over the weekend, on the Monday morning at 6am Les and I took responsibility for over 1,200 Police Officers and Staff. During the previous nine months the City had been restructured but we believed we needed to make major structural and organisational changes to better meet demand and to prevent and detect crime.

My position was Deputy Divisional Commander with responsibility for the implementation of our new plan. I was described by Les as his 'Rottweiler' which at the time I thought was a little excessive. But looking back a few of the less willing did get a necessary mauling. Despite the constant change for our officers and staff we found we were pushing at an open door as the overwhelming majority of our people recognised the need for and supported change. However I did have one immediate problem to manage. As a Superintendent my role required me to manage two other Superintendents which caused a few raised eyebrows. But as the plan unfolded it was evident why my position was essential. We divided the City into two Sub Divisions, North and South with a Superintendent at the head of each. They had responsibility and more importantly accountability for the day-to-day performance and running of their part of the world whilst I had oversight of divisional performance and the construct and design of performance improvement and management of change. As if this wasn't difficult enough we had critical incidents kicking off on a weekly basis. The definition of which is 'an occurrence of such magnitude where the effectiveness of the police response is likely to have a significant impact on the confidence of the victim, their family and or the community'. We had a large number of shootings and stabbings many resulting in fatalities.

The City was almost tribal with rival 'gangs' from a number of inner-city areas at war with one another, the hostilities were usually related to the struggle for drugs dealing areas or 'turf' or just personal historic beef. The rivalries and animosity ran deep across five large predominantly council estates. One thing for sure was the propensity for extreme violence had grown quickly from fist fights and baseball bats to knives and guns and for the sake of everyone, the public, police resources and the reputation of Nottingham it had to be stopped. The term 'gang' is interesting as in reality there are few real gangs or gang members but more a bunch of people who reside in a certain area who come together, not under some banner or flag but to defend their territory or one another against the threat of violence or the threat to their business, usually drugs or prostitution.

Whilst we were involved in the day-to-day firefighting of the consequences of this turf war we also devised a longer-term strategy for disrupting and dismantling the gangs and their criminal enterprise. The disbandment of the Drugs Squad had left an intelligence void and the Force had no handle on the organised criminal activity in this key area which had proven catastrophic for Nottingham City in particular.

In 2003 Operation 'Stealth' was established to be overseen by me with an experienced team of officers lead by an excellent Detective Chief Inspector Ian W. Building upon the intelligence work done previously on Operation Real Estate their job was to identify and target all key organised crime groups and their members. Through source led intelligence they would focus on taking out the foot soldiers and middle tier operators of the gangs forcing the top men to get 'hands on' drugs and dirty money. In theory it is organised crime Jenga. Taking away the lower part of the structure would ultimately lead to its collapse. It was a long game taking three years but piece by piece Stealth took out the gangs, eventually dismantling five Organised Crime Groups (OCG's) from the City and its conurbation, some serious heavyweight villains were brought to justice. Serious violent crime was reduced and shooting and stabbing virtually eradicated. But be under no illusion, operations of this kind are very resource intensive, because once you've lost policing control of the territory through either a lack of knowledge, understanding or commitment you are left with no option.

My first year at the City flew by, I was in the office for 5:30am usually seven days a week leaving around 7pm because rush hour traffic was an absolute pain. I accumulated 38 rest days owing over that period, that's 19 weekends. I was fortunate that my wife and family were so supportive. We knew it wouldn't be forever and I had my sights set of taking over from Les when he decided to retire. We had a great Senior Management Team delivering long term sustainable solutions to the issues facing the City.

One thing that was immediately apparent on our arrival was the lack of partnership working with the City Council. They had a one-billion pound budget and invested very little into securing the safety of their communities. Les and I met with the leader John Collins who from day one was incredibly focussed and supportive. We secured millions in funding for crime reduction initiatives including setting up a community protection scheme with Police Community Support Officers and Neighbourhood Wardens with the infrastructure to support it. We were able to buy technical surveillance equipment to reduce burglary and we agreed a policy with City housing where when we had charged a suspect with a gang, drugs or firearms offence the council would serve notice of eviction and repossession. There were lots of little elements in our joint enterprise which when added up made a huge impact.

It wasn't all about organised crime. When we started there were 100+ visible beggars on the City's streets which is socially unacceptable and deters people from visiting. Taking a multi-agency approach we eradicated the problem in weeks, providing housing, dealing with addiction or mental health problems in a victim centred approach. No one really wants to live on the streets. There was never a slow day in the City, always some issue to deal with and I loved it. It was like playing football but in the Premier League.

In October 2004 and having been trained to manage major events such as football matches and concerts I found myself as the 'Gold' Commander for Goose Fair, an annual event lasting four days, it is the largest fun fair in Europe, attracting tens of thousands of visitors each day. Every year without fail the weekend would be marred by gang related violence. At this time, tensions between the street gangs of St Ann's and the Meadows ran deep and we expected large numbers to attend the fair. It was dark in the evening, making surveillance difficult. I had a Police helicopter on standby should I need it and dozens of plain clothes and uniformed officers in fluorescent jackets on the ground looking for potential problems and to provide reassurance to the public. It was Saturday the penultimate night of the event and as I walked around the site early that evening I could feel the tension in the air. The fairground was enormous with thousands of revellers on site, the noise almost deafening, illuminated by the light of a million bulbs. Then around 10pm I heard a radio message from an officer who had come across a brawl within the fair, his colleagues were on scene immediately and the gang starburst in every direction. A quick search of the area and officers found two knives that had been discarded by the gang.

Goose Fair closed later that night without further incident and I felt relieved that there had been no major incidents, no real drama. I got home just after 2am and went to bed. I hadn't been asleep long when I received a call informing me that a young woman had been shot and killed in St Ann's in a drive by shooting.

I got dressed and headed for the City. By the time I arrived at the incident room it was established that two men in a vehicle had been seen driving around St Ann's and as they passed a crowd outside a row of shops the passenger had leaned out of the window and fired a single shot towards them. A 14-year-old girl, Danielle Beccan from St Ann's sustained a fatal bullet wound, dying in the ambulance. The media had a field day and community tensions were high. I met with family and residents explaining our response. A Homicide investigation was up and running and visible police patrols on the streets to deter tit for tat attacks and reassure the community. The murder team quickly identified the vehicle and occupants, and charged them with Danielle's murder. Apparently they had gone to St Ann's to shoot a male target but missed him killing Danielle instead.

Goose Fair on the final night which is traditionally family night went off quietly and I returned to the City and my day job to pick up the fall-out from the shooting. Never a dull moment. The prevalence of gun crime was a major political issue and changes to legislation were introduced. Being caught with firearm meant a guaranteed five years in prison and three strikes for drug offences resulted in automatic lengthy prison terms. This made a tangible difference combined with relentless covert and overt drugs operations taking out numerous drug dealers across the City.

Stealth became very successful winning a National award and over a three-year period virtually eradicated organised crime groups and massively reduced serious violent crime, firearms discharges, gunshot injuries and homicides. The ongoing success of Stealth was causing waves amongst those criminals whose livelihoods were under threat. So much so that we received intelligence that a convicted killer in possession of a handgun had been contracted to kill a senior police officer working as part of Stealth. It was clear that was either directed at the head of the Criminal Investigation Department, the head of Operation Stealth or myself as the officer with overall command of Stealth. Risk assessments were conducted and various measures implemented to mitigate the threat. I was issued a covert ballistic vest and implemented a number of counter measures. Reading this you might think it a little far-fetched and unrealistic but two things confirmed our suspicions. A man was seen acting suspiciously at the rear of one of the targets home addresses but was disturbed. Footprints were found to confirm this. The name of the 'hitman' was established as John Paul McSally a convicted hardened criminal with a previous conviction for murder.

Substantial assets were committed to locating McSally who was storing his firearm in a pub in Nottingham. In May 2004, the operation led to the arrest of McSally, hands on with the weapon. This firearm was linked through forensic ballistic analysis to two murders and one attempted murder in Nottingham. These were all contract killings, believed to have been conducted on behalf of the two brothers I had dealt with for wounding at a Christmas party back at Bestwood as a uniformed constable in 1988. It was a relief to hear McSally had been arrested and charged with two murders and one attempted.

By 2005 Les and I had resolved most of the City Divisions major challenges and we were making good progress, the pressure was diminishing with every month that passed. As part of my own self development I kept a record of my personal and professional achievements. I would often reflect upon those experiences and identify my strengths and areas for improvement. Patience was definitely one at the top of the latter list. But what I did have was determination, personal drive and discipline which were vital in moving forward change. Self-belief is critical when designing and implementing change. As a leader you frequently come up against the naysayers and the blockers who just don't want to work hard or take additional responsibility. In my experience change is best effected when you embrace your team and secure their personal commitment and investment. Making time to hear their thoughts and concerns and including them in the decision-making process is therefore key.

Personal contact, making time for people is the best investment of any leader's time. Understanding their position and the issues they face and problem solving with them creates a common bond and shared goals and with that comes loyalty and trust. We had created a strong, loyal team in the City prepared to go above and beyond for the cause, and I was proud to be part of that.

I had established my credibility as a leader in the most challenging circumstances and it felt good. Then out of the blue Les came from his grand, oak panelled Victorian office and into my significantly smaller one opposite. It was then that he told me he had decided to retire six months early. Furthermore he had spoken with the Chief and I would be taking over subject to passing the Chief Superintendent selection board. This would be the pinnacle of my policing career, Commander of the largest Policing Division in the UK and I was elated.

The promotion assessment centre was back in Wakefield and by now I knew the drill. Prepare, Prepare, Prepare. I had a fairly simple formula for success which had served me well in previous assessments. I dissected the core competencies and behavioural traits of the role and developed scenarios that I would face in the role of Chief Superintendent. By cognitively thinking through scenarios putting myself physically in that position proved a winning methodology. As soon as I started the assessment scenarios all the cognitive rehearsals kicked in and if I'm honest it was fairly straightforward. Sure, there's a lot of pressure but if you want to operate at this level of management then that's just part of the job. I had a mental tick list of behaviours and competencies I had to demonstrate and just worked through them imagining the assessors watching and listening via CCTV, furiously ticking away on the evaluation sheets. At least I hoped they were.

I passed the assessment centre process and just had a formal interview with the Chief and two other Chief Officers to ensure promotion. Historically interviews were my strong point and although I was nervous I was pretty confident. However I performed badly. It was just one of those days where it didn't click. You have to put it behind you and move on.

I didn't come top this time which was annoying but fortunately overall I had exceeded the required pass mark and now just had to wait for Les to retire and I would soon be sitting in the big chair in the even bigger office in the City. But life has a way of keeping your feet on the ground and simultaneously kicking you in the balls, sometimes when you least expect it.

Les had a fixed leaving date and the Chief had confirmed informally that I would be taking over as a reward for all of my hard work and of course it made perfect business sense to have continuity and a new leader who knew every nut and bolt of the division and who had established relationships with the staff and critically the City Council Leader and wider public sector partners. And then two months prior to the changeover I took a phone call from a friend informing me that a Chief Superintendent was coming back from a Home Office attachment and was replacing Les.

Marcus, the Chief Superintendent in question was a fast-track cop who had flown through the ranks but in his haste to enter the Chief Officer club had failed to secure the experience and credibility of Divisional Command. He had applied for numerous Assistant Chief Constable positions whilst on secondment and had failed to secure a position.

On hearing the rumour which I didn't doubt was true I made the short journey to Les's office and told him what I'd heard. He was genuinely shocked.

Fuck, I thought, *even Les doesn't know.*

'Sit down, Nick,' Les said. 'I'll call Steve.'

It was 7:30am but the Chief answered. Les had the desk phone on speaker and asked Steve to confirm or deny the rumour.

He confirmed and what followed was a man with years of pent-up frustration with Chief Officers and only two months away from retirement with nothing to lose letting rip. Why didn't he know? Why wasn't he consulted on the change of replacement? What about the impact upon the division? All valid concerns, I thought.

Steve had to suck it up and apologise, explaining that Marcus would only get promoted if he gained more experience as a Divisional Commander. He finished the call promising to call me. True to his word Steve called me. All I asked for was an explanation of his thinking and why he would risk the performance of the Division by changing its leadership, taking on an unproven leader and losing the two most senior people who had built the Division and knew every aspect of it intimately. It made no sense then and fifteen years later still appears a massive and unnecessary risk to take.

Of course he didn't have an explanation that stood scrutiny so I told him of the history between Marcus and I, which wasn't good and that I felt sure he would want to replace me and I sure as shit didn't want to stick around playing second fiddle especially as I was waiting for my own Command. To his credit Steve said he fully understood and asked me what I wanted.

There were no Chief Superintendent vacancies available as there were just six in the entire force, but I knew there was a Detective Superintendent slot free in Homicide. The Operational Head of Homicide was a plum job and ordinarily I would not have been considered for it as my Detective experience was limited to Operational Detective Sergeant and Intelligence Detective Inspector. In fact I had never even worked on a murder enquiry. 'Yes, Steve, I know exactly what I want,' I replied.

CHAPTER TWENTY-SIX

Homicide

So three weeks later, well and truly outside my comfort zone I started my learning curve as the Head of Nottinghamshire Police Homicide Department. In truth it was more of a learning cliff face. However it is my firm belief that personal growth can only be fulfilled by pushing mental and physical boundaries. Within Marines Commando training with the physical and psychological challenges faced I began to appreciate I was capable of so much more than I thought possible. Since that time I have developed a much greater awareness of who I am, and what I am able to achieve.

But more about that later as this was the first of several major personal mountains to climb. I had real self-doubt and reservations about leading a Homicide Department made up of several interchangeable teams each with their own established hierarchy. The CID and its specialist units such as Surveillance, Drugs Squad and Murder Teams were historically by and large a closed shop riddled with cronyism. If you weren't connected or playing the right sport you would find it almost impossible to permeate the 'club'. My experiences attempting to break through that barrier on the Drugs Squad, Force Support and later CID for promotion had reinforced that view. I can only describe it as a series of ladders. When one senior club member moves up a rung he (and it usually was a he), pulls up his mates on the other ladders. Please don't misunderstand, there were some very talented detectives on those units but it stifled growth, fresh ideas and suppressed freedom of thought and expression, as no one wanted to rock the boat and show out.

I was never a club guy and in truth I was always anti-establishment. I hated monolithic structures and processes (that's the way it's always been done!) and had no time for jobs worth cops or those that couldn't see beyond 'the job'. It defined them and their personality and I hated that. I believe the greatest attribute to be demonstrated by a Police officer is discretion, knowing when to act and when not to. Just because you can, should not mean you always do. Life is not black and white and working through the shades of grey is a skill and takes courage and judgment.

I always challenged convention and tried to create more positive productive alternatives, which in a world of mainly conservative, risk averse thinking was rarely welcome. One thing I learned however was that if you are intent on criticising the established norm then you had better have a well thought through alternative solution. This is illustrated clearly in modern society as all you seem to see through the media is journalists and detractors criticising Government or other institutions and politicians can be the worst. They pick away and undermine but rarely if ever offer an alternative solution. Why? Because they don't have one. It's attritional, damaging and unproductive.

So I broke the mould and stepped into the closed ranks of the Murder Squad. My apprehension was palpable and I'm sure some of the old lags could smell my fear. I can't say I was looking forward to the moment when I would get the call to be Senior Investigating Officer (SIO) for an unexplained death.

I was back in a suit and although full of self-doubt (again) felt proud of my achievements. I knew that if I projected self-confidence then most of, if not all of my colleagues would believe in my ability. I wasn't a complete duffer and my knowledge was pretty good but there was that nagging doubt due to my lack of experience as I hadn't even attended a murder scene before. I was a long way from the comfort of my office in the City and I missed it. It was a cruel blow having the Command taken from my reach. But as Forrest says, 'shit

157

happens' and you have to suck it up and move on.

My first day passed uneventfully and I spent my time meeting as many of the staff as possible. I had a nice office reasonably close to home with no City traffic, so all was good. Day two and I was in the office, early as usual. I had joined the local gym and was looking forward to a workout about 5pm. At 11am my work phone rang and I knew straight away this was it.

Uniformed officers had been contacted by the family of an elderly couple worried as they could not contact them. Officers attended the house finding the door was insecure so they entered and searched the house. In the main bedroom they found two bodies one male the other female, both were one oblique one or in layman terms 'deceased'.

I told the Control Room to instruct the officer attending to secure the scene not let anyone in without my permission and for the officers to remain there pending my arrival. I asked for a pathologist to attend but knew this might take a while. The operator said that officers had found no sign of forced entry and the house did not appear to have been burgled. On my arrival I made sure a log was started detailing everyone attending the scene. I went into the house and made my initial assessment and started a running log of all my thoughts and actions. I found nothing suspicious downstairs but in the bedroom lay the bodies of a married couple. Bottles of sedatives were on the bedside table, empty.

I pulled the team together and we met a couple of hours later in the local police station in Sneinton. In the interim period I had spoken to the son of the deceased and he had told me that his mother was terminally ill and in constant pain and his parents had been married over 45 years. It became clear that the deceased husband had administered the controlled drugs to his wife out of sympathy and a compassion for the woman he loved and that once she had passed away he had taken his own life in the same manner.

The term for this is murder/suicide which perhaps seems dispassionate and callous and I doubt there aren't many of us who do not have the deepest sympathy and empathy for their situation and perhaps if you found yourself in their position may well make the same choices.

I certainly didn't judge them and tried to manage the inquiry as sensitively as possible. Dealing with the unexplained death of a fellow human being requires not only the skills of a detective but also compassion and empathy. I believe that treating the deceased and their loved ones with dignity and respect was central to what we did. Keeping survivors and family informed of events is an essential part of the grieving process which is why I appointed a Family Liaison Officer (FLO). The finding at the Coroner's Court was as expected, murder/suicide. At the closing of the investigation the family thanked myself and the team for our work and the care provided by our team. It was my gentle initiation to the world of homicide but there was more to come and it would be harrowing. I had taken the first important steps way outside my comfort zone and had navigated my way through successfully. It felt good to be hands on again and involved in something of real value.

Perhaps unsurprisingly the murder team veterans were not hostile or suspicious as I expected them to be. They were welcoming, supportive and professional. Elite teams have a sense of pride in what they do and rarely do you find a slacker as part of these units as they are usually to be found avoiding responsibility and commitment like the plague. I was really enjoying leading and working with the homicide team but I was a Divisional Commander in waiting and was eager, as ever to move on and get started.

During my 12 months or so on Homicide I developed a homicide reduction strategy much of which was adopted by other police forces, I studied best practice from around the globe and visited Glasgow as they had faced a huge violent crime and murder problem. I led six murder enquiries, all different but all requiring absolute commitment and focus. There is no greater responsibility as a Police Officer than being asked to lead the investigation into the untimely death of a fellow human being. All victims have loved ones who rightly expect the perpetrators to be brought to justice. That expectation and the pressure from the media, community and the police hierarchy weighs heavy. But it's a responsibility I was proud to shoulder and in every case the offender was brought justice. Two cases in particular stand out in my memory.

The first was in Mansfield. Having worked my usual day in the office I was the out of hours on call SIO (Senior Investigating Officer) and at about 8pm was asked to attend a council flat where a body had been found in suspicious circumstances. Scenes of Crime (SOCO) were in attendance and a suspect was in custody having called the police to hand himself in.

Having gloved up and wearing a white coverall and shoe covers to protect the scene from contamination. I met with the senior SOCO at the doorway to the flat. He explained that the victim, a twenty-something white male was face down in the kitchen and there was blood 'everywhere'. I gave my details to the officer keeping the movement log at the scene and entered through the front door. I wasn't quite prepared for what I saw next. The victim lay spread eagled on the linoleum kitchen floor which had been transformed into an enormous pool of blood. If you have ever spilt a pint of milk on your kitchen floor then you'll know that it looks more like a gallon and this poor young man had exsanguinated every drop of blood in his body. It was like a horror film. Using the protective stepping plates placed by the SOCO I entered the living room and by all appearances it was the scene of the initial assault on the victim. A table was overturned and there was a knife on the floor with blood splatter patterns on the sofa and wall directly behind. Then I noticed words written by hand in blood on the wall opposite.

It appeared to be in Arabic, as it transpired that it was a passage from the Qur'an.

Over the following days I met with the twenty-seven-year-old victims parents who lived in the same village as me. It was terribly sad and I felt so sorry for them, such a waste of a young man's life.

Interviews with the suspect revealed what had happened and why. He was a former soldier from the middle-east and had settled in the UK. He was friends with the victim and they both used and dealt marijuana in the local area. They had been cultivating cannabis plants in their loft which had been harvested for sale. The suspect had become aware that the victim was dealing on the side and had not shared the profits. He said he had challenged him on this twice but the victim denied any wrong doing. He had decided on the day of the attack to wait in the living room of their flat and give the victim one last chance to tell him the truth. When the victim returned he sat down on the sofa and the suspect sat opposite on a chair.

The suspect asked him if he had been dealing behind his back. He denied it for a third time. The suspect then kicked him under the chin, moved towards him and grabbed his ponytail forcing his head back. He then took his knife and cut the victims throat open from ear to ear.

He told me he watched the victim clutch at his throat trying to stem the uncontrollable blood flow as he staggered to the kitchen where he collapsed on the floor. Using the victims blood the suspect wrote the Arabic passage on the wall. I asked a Professor of Islamic studies from The University of Exeter to interpret the text. It read as follows: *If you treat me as a fool then do not be surprised if I act like a fool.'*

The suspect then went to the local pub drank two pints of lager and called the Police to admit to his crime. It is there he was arrested and made his initial confession.

In my view and that of the Crown Prosecutor this was as clear a premeditated murder as you could possibly have. In the courts they took a different view finding the offender guilty of manslaughter by reason of temporary insanity. Well, that's the justice system for you. I know that the victims parents who were in court to hear the verdict didn't think justice was served that day.

Some weeks later on 9 March 2006 towards the end of my time with Homicide, I felt established in my role and confident in my ability to take on anything that came my way. I was fortunate that the degree of complexity had steadily increased along with my experience and confidence. Murders rarely get reported at 8am and I was on call again when at around midnight my work phone rang.

'Boss, there's been a stabbing in Radford and the victims 1/1 (deceased).'

I followed what had become my routine, I asked them to call me back in 15 minutes. I got dressed in my suit, collected my briefcase which contained my Dictaphone, daybook diary and policy log. In my car boot were wellington boots, a raincoat and forensic protective attire. I made a note of the time of the call and got in the car. When the officer called me back I was already en route to the scene and on hands free. I gave the detective at the scene instructions to call out the on-call homicide team and for SOCO to cordon off the wider crime scene which was outside a block of flats. I asked him to seize and view any immediate area CCTV, collate witness details and gather as much information about the circumstances of the stabbing as possible.

The victim was identified as Daniel Williams a 20-year-old man but it quickly became clear that we had no suspect and that this was therefore a category 'A' murder enquiry. At this point in time there were three categories of murder A, B and C each requiring differing levels of resources and of course community and media attention. Cat 'A' was the most serious and this was my first and would be a real test of my abilities and resolve. I set my strategy as the SIO... The immediate priorities were to secure and gather evidence from the scene including CCTV and eyewitness accounts. Officers were tasked with numerous actions and quickly the homicide machine was in motion. Clearly it was vitally important we identify the assailant quickly in order to preserve evidence, prevent flight and minimise the negative impact on the wider community and the victims family.

I met Daniels mother and his younger sister Chanell. I explained that I would be leading the investigation into Daniels murder and tried to reassure them that we would do all we could to bring his assailant to justice. I didn't know it then but Chanell and I would meet again 13 years later.

Radford was an inner-city area of Nottingham with a working class ethnically diverse community with significant amounts of drug related criminality. Very few people were prepared to speak to our officers on the record but after two days we had a name for our suspect, Cornelius Messam. He was a known drug dealer with a propensity for violence and had long standing 'beef' with Daniel. They had run-ins in the past and Messam had robbed Daniel in Daniels flat and on a separate occasion threatened him with a handgun at a house party. Daniel was just a normal kid but making a living dealing cannabis.

On the night Daniel was killed, Messam had driven past a chicken shop where Daniel was ordering take out with friends. He knew Daniel lived nearby and had hidden in bushes outside the block of flats where Daniel lived. When Daniel appeared Messam threatened him. They fought and Daniel was stabbed to death. Once Messam was identified as the primary suspect the hunt was on. We heard that he had left Nottingham almost immediately assisted by his girlfriend who had picked him up close to the scene and driven him to a location as yet unknown to the team. His girlfriend was uncooperative in the extreme. She was on a student visa from Jamaica studying at Nottingham University and was told in no uncertain terms how fragile her status in the UK would be if we proved that she had assisted an offender and had been uncooperative with the investigation. She still refused to cooperate. But I knew she would stay in touch with him wherever he was.

Utilising mobile phone data we could identify the location and cell traffic from Messam to his girlfriend. Messam was changing his mobile phone sim card every few days to avoid detection but three weeks into the investigation it was established he was living in Brighton. He had already set up home with a new girlfriend and was dealing drugs that he collected from London by train.

After weeks of painstaking work I was in a position to send a team to arrest Messam in Brighton. We didn't know if he was armed so they were assisted by a Sussex Police firearms team. The arrest was text book and could be viewed on the surveillance video. Messam got off the London to Brighton train having resupplied with drugs and as he left the station received a phone call from me which went something like this:

'Cornelius Massam?'

'Yeah, who's this?'

'Police, stand still and put your hands on your head.'

'What?' Messam looked at his phone with a confused look on his face whilst at the same time a police firearms officer approached him and pointed his Heckler and Koch MP5 at his head. Messam was finally in Police custody.

His new girlfriend another student had no idea what he was doing or what he had done. Her flat was searched by detectives and a forensic team and evidence seized. Messam refused to answer my questions in interview but the evidence gathered from eyewitnesses and from forensic telephone and DNA analysis was sufficient to charge him with the murder of Daniel Williams. We proved his Nottingham girlfriend had known of his crime and had nevertheless assisted him from the time of the murder when she picked him up in her car and had continued to do so until his arrest. She was found guilty at Court and deported to Jamaica leaving behind a promising career in Engineering.

Messam was found guilty of murder and given a life sentence. My team and I received Crown Court Commendations from the presiding Judge which as an SIO I was proud of as it supports the view that the investigation was of the highest standard. I met with the bereaved family to inform them of the outcome of the trial but was sure it was little consolation for a loved one's life lost but we had done our best.

It was to be my last investigation as the post of Divisional Commander for Mansfield and Ashfield became available and I was promoted.

CHAPTER TWENTY-SEVEN

It's a small world

Fast forward to 2019, some thirteen years later. Out of the blue and long since retired from Policing I received a phone call from a TV producer who was working with a woman who had won a National Media Competition, her prize being to be provided an opportunity to film and produce a documentary. The film would be about knife crime and bereavement and would be based upon the murder of Daniel Williams. The documentary maker was Daniels younger sister, Chanell Wallace who I had last seen as an eleven-year-old in her mother's living room in Radford. Initially I was extremely cautious about committing to take part. Since leaving the Police I have never looked back only forwards, I don't attend leaving do's or reunion get togethers as I don't want to dredge up the past. I find it invariably ends up with ex cops moaning about how 'everything was better way back when' and now the 'jobs fucked'. Believe me old cops said that to me the day I started on the beat and nothing's changed. I don't like looking to the past and I spend little time celebrating my achievements as I am driven to find the next challenge. I'm not sure what that says about me, and maybe I'm just antisocial but that's the way it is.

I was years into retirement from policing with my knowledge of the event somewhat faded, but I agreed to meet the producer Steve and Chanell in my local pub for a coffee to sound things out. When we met there was an instant connection and as we spoke I knew that I had to do the right thing.

Chanell was still grieving and all of these years later she remained traumatised. I agreed to do all I could to help and a few weeks later having refreshed my memory of the events we met again at my home. I asked myself whether I should disclose all of the details of Daniels death but she was adamant that she wanted to know every detail, so I agreed. I told Chanell the chronology of events but when I told Chanel that Daniels attacker had laid in wait for him she became very upset as she wasn't aware of this. I didn't know if I had done the right thing and we had to stop filming, but when we had finished she gave me the warmest embrace and said she couldn't thank me enough. I am so pleased I didn't say no. Out of my comfort zone again at 59, I thought those days were over. I received positive feedback on the documentary but should probably have moved my Ducati Panigale race bike out of my kitchen before filming. But it did look good and anyway doesn't everyone have a superbike in their kitchen?

Back to 2006. I left the Homicide Department with good memories and a total respect for the staff who routinely went above and beyond for the public and I hoped that they shared that view of me.

The power and flexibility of the human brain is an amazing thing. There is a popular myth that we only use a maximum of 10% of our brain capacity which isn't true but we definitely don't use anywhere near all of it.

Before my time as an SIO on Homicide I felt that I was on top of my game, able to retain voluminous amounts of information on all aspects of my role. However as an SIO you are required to retain a huge amount of detail.

Names, addresses, dates of birth, time lines, sequences of events, relationships, management of resources, political aspects and that's just the tip of the iceberg. Of course the brains cognitive power allows us to retain data and form connections, but when I started as an SIO I had to work hard to learn and retain this information, twelve months later it had become a natural process. My brain had been reshaped to manage my situation which I found incredible.

CHAPTER TWENTY-EIGHT

The boss of bosses

However, I was over the moon with my new appointment. Mansfield, Ashfield Division was performing pretty well and it had an old school community feel, far different to that of the City which always felt a little sterile and impersonal, probably due to its sheer scale. One of the previous Divisional Commanders was the same kind-hearted soul who had black balled my application for promotion to C/Insp on two occasions. As I sat in my new office with en suite and conference table I swivelled in my leather chair smiling to myself. Oh, the irony, I knew he would be furious to think of me sat here and I derived a lot of satisfaction from that. I was master of all I surveyed. 850 staff and numerous police stations covering a large swathe of the county. I actually felt I could finally relax a little and enjoy my success. I had far exceeded my own expectations from when I first joined the West Yorkshire Police and had grown as a person with a great family behind me. I reflected back to that bar in Londonderry when Dave the Corporal said I was a loser and I now realised that was a defining point in my life. So, Dave, 'Thank you.'

You may have personal experience of occasions when someone has told you, you 'can't' achieve something and if you're like me that is all the extra fuel you need to drive yourself to succeed. When barriers are placed before you, find a way to navigate around them. I know from bitter personal experience it is a far better strategy than hitting it head on and expecting it to move. Regrettably given my flawed character I would sometimes enjoy butting up against the barriers or the individuals who created them. Of course I know confrontation rarely leads to a positive outcome but sometimes to be true to yourself you just have to tell people they are, well, 'twats'. I just had this burning urge to let people know what I thought of them. I had to learn how to play a political game the hard way and I didn't learn fast.

I thoroughly enjoyed being the boss and for a long time everything went well. I spent a great deal of my time meeting and talking with my staff and making sure they knew my game plan and priorities and importantly that I understood their world and its challenges and that I would be there to support them to succeed.

My eldest daughter Olivia had applied to join the Police, she had been successful and had been given a joining date. Two months prior to Olivia starting training I sat at the monthly board meeting to discuss amongst other issues, budgetary savings. The Force had its budget cut by the Home Office and it was Chief Steve's job to decide where the cuts would fall. As Divisional Commanders we all knew it would be the front line that would be hardest hit and we were right. Steve announced that future Police Constable recruitment would be frozen for two years which of course meant that any future vacancies at the front line would not be filled, but much, much more importantly for me was the immediate realisation that Olivia may not have a job as a cop after all. It was all she had dreamed of from the age of eleven years of age and I was gutted, how was I going to tell her? I looked at Steve and the realisation dawned on him.

'Is your daughter in the next cohort,' he asked.

'Yes, Steve, please tell me that one is going ahead.'

'No Nick, I'm sorry,' he replied.

To be fair to Steve he offered to speak to Olivia to explain the situation but of course it would have to come from me. I got home from work and sat with Olivia to break the news. Olivia is nothing if not resilient. Olivia was already a community Warden for the City Council and got a job as a Police Community Support Officer whilst waiting two years for Police recruitment to open up again. She reapplied a much more experienced and rounded person and of course was successful. She has since made Detective Constable has passed her Sergeants exams and is now a Uniformed Sergeant. When Olivia initially told me of her intentions to become a Police Officer I was not best pleased. I wanted more for her as she was bright and intelligent and I knew she could achieve anything she set her mind to.

When she was sixteen I fixed it for her to be attached to a beat cop for a few days, my sole intention being to put her off the idea of joining. It was snowing and I asked the beat cop to make sure she was freezing and walking the beat all day. It didn't put her off one bit. She is a natural fit and loves her work, sometimes things are just meant to be.

The Home Office which has responsibility for policing in all its forms, Prisons, Customs and Excise, Border Force and MI5, launched a development scheme for senior leaders and open to all in the public sector. I applied, travelled to London where I was interviewed, tested in various ways, personality, numerically, cognitive reasoning, etc. I returned to the Force less than optimistic, hundreds had applied including some bright young things from my own Force. A week later the Chief called me to tell me I had been the only successful applicant. This was another highlight, unexpected and a great opportunity if I managed it well. The scheme came with a cheque book but any external development courses would have to be funded 50% Home Office and 50% Force. I needed to stay best mates with the Chief and of course I knew he still felt bad for shafting me over the City Command post so I was confident in getting my own way. I was appointed an external mentor, a great guy from my home town. He had been a very successful businessman and now helped others to develop their skills, I'm sure the grand a day he was paid was just an added bonus.

I completed a series of self assessments, Belbin, Myers Briggs and others to try and identify areas of strength and others for me to develop. I already knew I needed to work on my strategic thinking and leadership and together we found two courses that seemed perfect. One small problem, they cost £14,000 per week. One was at Harvard in the States and the other at Oxford University. I met Steve the Chief and explained my position and thankfully he agreed to fund it. Result. I chose Oxford as the kudos and grandeur of this University is world renowned and I am so glad I did, and honestly it was life changing.

CHAPTER TWENTY-NINE

The Oxford choirboy

There were 25 students on the Strategic Leadership Development Programme and perhaps unsurprisingly I was the only cop. I looked at the list of names, various nationalities and job titles and immediately once again felt out of my depth. It was Chief Executive Officer, Chief Operating Officer, Executive Director, Vice President, etc. I felt more than a little intimidated. I reckoned that my salary was probably £100k less than anyone else in the room.

I arrived at Oxford early one Sunday evening in 2007. I drove a Porsche Boxster S at the time so at least I wasn't too embarrassed pulling into the car park alongside the Range Rovers. I checked in was taken to my room, a small but functional affair pretty much laid out like a hotel room. On the reading table I found a two-foot high stack of books on leadership and hoped I didn't have to spend my evenings reading them.

Bag unpacked I was shown to a large room with chairs forming a circle around its circumference. Each student stood in front of a chair and the course staff introduced themselves. They looked like what they were a bunch of academics but obviously very good at what they did, as Oxford isn't known for its mediocrity. I was excited and like a human sponge I intended to soak up as much as possible out of my time there. We did a few ice-breaker routines and introduced ourselves and I felt self-conscious. We were told that our experiences during the time there would stretch our imagination and thinking and that we would be pushed far outside our comfort zones.

I liked the sound of that but it clearly wasn't for everybody.

Then we got started. We stayed in a wide circle and one student was thrown a squash ball. It was explained that one person would leave the room and whilst they were absent the ball would be passed around the students stopping only when told to do so by the instructor, the person holding the ball would hide it from view. The first student left the room and the ball was moved around until told to stop. The absent student was recalled and told to identify the person with the ball. He looked around the room bewildered selecting one person and another only being told to stop after several incorrect guesses. This happened again with the next student and the next. At this point it was my turn and I was asked to leave. A couple of minutes later I was invited to return. As I walked in the room I subconsciously scanned each individual and their body language and after about 30-seconds pointed to a fellow student. She held the ball out in her hand and some of my fellow students actually gasped in amazement, I felt like Dynamo. Apparently this had never happened previously and even now I'm not quite sure how I did it. That said in my assessments prior to the course at Oxford I scored 100% on observation meaning I notice things that others perhaps don't, which is very unusual so maybe that's something to do with it and of course I may just have that 'coppers' instinct for noticing when something is 'off'. It certainly made for an interesting night in the bar afterwards, people actually thought it was a fix and I was a plant but I now had the attention of the group.

One of the first characters I met on the course was Mark Wall. Mark was a charismatic Australian and former firearms Sergeant with the Australian Police. He had left the Police after ten years to set up his own security company with another ex-cop, Peter 'Macca' McCommish. They started with just one contract with a Gold mining company, Placer Dome in Porgera, Papua New Guinea setting up security systems and staffing in an extremely hostile part of the world. Porgera is the land that time forgot with numerous indigenous tribes who are constantly in conflict with one another and the only thing they seem to agree on is they all hate the mining operations. But within months Placer Dome had been acquired by the world's largest gold miner, Barrick Gold which like many other gold companies was based in Toronto, Canada. Barrick were clearly impressed by Mark and Macca as they offered them senior roles within their company. Mark became Vice President for Security and he and Macca moved to Toronto.

Mark and I got on immediately and shared many common interests. We chatted one evening over an overpriced bottle of specially selected Oxford varsity wine and was joined by a woman from St Kitts, Jennifer Nero.

Jennifer was not only strikingly beautiful but also Managing Director of the Caribbean Bank. We bonded quickly and like me Jennifer was a fitness freak. It didn't matter what time we stopped drinking the night before, we always made it to the gym at 7am the following morning, me on the weights and Jennifer the treadmill. Little did I know then but I would work with them both in the years ahead.

As I had been promised on that first evening, I spent most of the course outside of my comfort zone. The activities included acting out leadership roles. Assisted by Mythodrama a company owned by Richard Olivier, son of Lawrence and assisted by actors from the Royal Shakespeare Company. We played out scenes from *Henry the Fifth* and discussed the leadership challenges he faced and how we would respond. It was definitely out there. One evening we had dinner in the 'Harry Potter' dining room in the Old University building and afterwards a Finnish composer resplendent in leather trousers and sporting a handlebar moustache taught us the basics of conducting a choir, baton and all. He informed us that this exercise was about exploring the intra-human connection and emotional intelligence, how we spiritually connect with others. It sounded bollocks to me as my mind was pretty well closed to the idea but I was so very wrong. After our brief introduction to conducting we walked the short distance to Christ Church College cathedral where around eighty choristers sat patiently waiting in the terraced pews.

In the splendour of the cathedral our maestro gave a demonstration on how it was done. Initially when the choir broke into song they were seated and focussed solely on the conductor. As the tempo and animation of the conductor increased they began to rise to their feet one by one as if motivated by an invisible force. It was surreal to witness, sending shivers down my spine witnessing the influence of that one individual over others. It was a beautiful thing, the atmosphere and grandeur of the cathedral and the aural perfection of the choir all led by our leather clad maestro.

We were quickly brought back to reality as it was our turn. Some students refused to even step forward. Mark volunteered but didn't seem to get the connection and the choir were vocal but remained seated and clearly unmoved, several others had a similar experience. I took a deep breath, raised my hand and volunteered to go next. This was so incredibly uncomfortable and unnatural for me, with all eyes focussed in my direction. I took up the baton and made eye contact with the principle chorister. What followed I can only describe as an out of body experience. My whole body tingled with the charge of electricity and I became totally engrossed in my role. I made eye contact individually one after the other with all of the choir as they looked to me for direction. As the piece moved on and the tempo increased I became more animated and the lead got to her feet, quickly followed one after another by the whole choir. I have rarely felt anything like that in my life, it was so emotionally impacting and rewarding. I could have carried on all night but sadly it was time for someone else to have a go. The lead chorister was asked to provide individual feedback and she said that I had made that emotional connection with her through my actions and our eye contact and she felt as though she and I were the only people in the room. Her colleagues all agreed. Such is the power and energy of the human spirit.

After the squash ball magic trick and now this, I noticed people looking at me differently and wanting to engage directly with me. Whilst I was at Oxford I was approach by the Vice President of Shell Oil and offered a very well-paid senior role. Of course I was flattered to be asked and did considered the proposal but I was a Chief Superintendent with a significant pension and commutation only three years away and it would have been a massive risk to leave the police with a much reduced payout. On this occasion I took the safe option and declined his kind offer.

Jennifer also approached me and asked if I would be interested in conducting a security review for the Caribbean Bank in St Kitts. I would have to seek permission from the Chief but agreed in principle. Jennifer said she wanted me to meet her boss the following night. He was guest of honour at the Said Business School awards ceremony.

On our final evening together we had a fancy dinner and Mark, Jennifer and I sat together and were soon joined by Jennifer's boss, Sir K. Dwight Venner. He was an imposing figure and exuded status and authority, commanding the attention of the whole room as he entered. He greeted me warmly and during our conversation he asked if I would work for him as per Jennifer's request in St Kitts.

Of course, I agreed and we had a wonderful night as new found friends. On my return home all I could talk about was my experiences at Oxford which had definitely changed me as an individual. Being able to work successfully outside of the police organisation had instilled more self-belief and confidence and I had greater empathy for others and awareness of self. It is so important that we understand who we are and the impact of our actions upon others. It also taught me the value of relationships and how personal positive interactions lead to more productive outcomes.

CHAPTER THIRTY

The big, bad, new world

Steve was happy for me to take leave and work in St Kitts. The Bank flew me business class, a first for me and rewarded me handsomely for my work but to be honest I was more interested in stepping outside of the policing world and into a new one to test myself. If I could make this work then there might actually be a life after policing. I flew British Airways from Heathrow to St Lucia fought my way through the airport chaos and onto a small, fixed-wing charter plane to St Kitts. St Lucia was absolutely beautiful and I had high hopes for St Kitts. It was my first visit to the West Indies.

St Kitts is an abbreviation of St Christopher the island named after Christopher Columbus who landed there in 1493. It has a history of Spanish and English rule and its legal system is founded on English law. Its capital is Basseterre.

I arrived on the Sunday evening having flown low over the islands international cricket ground where locals including Jennifer were playing a match. I was met at the hotel by Daniel King a six feet five inch giant of a man who worked security at the Caribbean Central Bank. Daniel was to be my driver and personal assistant/bodyguard for the duration of my stay. I didn't know much about St Kitts or the risks I might face but was comforted by the 9 mm Glock attached to Daniels right hip. He explained that the hotel bill was being taken care of by the bank and that he would collect me at 8am the following day. Happy days, time for a cold one by the pool, I thought.

As I sipped a locally brewed Carib beer, I ran through the scope of work for the umpteenth time. All I was required to do in the 10 days I was there was conduct a security review of the Bank and its assets including the Governors' mansion. Pretty straightforward I thought but as with almost every well laid plan things change dynamically.

Daniel arrived at 8am sharp and drove me to the banks HQ. It was a large, gated complex with chain link perimeter fence, CCTV at the gate and armed officers checking arrivals and departures. We drove into a large car park driving to the front of the grey stone building, parking outside. Daniel escorted me to the front reception desk where I signed in and was handed a VIP visitors pass. The bank was clearly doing well as the inside of the building was immaculate with an expensive finish. We went two floors up in the elevator and a right turn to the office of Sir K. Dwight Venner (CBE, KBE) the banks Governor. Daniel opened the door to let me in. Christ I was nervous but being met by a warm smile from both he and Jennifer made me feel immediately at ease. 'Commander' boomed the Governor which was to be my title from this point. Apparently Jennifer had told him my rank and position of Divisional Commander and he must have liked the sound of that. He shook my hand and we were all seated. He welcomed me and we discussed the plans for the next ten days.

On speaking to them it was pretty clear that my role and scope would morph somewhat. I completed the physical reviews of security, identifying numerous vulnerabilities and making recommendations to eradicate or mitigate the risk. There were some obvious and immediate risks such as the access procedures to the Bank front gates. There was only one lane in, access being controlled by an electronic barrier but there was no sterile area for vehicles to be properly searched or turned around should access be denied. As it was, the 'at risk' vehicle had to drive into the car park turn around and out of the exit gate via another barrier. I designed a plan for controlled access which allowed this to happen. The costs were minimal but safety and security much improved. Basic stuff, as lots of security issues are, but often these are missed, creating potential risks. There were more complex problems with technical solutions but the basics were easy wins.

I was also tasked with speaking with one of the Security Officers who had been shot accidentally by one of his colleagues during a transfer of assets from the bank to the airport. I studied their security procedures manual including the training, use and storage of firearms. The officer had a grievance and a legal claim against the company and it was clear that the Governor wanted me to persuade the plaintiff to drop his claim. I met with the aggrieved officer, Joshua and found him reasonable and somewhat justified in his grievance. We chatted about the incident and as we talked it was clear that he felt isolated and ignored which created the feeling of victimisation. He had taken a grievance and legal action as a last resort. He loved his job and wanted to return but wanted recognition that he had suffered and that training and procedures needed to improve. All firearms officers had been initially trained in the US by Smith and Wesson the gun manufacturer but many had not had any training or practice in years. I empathised with Joshua and listened to him providing supportive advice where I could, it was clear he would benefit from counselling, which had not been provided. In truth it felt to me that that's what I was doing at the time, just by allowing him to pour out his feelings and putting an arm around him. Getting shot is bound to have psychological consequences. Joshua and I spoke for maybe two hours and talked through his ideas to improve the procedures within the security team. I agreed to put forward his ideas with a few of my own thoughts and closed the meeting, parting as friends with a handshake. Joshua was a good guy and loyal employee who just needed to vent his emotions and feel valued and listened to. I'm sure we can all understand that. So often in my experience employee grievances spiral out of control due to poor communication when an honest two-way conversation could have resolved it at the outset. All too frequently pride gets in the way of doing the right thing. Sometimes we just have to admit when we get it wrong.

I debriefed the meeting with Jennifer and the soon to retire Head of Security, Kenneth and they agreed to support any changes required and to fund the counselling for Joshua. Jennifer asked if I would bring their security and firearms practices and procedures up to scratch, and of course I obliged. A quick phone call back to a friend running Nottinghamshire's Firearms Department and I had a Policy I could adapt for St Kitts. I was putting in the hours rising at 6am then an hour in the gym in the office for 8am usually finishing there at 6pm, a shower and then dinner for one in the hotel restaurant with an over-priced bottle of wine for company. Then I would do two or three hours work before lights out. My plan was to complete my final reports prior to leaving, present Sir Dwight and Jennifer with a copy and talk through the headline recommendations. I knew they wouldn't expect this but I wanted to impress.

The Governor had arranged a canapé and drinks event for me to meet the Heads of the Military and Policing for St Kitts and Nevis. The Military Commander was a great guy and we shared tales from our experiences in service. The Chief of Police was more guarded and I think suspicious of my motives for being there, maybe he thought I was there to take his job. Sir Dwight asked if I would meet with the Police Command Team to agree some response and security protocols. I had a frosty reception but worked through some ideas to agree police response procedures for attacks on the bank and its employees such as kidnap and ransom and armed attacks on cash in transit from the bank to the airport. I knew they would agree to everything within reason. Sir Dwight wasn't a man you said 'No' to, well not if you wanted to remain as Chief of Police. I formalised a Memorandum of Understanding between the Police and the Bank prior to my departure.

Jennifer called the following day to inform me that Joshua had withdrawn his legal case and the grievance. She was delighted as was

I. Joshua came back to work and helped to implement the changes we had both agreed.

Never one to miss an opportunity she also asked if I would interview candidates for the soon to be vacant Head of Security position and of course I obliged.

One of the applicants was Daniel King, my right-hand man. Daniel was a great guy, very laid back and he showed me everything St Kitts and its capital Basseterre had to offer, which to be honest wasn't that much. There are some historical sites such as Brimstone Hill Fortress, built over the course of 100 years by the British using slaves from Africa. It was the scene of a British defence against the French with the 1,000 British soldiers and slaves fighting side by side against an 8,000 strong attack force. The siege lasted a month ending with a British surrender. St Kitts was strategically important due to its key role and financial value in the sugar trade.

Sat at the promenade of the marina with a cold beer, we watched the enormous cruise ships dock. Daniel explained that as soon as they made port, local prices went up 50% for tourists. I made a mental note not to go cruising the Caribbean any time soon. The residents of St Kitts had a great lifestyle and didn't rush to do anything which could be frustrating. One morning as Daniel drove me to the office we sat behind yet another car driving at 20 miles per hour and at the bottom of the number plate was the slogan, 'What de rush man'. That just summed the place up.

After ten days living and working outside my comfort zone I was heading home. Yes, I'd banked a significant amount of cash, which was nice but more importantly I had a new found confidence knowing that I could perform well in challenging environments outside of the world of policing. Sir Dwight and Jennifer were delighted when I presented each of them with a bound copy of the final report. Each business area had a risk assessment and cost benefit analysis with several scaled options to improve their security and mitigate risk. They called me a couple of weeks later to tell me that the board had agreed to fund and implement all recommendations and that Daniel King was to be appointed the Head of Security to deliver the plan. I was delighted for Daniel. It had been invaluable experience and incredibly rewarding.

CHAPTER THIRTY-ONE

All good things

It was back home to the cold of Nottingham and business as usual for me but I knew given my recent experiences that I could thrive outside of policing. I was now keen to get out there and see what I could achieve.

However for here and now I had the responsibility of running a Division, I was enjoying life and things went well for a couple of years. As Divisional Commander I had found my *raison d'être* and I worked hard to build productive relationships with my staff, the public, media and politicians who are all essential elements in successfully delivering policing by consent. I had the freedom to lead my division and make all the decisions. I had a predominantly strong team of senior managers but with one or two challenging individuals but that's life. There's no perfect team unless of course you have the luxury of hand picking them. I believed that I achieved all I could given my situation and with hindsight that hasn't changed. I invested in my people with both my time and resources, I supported self-improvement and development. I took personal responsibility for mentoring those with ambition to succeed.

It is true that one of my failings is impatience and I had little time for those colleagues of mine who did not share my work ethic or commitment to the cause of public service. Many police officers didn't quite understand that it is the public who pay their salaries and they actually thought they had a choice on whether they delivered a quality service to the public. I would open each officer and staff training seminar in order to meet everyone, take feedback and make my position and priorities clear. Occasionally an officer would disagree with my instruction to keep victims of crime routinely updated on the progress of their investigation. A simple task you might think but some thought they had better things to do and complaints from victims were a problem. My response to those officers and for the benefit of others who might agree with them was to say, 'If delivering the priorities of the public isn't important to you then maybe you should consider your choice of career, because this isn't optional'. All I ever wanted as a cop was clarity. I left no one in doubt of my expectations as their leader.

All was going well, that was of course until the Force once again came under Home Office scrutiny. In national policing performance terms Nottinghamshire Police was compared to its most similar forces (MSF), these are forces of a similar size and demographic with similar crime and socio-economic issues. Nottinghamshire were performing poorly in a number of key areas. My own Division had issues around car crime and house burglary. I had implemented (indeed written) best practice and knew after analysing voluminous amounts of data that by comparison we were significantly under staffed. As a member of the taxpaying public you might ask yourself as I did why Chief Officers do not allocate resources scientifically to meet and suppress demand whilst devising longer term strategies for continued suppression of crime and disorder. In order to understand why, one needs to appreciate the politics of policing at its most senior levels.

It was clear to all that the ACPO team (Association of Chief Police Officers) in Nottinghamshire were not team players, rather acting out of self-interest, striving for that next rung up the ACPO ladder. Agreeing to share or lose resources rarely results in a positive outcome for those giving them up. They may also mistakenly believe that if they did so this would make them appear weak to those whom they lead. For strategic leadership to work effectively there has to be a common understanding, a shared goal with each leader playing their part toward the attainment of success. And that of course is why we have a leader at the top of every pyramid to take the difficult decisions.

Dysfunctional and often therefore poor performing teams, jealously guard 'their' resources forgetting that it is the public they serve and who fund those resources. Confident and competent leaders are not afraid to make decisions that are clearly informed and risk based. They encourage entrepreneurialism and creative solutions for it is the shared outcome of success that inspires and drives them.

Regrettably our ACPO team thought in silos and protected themselves from risk. I would sit around the boardroom table being instructed to improve performance by reducing crime, but not once did I receive or was offered any tangible support in achieving that goal. Always a problem with no offer of a solution. It was clear I was on my own and therefore vulnerable.

I prepared a business case drawing on all the data and information available. I could clearly show that the division was short of around 80 staff that its profile demanded. I asked for 21 as I knew I could make this work by placing them in critical areas and I could reduce crime through the targeting of high-risk offenders through partnership working and surveillance. It was a basic Pareto principle 20% of our criminals causing 80% of the harm. Target the 20% and disproportionately reduce crime.

It was the annual budget meeting and I had (I thought) secured support from my ACC line manager. I had submitted my business case in advance and as Divisional Commander and Heads of Department we were told that the meeting would review all requests for resources openly and if merited force resources would be reconfigured and reallocated. And I, in my naivety actually believed it. The four Divisional Commanders were optimistic that resources from HQ and Support Departments would be moved to the front line to meet and suppress the demands of crime and disorder. How else would we deal with the problem and satisfy the HO that we had our act together as a Force? Chief Steve chaired the meeting and the Heads of Service each put forward their plans for the following twelve months supported by costs, benefits and risk.

The ACC in charge of support services put forward her bid which included replacement command and control vehicles and a new replacement boat for patrolling the River Trent. As she presented one new bid for increased spending after another, myself and my fellow Divisional Commanders looked at one another with incredulity. Surely the Chief hadn't agreed to fund this nonsense when the Force were in crisis! Believe me, there aren't too many pirates on the River Trent these days.

I presented my business case for an extra 21 officers and staff at a cost of £900k per annum, it was as clear as day that the case should receive support and this was immediately acknowledged by many present. The meeting drew to a close and Steve summed up his decision. My business case was refused with zero growth to my budget which in real terms meant a budget cut as running costs always rise year on year. The Operational Support Department were handed over one million pounds in growth to buy a boat, van and some other non essential toys. It was a defining point in my career as it was clear I would be criticised for a lack of performance improvement. I knew I had done all I could with the resources at my disposal and it was also clear that my business case was valid and justifiable, but that ultimately when the blame game started the buck would stop with me and I would be held accountable. I had received absolutely no support from my line manager or ACPO team to improve performance. The future looked pretty grim and I had learned a very hard lesson.

No matter how irrefutable you think your case or argument may be, unless you have secured support from the key players in the room prior to any decision making you will most likely fail. I should not have assumed my boss would have secured Chief Officer support and I should have worked harder to secure support from the Chief prior to the meeting because in truth it was clear the decisions on budget allocation had been made behind closed doors well before the meeting. I believed my line manager who was a part of the ACPO team would fight my corner, I was wrong. As a leader the frustration of not being able to support my officers and staff with the resources we required to deliver to our potential was huge. In reality the overwhelming majority of our people in Nottinghamshire Police worked hard and usually above and beyond the call. My job as their leader was to provide not only clarity and direction but the support they required to deliver on those goals. When you begin to doubt your own ability to provide that support, it's time to leave. I am not a hypocrite and I found myself in a conflicted position where I was asking people to deliver the impossible.

Ironically but unsurprisingly as performance of the Force declined further the Home Office intervened and sent senior ACPO officers into Force to provide 'support'. This support was clearly Home Office intervention and they were now pulling the strings having lost confidence in the ability of the command team to deliver. I met with Deputy Chief Constable Chris Simms who came from the West Midlands Police and he was fully aware of the planning and resourcing debacle amongst numerous other failures of leadership. He also told me I had been scapegoated by ACPO as part of the problem. Unbelievable, trying to pass the buck of responsibility when it was crystal clear who was culpable. But I was on my way out from division to make way for the latest 'Marcus'. Simon was an accelerated promotion 'flyer' who needed Command experience. Divisional performance was used as the argument for me to be replaced. I was so frustrated by the lack of support but having only two years to go before I could retire I did not push back, what would be the point? In truth I was relieved to be able to take the burden of stress and responsibility from my shoulders. Stress is part and parcel of any leadership role and I believe stress is usually productive, it creates adrenaline and when the challenge is deliverable it is a positive emotion. When the challenge is not achievable it creates a damaging psychological stress born of frustration and this is the stress that kills. As I left my office for the last time I thought, 'See if he can do any better.' If only I could have seen a couple of months into the future I would have pushed back at the decision with everything I had.

With external intervention at the Chief Officer level resources were reviewed and eighty-six, YES, 86 officers were tipped out of support departments and sent to my former Division. Vindication if it were ever needed I thought. At the subsequent Board Meeting I received an open apology from the new Chief Julia who clearly had no part in the original decision. They actually openly declared that my business case for resources was the most compelling they had seen. To be honest it was far too little, too late. I had lost my Division, some credibility and felt bruised by the treatment I had received and was now sat behind a desk as Head of Corporate Development. I felt like I had been kicked in the teeth but that's politics. I did derive some satisfaction from seeing the contrite faces of those who had driven the nails in my coffin eating humble pie in front of my colleagues and their new Home Office masters.

CHAPTER THIRTY-TWO

The countdown

I was now even closer to the command team at headquarters and a fish out of water. In my own mind it was over. I had twenty-four great years of Policing and now I was working with a bunch of people who were supposed to be a team but seemingly couldn't even agree on what day of the week it was. There was much discontent between them and they were under pressure. As ever, I tried to stay positive and find the silver lining, after all, two years and I was out of there anyway. Certainly, I found I had more time on my hands and I could structure a routine, I wasn't even on call for the first time in as long as I could remember. I could go to the gym or for a run around the country park in which I was situated. I worked days with no evening, weekend or public commitments which you'd think sounds great, but I felt unfulfilled and bored. After six months a new Deputy Chief had also started as part of the shake up and I was to report directly to him. Chris Eyre was a great guy, very talented and experienced and I felt that working with him to move things forward at the corporate strategic level might actually make my last 18 months bearable and possibly even enjoyable. And so it proved, we worked well together with a shared disregard for his ineffective senior colleagues. Chris was on a promise for the Chief Constable position otherwise I am sure he would have stayed in his Deputy Chief role at Leicestershire, a Force of comparable size and without the drama. He was surprisingly open with me some would say indiscreet but I welcomed being drawn into his confidence. How I wished he had been Chief Constable five years earlier, my time as a Divisional

Commander would have been so much more positive and enjoyable. This was the kind of leader I tried to emulate, forthright but compassionate, intelligent and totally focussed on the end game.

I was tasked with developing a performance dashboard that would provide real time performance metrics, providing transparency to enable dynamic resource allocation. I worked with the IT developers and pressured them daily to deliver much to their displeasure. IT certainly in my experience works to a different temporal dimension than the rest of the world and they don't much care for close scrutiny and challenging timescales. But they came through and successfully delivered. I had to create a planning framework for the Force and fully understand business and finance once this was established. At this point I had twelve months remaining of my thirty 'pensionable' years I needed to retire with maximum financial benefits. Fortuitously four of my five military years had transferred across as pensionable. I could retire with 26 years' service. Thank God.

Austerity loomed and first to be targeted by Government were public services and first in line were the Police. Predictably Chris was ahead of the game and I was tasked with reviewing the operational policing structure of the force. This included the Divisional and Departmental construct and rank structure. My simple task: 'It must be effective in service delivery at a significantly reduced cost.' At that time Chris expected to lose up to 30% of the police budget in the years ahead.

When faced with a financial crisis imperative it is much easier to move mountains. I had to think what would have been unthinkable just months been before. I challenged conventional thinking and took significant numbers of supervisory ranks out of the structure including those at a very senior level and reduced the Divisions from four to two. My plan was for the Force to have a City and County Division coterminous with the local authorities and City and County Councils. Of course if you have only two divisions you require two less of a lot: Chief Superintendents, Superintendents, etc, and only two devolved Human Resource Departments. But my proposal was to centralise all support functions such as HR and Finance to save costs. Furthermore I recommended reducing the number of Police Stations immediately by 40% and subsequently 60%. My decisions were not merely cost driven but service based. There were numerous small stations owned by the Police Authority and housing only a handful of locally based community staff. My proposal was to relocate these officers to shared local authority managed and paid for accommodation. I was amazed at how quickly the Chief Officers and Police Authority agreed to a plan that took less work than my doomed Divisional business case. I consulted with leaders of the two County Councils who supported the plan and presented the final draft to various committees. All accepted the changes. I had a suspicion that I was given this poison chalice because I was about to retire and would take the blame away from others who remained. In truth it had to be done and at least I had the operational experience to understand and apply the most effective plan that would best protect front line staff and service delivery to the public. I suppose with hindsight I achieved a lot at Corporate Development and I learned things I wouldn't have otherwise and these served me well going forward. As they say, 'Everything happens for a reason.'

I was six months from retirement and the job owed me about three months in time owing for all the rest days I had worked and I was taking them. This meant when added to my annual leave I could finish in April instead of September, but what would I do next? I didn't really have a plan, I would get a pension that was more than most people's salaries and a significant lump sum to pay off the mortgages on the two properties we owned and even provide some savings. I didn't need to work but I was only fifty-one, full of energy and looking for a new challenge.

CHAPTER THIRTY-THREE

Opportunity Knocks

And then one sunny evening I was out for a ride on my mountain bike when my phone rang, 'number unknown'. I don't usually answer calls I don't recognise but had a feeling I should. I answered and it was my old Oxford Uni mate Mark Wall, Vice President at Barrick Gold. After exchanging pleasantries he explained that he knew that I was coming up for retirement (I don't know how but his team had definitely done their homework on me) and had a job for me if I was interested. Of course I was keen to hear more and he explained it was working for Barrick in Africa, specifically Tanzania. I told him I was interested and he said his colleague Glen Salt would be in touch to discuss matters in more detail. Soon after I arrived home Glen called. The conversation was pretty brief and went something along the lines of. 'Nick, can you jump on a plane and get over to Dar es Salaam this week?'

It was Monday. I said I would seek authority from my boss (Chris Eyre) and get back to him if he could check out flight arrangements for Thursday and Friday. He explained that Barrick were in need of a Corporate Investigations Manager but all employment terms were up for discussion. I wasn't sure what that meant but from that point I was so excited at the prospect of new opportunities, I couldn't even sleep. I discussed the possibilities with Jenny who was now employed full-time as an intensive care manager and the kids, Olivia now 21 and Savannah 15. It was a great opportunity but I would be spending a considerable amount of time away from home which I hadn't done before and we are a very close family. We agreed that I should go to Tanzania, get a feel for the place and people and establish more details of the contract which I hadn't yet seen. I had no idea what the offer might be but Jen and I discussed it and agreed it had to be worth a shot if they offered £80–90k on top of my pension. On the Tuesday I saw Chris Eyre and briefed him on my news. He was genuinely delighted at the prospect and I asked his advice.

'My advice, Nick, is to jump on that plane with my blessing and seize the opportunity.'

I was even happier I had his support. I didn't bother speaking to the new Chief Julia as I wasn't really interested in and nor did I value her opinion. We had never really hit it off and were on completely different wavelengths. Experience had taught me that her response would only be negative. I would be proven right a couple of months later.

With all of the family on board and excited to hear what was on offer I flew to Dar es Salaam with KLM via Amsterdam airport, Schiphol. KLM, Royal Dutch Airlines is a great airline. The cabin crew were and how can I say this politely – mature but the service and food was always outstanding. The business lounges and there are two of them in Amsterdam airport are the size of two football fields. I hadn't flown with them before, I was flying economy and ordered a gin and tonic with my lunch. The male flight attendant gave me a bottle of Bombay and a tonic. I held out a £10 note and he smiled.

'Sir, drinks are complimentary, you're flying Royal.'

'In that case,' I said, 'make it a double,' and he was only too happy to oblige.

It was a long day and one I would become accustomed to. Leave home at 5am to arrive at Birmingham airport for 6:15am, 7:30am city hopper flight to Amsterdam and 10am take off to Dar Es Salaam via Kilimanjaro arriving finally at 10pm which was 8pm UK time.

When I arrived in 'Dar' I followed the narrow corridor to the arrivals visa desk which was bedlam. I needed a tourist visa before I could collect my case and there was absolutely no organisation to it.

New arrivals all crowded around a glass fronted desk waving cash at a solitary figure who looked incredibly bored. Just then two men arrived and having taken cash from the new arrivals stamped their passports and allowed them through. I soon learned that this was all a scam and every time someone arrived in Dar they would be asked for a different amount. It should have been $50 USD but was sometimes $200. I handed over my $50 got my passport stamped and collected my case. I exited the airport and was met by Glen Salt an Australian from Perth, he looked just like Larry Fishbourne but white. He was a good guy, another ex-cop and we got on well. As we headed to the hotel he explained that there were two options on the table to try and make the job work for both me and Barrick. My job was to take over from him as Corporate Investigations Manager which translated meant overseeing all investigations across all corporate entities, the Companies African Headquarters, one in Johannesburg and another in Dar and the companies four active mine sites and additional exploration sites. The Security team was led by a Director who was to be my line manager. I would report to the Director for day-to-day matters but the real power and leadership direction came from the Security Vice President, Mark Wall in Toronto. Effectively I had two bosses. This concerned me as a dog can only have one master. In my new position I would have two expat Investigations Managers at each location and they were supported by trained investigators who were Tanzanian nationals. The security apparatus included a training school based at Bulyanhulu mine site which ran courses on everything from firearms to investigation. Until accommodation could be found for me I would be living in a hotel, the Double Tree Hilton situated on the seafront. All the guys I would be working alongside had flown in from Canada, Australia and elsewhere 'in country' to give me a grilling over drinks and dinner. It was all very informal but it was definitely a job interview. These guys, mostly Aussies all knew and trusted one another and it would be important, given the loose structures and interoperability, that I fit in. We had drinks before dinner on the terrace of the Sea Cliff Hotel and one after another the guys came over for a chat. I was that preoccupied chatting I hadn't looked at the dinner menu so when the waiter came to take my order I hadn't a clue but overheard Andre Claasen one of the site investigators order a steak so I just said, 'I'll have what he just ordered.'

'And how do you want that cooked sir?' he asked.

'Medium rare please,' and with that off he went. I love a medium rare fillet of beef. When dinner arrived a plate with what can only be described as an uncooked lump of white flesh the size of a forearm lay before me.

I nudged Andre. 'What the fuck is that?' I asked.

He laughed, 'Octopus steak man.'

I just couldn't eat it, it was tough as rubber and slimy as tripe. I resorted to hiding bits in a napkin and chucking it under the table. I was bloody starving.

So that's just the way it is, no advert, no short listing just a chat over a dinner without the dinner and the jobs yours if you want it. The Police HR department would be apoplectic to think any businesses let alone a really successful business operated this way. In the real world if you don't know the jobs yours when you pitch up for the interview it's very likely it isn't.

Having googled Barrick prior to my departure I found that this multi-billion dollar company was having some public and investor relations issues. It was in the public domain that 21 people (trespassers) had been killed at Barrick's North Mara mine site by the Police who were protecting the mine on behalf of Barrick. As a consequence of the negative publicity some of the heavyweight investors had withdrawn funds. There were human rights protests outside Barrick's offices in Toronto and Human Rights Watch were monitoring Barrick's response to the situation in Tanzania. It was made clear part of my role was to reduce the number of fatalities and improve relationships with the Police and communities surrounding the mines. It was explained that theft and other losses from the mines was a huge problem with the company losing multi-millions of dollars in assets from fuel to vehicles and of course the prized commodity, gold, on a daily basis. It seemed like a mammoth task but I felt sure I could add some value and it certainly didn't appear that it could get any worse.

Fuel theft was so far embedded that three filling stations had set up in Kahama the town local to Bulyanhulu. Kahama had grown in size and population largely on the back of property stolen from Barrick Gold. It was estimated during the previous two years Barrick had lost over $20 million in stolen assets. Kahama had burgeoned in scale from a small village into a town of thousands.

In response, Mark and Macca had introduced a set of Gold Security Standards which were at the cutting edge of Global Mining Security, but it needed to be implemented and monitored to ensure the maximum effect in reducing company losses.

Over the following couple of days I got to meet some of my prospective colleagues. My new boss in country would be the Security Director, Tex, a kiwi and former New Zealand SAS sergeant. Tex had brought in a few of his mates including a former MI5 operative Jonathan and an analyst Dr Reece to manage intelligence.

My first encounter with Tex didn't bode well for our future relationship. Out of courtesy I went to his office to introduce myself and to thank him for hosting my visit and the opportunity to potentially join the team.

His reply was: 'Don't fucking thank me mate, I didn't bring you out here.'

'Nice guy... not much point in continuing that conversation,' I thought, so I left and found Glen. It was clear Tex did not want me out there and at that time I wasn't sure why, but I would find out later.

Clearly I wanted to know more about the terms and conditions. I was out there and Glen was looking for my level of commitment but I still didn't have any idea what I would be paid. I broached the issue which I found a little awkward but Glen explained that I had two options.

Option 1, fly-in-fly-out (FIFO) six-weeks in-country followed by three-weeks leave at home. I would be offered a two-year contract with all company benefits such as flights, family medical, dentistry, life cover, accommodation and personal living expenses all covered by Barrick. Tax would be paid locally at 30%.

Option 2 was to work as a self-employed contractor without the benefits or security of a Barrick contract, tax and domestic arrangements would be down to me. The salary for Option 1 would be $160k USD which was way more than I expected especially given that I would have all my costs covered. As a contractor I would be paid £10,000 per month.

I said my goodbyes to Glen at the airport feeling nervous but excited. 'Here we go again, Nick,' I thought to myself, 'another bloody mountain to climb, what do I know about Gold mining security?' and to do it in a totally alien environment was incredibly daunting. I wondered if occasionally I should try staying in my comfort zone for a little while and try it out for size. I might actually enjoy it! But not this time, there were adventures to be had.

In reality Managerial and Leadership skills are the same no matter what business you are in, soldiering, Policing or Gold Mining and are transposable. There is however no substitute for experience.

Jenny picked me up from the airport the following morning at 10am. We talked all day and then later in the pub that evening. What decision should I make? I had to consider the kids of course. Savannah was only 15 and whilst everything seemed ok with her, she was coming up for GCSE's which would be followed by 'A' levels the year after and I worried what effect me being away for six weeks at a time might have on her. Olivia was fine and much more independent, living with Ben, my son-in-law in their own home nearby. In truth I wasn't convinced that I would be happy being away from the family for six weeks. I had never been away from home and family for more than a week or so before and it would all be new and very demanding and of course I didn't want to fail. The money wasn't a major issue, I was comfortable financially and really didn't need to work but the additional cash could make a huge difference to all our futures. Having weighed everything up, we decided as a family that I should give it a go.

After all I wasn't in prison, I could pack it in and come home anytime I chose. I told Chris Eyre and human resources my leaving date of 7 April but knew I would still be legally employed, by Nottinghamshire Police until 11 September 2011. Chris had no problem with my plan and I never even discussed it with the Chief as I knew she wouldn't add any value and I had Command approval from Chris. When I walked out of Police Headquarters for the very last time I never looked back. No regrets, no remorse, no sadness at leaving. It was time to open a new chapter. Africa was calling.

CHAPTER THIRTY-FOUR

Out in Africa

I was required by Barrick HR to complete numerous forms, submit to several medical examinations, blood, eye and hearing tests. I bought a scanner as I got so fed up with going to the library every day to send yet another form or certificate to Johannesburg. It took six weeks to complete the 'on board' processes but I finally had my airline tickets and start date. Jenny and I had decided we would help Olivia and Savannah get on the property ladder so that was a sizeable chunk of our savings gone but Africa would refill the coffers. Like many people we had struggled financially when we were younger and had decided that if we could help the kids avoid that pain then we should. Better to have the cash now and see them flourish and enjoy life than have it when we were dead and buried. We were lucky to be in that position and not everyone is. It felt good though, a real achievement. We always worked hard for what we had and had never been given a thing. This made it all the more satisfying because of that.

I decided upon option 1, a permanent contract for greater personal security. I was on board and excited but knew I would miss my family, friends and lifestyle terribly. In my mind I had convinced myself six weeks wasn't that long. I was wrong.

I said tearful goodbyes to the family and off I went. I had bought a Macbook Pro to keep in touch with them and some new suitcases. I had loads of smart casual summer gear, some desert boots and even a new pair of Oakley Flak Jackets. I definitely looked the part.

For the second time Jenny dropped me at the airport and I headed for Tanzania. The whole transition through airports would become second nature and a breeze but on this occasion my head overflowed with emotion and I even left my bum bag containing my wallet and passport at security. Having recovered it I had a couple of drinks to steady the ship and looked around at the travellers most of whom wore happy faces beaming with the anticipation of a holiday abroad. It is a very different sensation when travelling for business. It is a lonely experience and I was already missing the family and the prospect of six weeks away was disconcerting. I told myself to 'man up' and made my way to the boarding gate.

Birmingham to Schiphol takes about 35 minutes and by the time the pilot makes altitude and cruising speed it's time to start the descent and pre landing checks. Schiphol is a huge airport and it took me 20 minutes to walk to the departure gate. I sat waiting to board the fight to Tanzania and looked around the waiting area at my fellow passengers. Who was travelling for work? Well some Africans in ill-fitting suits and a couple of ex pats like me with back packs and the nonchalant confidence that comes with frequent flyer status. There were a number of guys in full camo and I guessed they were going hunting. They were all American, probably dentists intent on slaughtering some endangered species. And then there were the groups of fifty-something women with bandanas and flowery flowing dresses clearly going to climb Kilimanjaro and to find their inner self. They honestly looked like they had just come from a Californian film set in the 60s. So it was a bunch of tourists, hunters, African politicians and expats, and in the thirty or so flights I took to Tanzania it never changed. We stopped for an hour at Kilimanjaro to let most of the passengers off and to have a meal, then off to Dar es Salaam which translated means 'The City of Peace'.

Tanzania has a population of around 57 million with Dar es Salaam the largest city with over four million people. It was formed in the early 1960s when Tanganyika and the island of Zanzibar united after independence from British rule. Their legal system is based upon that of the UK and their currency is the shilling, but most transactions are undertaken in US dollars. Swahili is the widely spoken native language as is English, which is taught in schools. Religion is divided with over 60% being of the Christian faith and 35% Islamic. The island of Zanzibar is 99% Muslim.

Tanzania is one of the more advanced and developed countries in the African continent but still has poor infrastructure. Transport routes are dire and electricity power outages frequent. Corruption, as it is elsewhere in Africa is commonplace. It is a beautiful country with Africa's tallest mountain, Kilimanjaro to the north close to Lake Victoria and boasts the Serengeti national park which hosts the 'Big Five' of the animal kingdom, lions, leopards, rhinoceros, elephants and cape buffalo.

I was told Glen would stay for a month to ease me into this new world and hand over the reins. I was to meet him at 7am the following morning at my hotel and took a taxi from the airport to the Double Tree. My ground floor room was spacious and modern with views out over the Indian Ocean. I had a shower and after calling home, hit the sack around midnight local time. Glen arrived on time the following day and we drove the five-minute commute to the security office villa. It was a former embassy and came complete with kitchen and even a swimming pool which I never got the chance to use. The bedrooms were all now offices and I went with Glen to mine. I was grateful for the air conditioning as it was already over 75 degrees outside. The weather in Dar changes little during the year, ranging from sunny 80 degrees to sunny 90 degrees, rain is occasional and tropical in scale.

Tex was in when I arrived, I thought he might come and say hello or even just welcome me to the team, he didn't. So I went to see him and right from the off it was clear he didn't welcome my addition to the team. 'Why I wondered?' Was I a threat to his authority? If that was true maybe it was because he wasn't qualified for the role he had, with no degree and his military and managerial experience was limited. He had worked at Papua New Guinea as a security officer and had been promoted to Tanzania.

Maybe I was a threat and he had good cause to fear for his future, particularly given my close relationship with the VP Mark and his deputy Macca. Either way he was as cold as the air conditioning. I knew he was going to be an issue but I would report to Macca and Mark and they would have my back if things became difficult for me to manage alone or at least I hoped they would. I decided to minimise my contact with him and crack on and if he wanted to know anything he only had to ask.

At this point I didn't have a phone or laptop, vital tools when you're constantly on the move and your staff are scattered to the four corners of Africa. I was pissed off this hadn't been sorted by Glen, but I resolved this by making my first visit to the Dar offices of Barrick. The offices were set in a gated compound with a huge eating/social area in the centre, open sided but with a roof thatched with palm leaves. I made my introductions and was warmly greeted by the local Tanzanians employed there. The first piece of advice Glen gave me was to let the Tanzanians know I was from the UK and I would be well received. He said, 'If they think you're from SA (South Africa) they will do everything in their power to fuck you over. If they know you're a Brit they will look after you', and he was right. They despised the SAFA's and had a phrase in Swahili for them: 'watu wasio na nyumba', which when translated is meant as a pejorative and means 'people without a home' this was in reference to them occupying South Africa which was the true home of native Africans.

I had a great relationship with the nationals and more often than not got what I needed from HR and the tech guys. I got sorted with a Blackberry and a laptop and onto the intranet within three days and I should have been good to go, but I had ongoing issues with the laptop and couldn't connect to the Barrick email system. As soon as I had my essentials Glen told me to pack a bag as we were flying to Jo'burg on a job. I went back to the hotel packed a 'carry on' case and my back pack which in the months that followed went everywhere with me and was en route to the airport with Glen. I was excited to see Johannesburg. It would be the first of several visits.

When we left the airport at Jo'burg the first thing that hit me was the cold. It was 85 degrees back in Dar and 55 degrees here. I'd taken all my summer gear, no hoodie, jacket or sweater just polo shirts. I was freezing, we took a taxi to the hotel and past the townships of corrugated shacks. The view was depressing and the poverty looked extreme. I was told there were worse places than these where the Somali immigrants lived. I made a mental note to give that a miss on my sightseeing trip.

We had accommodation in the Barrick office complex which formed part of a large office and apartment building integral to a shopping mall. After sorting the apartments heating system my first job was nipping to the shop to buy a fleece.

We were in Jo'burg to interview a potential witness, a former employee who said she had evidence of corruption by a specific General Manager (GM). To explain; each mine site has a GM and they are God. Salaried at around 400–500k USD, they hold all of the power on site, controlling every facet of the mining operation and we had one in our crosshairs. A big fish and a big risk of negative blow back. Great first job, I thought, get this wrong and my stay in Africa might be short lived. But get this right and my reputation as a professional investigator and one to be respected was assured. We got what we needed from our witness a statement detailing explicit financial transactions, we gathered supportive financial information from the Finance Department which confirmed our suspicions. This was looking very serious for a number of people and I would need to tread carefully. That night Glen and I sank two bottles of Cape red and feasted on springbok and antelope, both a first for me and delicious.

We headed back to Dar and I was still having problems with my laptop and emails. Glen was bouncing dozens of them from his to mine as I was now 'in the chair'. I had loads of things to action but couldn't move on them as I couldn't get access. I was reassured by Glen's presence as he could manage the flow of information required by the sites, London, Johannesburg and Canada. Then just over a week into handover Glen announced he was flying out. 'No, no please don't abandon me,' I thought and asked, 'when will you be back?' His reply, 'Never, I hope!' Brilliant, I'm climbing a mountain and the safety ropes just been cut.

Glen was being sent by Mark to South America, Chile to be precise where Barrick it appeared had big problems with multi-million dollar frauds. I was on my own. I felt exposed and the learning curve just became a little bit steeper. I decided to get the IT issues sorted and door-stepped the technician. Problem solved I was on line and I booked a charter flight to North Mara the site managed by our corruption target GM to see for myself what the issues were and also meet the security team and my investigators.

Barrick had its own £20 million, 70-seater plane which took people back and forth between site and Dar via Mwanza airport. Glen told me to avoid this if possible and book a direct charter plane or if none were available and it was urgent a helicopter. The problem with the company plane was the hours of waiting around for other passengers coming back from rotation with the flight stopping at Mwanza and every other mine site so you could end up stopping several times before reaching your destination. I had a great deal of autonomy and a budget to go with it. Tex was palpably disinterested in what I was doing so I just got on with it. I learned quickly to work on the move and my laptop and phone went everywhere with me.

It was my first charter flight and the fixed wing twin prop 'executive' aircraft had clearly once been a top-of-the-line carrier but 40 years and no doubt a million miles later it was battered and bruised with split and faded blue leather seats, broken or missing cup holders and seat belts that appeared to have no other use other than decoration. We flew low over the Serengeti and I was blown away by the expanse and majesty of the Savannah. I had bought a new camera for just this occasion and clicked away furiously taking images of elephants and rhino and thousands of wildebeest making the annual migration in search of water. We flew even lower at about a thousand feet over Lake Victoria and it was more like an ocean as you couldn't see the edges of the lake. There were dozens of small fishing boats who made their living from catching the Nile Perch and Talapia which were abundant in the lake. As we circled North Mara's airstrip I saw the villages made up of small domed wattle and daub huts forming a circle around the livestock in the centre, it looked prehistoric.

The pilot made a perfect landing, lowered the rear steps and I grabbed my backpack and go bag and walked down the steps taking in my surroundings. I was met by the Security Manager, Johannes 'Jonny' Barwise a South African former special forces soldier who had worked as a contractor in Iraq and Afghanistan prior to Tanzania. Jonny like all Afrikaners I met in Tanzania was a massive bloke with a twenty-inch neck and hard as nails. Jonny and I would become good friends. I asked for a tour of the mine site before heading to the security compound. It was akin to a war zone. North Mara is vast covering five square miles with four open pit mines which were, half a mile across and 600–1,000 feet deep, this enormous crater had steps cut into the sides called 'benches'. In the base of the pit I could see a hundred or so ant like figures. 'Who are they?' I asked.

In his strong Afrikaans accent, 'Intruders, stealing the ore man,' was Jonny's reply. He explained that several times a day mining operations would lay charges and blast the pit base, this would break up the rock base layer into pieces small enough for the enormous excavators to lift into the 450-ton capacity haul trucks.

Before the dust had even settled up to a thousand trespassers came onto site to steal whatever they could from the base. The area of mining operations was the size of a large town and difficult, borderline impossible to secure.

Sure Barrick had its own security officers but no longer had firearms with lethal force, just bean bags fired from shotguns and flare bangs. Given the sheer numbers of trespassers and the violent threat they posed, to mitigate the threat the local police were paid a 'per diem' (day rate) to provide additional armed security. The police were armed with AK47 Kalashnikovs. It was clear why so many trespassers had been killed and injured. Faced with hundreds of intruders usually after dark and some armed with pangas (machetes) must have been terrifying. Soon, I would experience this first hand. There was CCTV coverage with night vision (Forward Looking Infra Red) FLIR cameras and sixteen-foot walls were being built to keep them out but it was a work in progress costing tens of millions of dollars. I headed to the security compound to meet a few of the guys.

I met some of my investigators Andre Claasen another Afrikaner and the one I had sat next to at that first octopus steak dinner and four of the Tanzanian nationals supporting him. It was clear Andre an ex-Police Detective was boss and the Tanzanians were a mixed bag with differing skill levels. Also on site were a handful of external contractor investigators. Initially I was confused by their role. They answered to Mark Wall and the company lawyer and General Counsel Katrina White and had been working for Barrick for as long as Mark and Macca. The leader of the private contractors was another Australian ex-cop Peter Coombes. Coombsy was a charismatic individual and former undercover operative and I instantly liked him. He and his team were acting as independent investigators looking into the civilian deaths at North Mara in an attempt to prove to the Human Rights lawyers that Barrick had acted appropriately.

North Mara was almost sensory overload, so many new and different sights, sounds and smells and the sheer scale of everything, right now I felt a million miles from my comfort zone.

I was pointed to my room, which was one of a series of corrugated tin sheds, like a terrace of cheap garages. I saw a pair of enormous stork-like birds of the rooftop. They were the ugliest living things I had ever seen. I learned that these were Karibou storks, a mix between a stork and pelican with enormous beaks and yellow straggly legs, yellow because they urinated on themselves. I came to despise these creatures as they would wake me at 5am in the morning tap dancing on the tin roof. I was sure it was deliberate.

My accommodation was worse than shit. It was obviously a security officers room who was home on rotation. Twelve-foot square, two cot beds nylon sheets and a Tazmanian devil duvet that had seen the sort of action only single men know about. I was dusty and sweaty so turned on the shower. The overhead sprinkler fell off and water shot over the screen soaking me, my clothes and the toilet roll. I looked in the mirror at the dripping, dusty figure and thought. 'What the fuck am I doing here?' It seemed to all come on top at once. Homesick, abandoned by Glen, in the middle of nowhere surrounded by armed strangers and potential threats everywhere and I forgot to mention the numerous insects and reptiles whose only mission in life is to kill you. I knew nothing about anything in this new alien world and to top it all off I couldn't even have a shower.

If I could have pressed a button to teleport me back home right there and then I would have done it in a heartbeat. I was overwhelmed and miserable.

But as the days passed things became more familiar and I got into the routine. We humans are nothing if not adaptable and after a few days I actually found myself enjoying the experience. It's quite amazing to me that one minute I felt so out of my comfort zone and bereft of the comforts of home and all that is familiar and the next I felt at home, immersed into this strange new life. Two years down the line I actually preferred being on site to my penthouse in Dar. But we'll get to that.

I familiarised myself with the practices and procedures and practiced with some of the ammunition and firearms. The armoury was very well equipped with shotgun launched flash bangs and bean bags as a less than lethal option. PPE (Personal Protective Equipment) full body armour was military standard so the security guys were well looked after. The expats, all from SA occupied all the managerial positions but the front line 'soldiers' were Tanzanian. They were well trained, disciplined, well fed and paid much more than their police counterparts. I'm not suggesting it was an easy life for them but compared to the alternatives available in Tanzania it was a revered position. The South Africans (Safas) were all ex-military and most had worked in Iraq and Afghanistan as security contractors. When I mentioned the state of the accommodation to Jonny he smiled and described Afghanistan to me. Three years of 14-week tours 'in country' living in a shipping container with no A/C or running water. I made a mental note not to moan about the accommodation again. They were all huge, hard men, toughened by their experiences and bitter about their current position back in SA. They repeatedly spoke about being the new victimised minority with no jobs back home as 'blacks' had priority regardless of skills, qualifications or experience. They were effectively unemployable back home and naturally they feared for their families futures. They worked hard to suppress their inner views on race but occasionally could not contain it. I guess when you are brought up in a system of apartheid and indoctrinated by the society you live in it must be difficult to view the world differently when it is all you've ever known.

I gathered more evidence in relation to the GM investigation utilising Coombsy who seemingly knew everyone and had access to everything. Like Glen he hated the GM as they had previously crossed swords and it hadn't ended well for Glen or Coombsy so he was only too happy to help.

I returned to Dar more settled and I got to grips with the new systems, processes and the IT. I was fortunate to have a great ally in Margaret Stoker. Margaret was from SA and was stoicism personified, she was strong, resolute, and knowledgeable and she became a good friend to me. Without her I wouldn't have lasted six months. She was a great sounding board and understood all the politics at play, she had worked for the company for some time having previously worked in SA for De Beers the diamond miner. Margaret ran the recruitment, training and selection process for CCTV staff across the organisation. These employees had to be trusted with highly sensitive information such as the inner workings of the gold processing plant and gold room and they had the opportunity to ensure CCTV might not pick up on suspicious activity in high-risk areas. All of our CCTV operators were Tanzanian and sadly corruption is just accepted as part of the culture. So to counter this Margaret employed a polygrapher to conduct lie detector tests on potential candidates.

When she went home she was a true Afrikaner wife, her husband would go hunting on their land with his mates, shoot whatever couldn't outrun a bullet and bring it back for Margaret to skin and butcher whilst they drank beer and watched rugby. I know that she enjoyed the independence and freedom her job gave her from the domestic bliss of SA.

For the first six months I stayed at the Double Tree. Don't get me wrong it was a lovely hotel with decent food, a pool, great ocean views and gym but it was isolating and I was lonely. I was the only one of the security team staying there as the others all shared a villa further down the coast.

I would regularly have dinner with Margaret, usually at The Slipway, a lovely open air restaurant by the Indian Ocean and two minutes from my hotel. The hotel food was ok but rarely did I get what was ordered.

Communication wasn't their strong point but I had started to learn Swahili which helped and ensured I wasn't treated like a tourist. And of course my first phrase learned was, 'Kaka, naweza kunywa Bia tafadhali.' Brother can I have a beer please.

Whilst I was employed as the Corporate Investigations Manager I wanted to develop the role and the capability of the team. I needed to make sure I knew as much about what was going on across the organisation as possible in order to manage the risks it faced and to reduce the possibility of repeating the negative exposure it had suffered from previously. I put a plan together, another business case, but this time I would ensure I had support before any decisions on budgets were made.

Glen dropped in from Chile after a couple of months and I ran it past him. I wanted three elements to my team. Intelligence, Investigation and Proactivity. I knew this would be stepping on Tex's toes as he had Jonathan and Reece managing informants and intel but frankly they were playing at it. I took Glen through the Intelligence Cycle which I had implemented as a DI in the Police and he got it, fully supporting the proposal. I told him I needed another fourteen guys, a mixture of expats and Tanzanian and Jonathan and Reece could be a part of that.

I needed a few million dollars to make it happen but knew I could guarantee results. We had three excellent Tanzanians in Peter, Chacha and Tobias. They had different roles within security at that time and I would need to have them released to my team. Glen and I presented the plan to Mark and he agreed to provide support. All that remained was to gain approval at the annual budget meeting in Jo'burg two weeks later.

Fortunately, Tex was on rotation back in New Zealand and his deputy Arthur another Safa was in the chair for the security budget presentation. I didn't know Arthur well but I briefed him, told him Mark and Macca were relying on him to secure my funding and off he went. 'Don't comeback without my cash,' I told him. It was a relatively straightforward process or so I thought but Arthur just wasn't experienced in presenting business cases or budgets and I'm not sure he understood my proposal well enough to represent. Another difficulty was Tex had given him only one instruction.

Same plan as last year, plus 5% for inflation. Jesus, I guess New

Zealand SAS Sergeants didn't get too involved in strategic planning. He had just used Maccas old plan plus 5% there was no creativity and no development or performance improvement plan. Arthur came back and when he walked in to my office he looked at me sheepishly and said, 'Nick, sorry man, they didn't understand your plan.' He was a good man but lacked the experience at this level and I felt for him, he just didn't want to expose himself or take any personal risks and I understood that.

Arthur hadn't secured the funding I needed so now I would have to do it myself or let the plan slide and that would be that for another year. So I set up a meeting with the key decision maker, the Chief Operating Officer, Marco Zollezi. It was my first meeting with Marco so I got Mark to call him to get him on side and give me some credibility. Marco was a former South African 'Special Operations' military officer but you'd never know it from looking at him. He was six ft one tall and about 60 years old and he had put on weight since leaving the 'Scorpions'. He presented as a gentle, softly spoken and kind person and I immediately liked him.

We exchanged back stories and bonded immediately and then I took Marco through my plan explaining everything in detail. I would have staff in Dar managing and developing intelligence from informants and information sources such as employees, police, military, or civilian. My team would develop the information into actionable intelligence or better still evidence and pass this to our proactive team in the form of target packages for prosecution by skilled investigators. I would utilise my Tanzanian assets to manage and cultivate sources in the field and to liaise with the Police and Secret Intelligence Services (SIS). The SIS were trained initially by the Chinese and latterly the CIA, the USA becoming involved after the American Embassy bombings in 1998 in Kenya and Dar es Salaam. Both attacks were simultaneous killing 224 and injuring over 4,000. Al Qaeda under the leadership of Usama Bin Laden took responsibility and followed up in 2001 attacking the World Trade

Centre in New York. So our allies in Dar were trained by the best, experienced and willing to work with us.

Since our surreal first meeting in the hotel lobby where I handed him $25,000 in a brown bag I had met the Director of Intelligence Mr Ngowi several times and we had a mutual respect and had shared information relating to the threats to our mining operations. These ranged from armed criminal gangs intent on attacking the gold mines gold room to large scale fuel theft. Gold rooms are where up to $40 million in gold bullion dore bars are stored prior to transportation by helicopter and aircraft to Switzerland.

The threats were real and immediate but lines of communication and our operational capability could be much improved. Having heard my pitch Marco completely supported the plan, he understood the synergy with the component parts and the operational imperative for this resource. It would potentially save millions of dollars for the company whilst making its operations much safer and more secure.

CHAPTER THIRTY-FIVE

Politics and subterfuge

Plan and finances secured I left it to Mark to break the news to Tex. It was his show after all but he would no doubt think I had pulled the rug from under his feet. I knew he would be seriously pissed off but I couldn't care less, the guy made zero effort to engage with me or understand my role. I'd had loads of conversations with Jonathan the former MI5 spook. He was a big man six feet five and built like the prop forward he was. He was typical ex-public school, confident, borderline arrogant and very switched on. It seemed to me that Johnathan was one of those creatures that simply glides through life. He did what he wanted, when he wanted. Tex would tell him one thing, he would do the other. I was just glad I didn't have to manage him.

From my investigations into what he and Reece did I could find little that added any value to corporate security. They travelled a lot – and spent absurd amounts of cash on potential information sources that produced, as far as I could tell, Jack shit. I knew under the new world order Jonathan and Reece would be surplus to requirements, a luxury we couldn't afford. Reece the 'analyst' had a doctorate – good for him but all he produced were an amalgamation of open-source newsfeeds talking to the political landscape of Tanzania and super high-level socio-economic rubbish that had little to do with the core business of security in all its forms. Whilst it may have been an interesting toilet read it added little value.

From the outset in Tanzania I would have an almost daily

conference call with Mark and Macca to work through the latest crisis. They were in Toronto and seven hours behind Dar so calls would usually start at six or seven in the evening. As I made progress and got on top of the critical incidents on site, nipping problems in the bud with early intervention or effective investigation confidence grew and after twelve months I rarely got a call.

No doubt, Macca gave Tex the good news that I was moving things forward and once he knew of my plan Tex came to see me and asked for an explanation. I took him through the machinations of intelligence and investigation and I actually think he understood the benefits. But Tex could see the writing on the wall, I was a real and immediate threat to his authority and he set his sights on me. He went from being passive to actively making my life as uncomfortable as possible, picking up on obscure details of security incidents demanding unnecessary reports when he knew I was snowed under with work. He would order me to fly out to the mine sites for bullshit reasons when he knew I needed to be in Dar or Jo'burg to continue my investigation into the North Mara GM. His plan was working, I was getting really disillusioned and more and more homesick due to the isolation. That said it didn't dampen my resolve to build my new team.

With the funding for my plan in place I began recruitment. I had inquired through the grapevine back at Notts if there were any qualified Senior Investigating Officers (SIOs) that fancied a short-term contract in Tanzania. I was amazed by the response or lack of. I called recently retired Detective Inspectors thinking they would jump at the chance of earning £600 a day, all flights and expenses paid, but much to my frustration I had no takers. It surprised me that they were so set in their public sector conservative ways that they were frightened to make that step outside of their comfort zone. I was frustrated and I needed immediate support and then out of the blue one Friday evening, Bill called. Now Bill and I had history, he was an established Detective Inspector at South Notts Division when I was newly appointed as the Intelligence DI. Bill wasn't too happy because to that point he had managed all information sources (informants) and didn't want to lose control of them as his staff ran them (handlers). He told anyone who cared to listen that it was impossible for one DI to manage his and the other divisional DI's sources. After all, he said, they had 112 between them. That did seem a lot but I had no idea at that time and nor did anyone else how productive they were so it might not be as much work as it first appeared.

The process with source management is straightforward. The source handlers would meet a potential source make an assessment as to their value in a particular area of crime or criminality. Assess their reliability and submit that for my consideration. I would meet the potential source and talk through the rules of engagement and method of communication and payment. I would conduct a risk assessment and if they seemed of value I would register them and provide a pseudonym by which they would be known. No one other than myself and the handlers would know their true identity. Sources would be paid on a sliding scale for information based upon risk and value and would be tasked by me into areas of criminality where we had information gaps.

It made sense for a dedicated Intelligence DI to manage intelligence and dedicated handlers to manage sources. Prior to this the Investigative DI (Bill) and their Detective Constables would do this around the demands of criminal investigation so it was rarely a priority. I took possession of Bill's informant files and those of his DI opposite number on the other half of the division and I conducted a review of the 112 registered sources. Most had provided no information at all in the past 12 months and only 22 were of real value to our priorities. I took satisfaction from presenting my findings to the senior management team which showed Bill for the bullshitter he was. He lived at work did 11 or 12 hours a day but spent five or six of them drinking tea and chatting with his mates in the office. So many times in my career I have seen these people who on the surface appear to be real grafters staying after the boss has left to show their commitment when in truth they produced little. People are easily fooled. Coincidentally Bill was also the DS who got the job I applied for on the Drug Squad and had played rugby with the boss. The irony is, he only stayed six months as he and I quote, 'couldn't get excited by a bag of powder'. Maybe he did me a favour Chief Steve shut down the Drugs Squad soon after.

Back in Dar I said, 'Bill, I'm surprised to hear from you,' and I was. Bill was probably the last person I expected to hear from and I'm sure he picked up the irony in my tone.

'Yes pal, I know we were both strong characters and it was never personal.'

Then Bill asked, 'I hear you're looking for an SIO?'

We chatted for a few minutes as I sat on the promenade of the hotel on a glorious sunny evening looking out at the Indian Ocean. I must have felt generous spirited or maybe and more truthfully I was just desperate for someone to lighten the very heavy investigative and managerial load I was carrying. In the first four weeks alone I had made 21 flights across various parts of Africa.

So I said, 'OK Bill, let's give it a try. How soon can you fly out?'

I put Bill on a day contract so I could part company with him if that was necessary and with no fuss. It also meant I could get him out to Dar quickly with minimal HR interference. Perhaps unsurprisingly nothing was ever straightforward with Bill. He came out for a few weeks and then had to return home to get married, for the third time. But during his time in country we worked and got on well together and I took him with me to SA to further the GM investigation and to build our relationship so I could depend upon him to hold the fort whilst I was home on rotation. Bill was Bill, he played the game and we got on well both socially and professionally but I always knew he was all about – Bill. But I needed help, badly so was happy to take the risk. I had taken numerous statements and had copies of employment contracts and salaries. It was clear the GM had set bonuses for his staff way higher than the norm including for himself and had enhanced payments by more than double the permissible amount by significantly more. This ran into millions of dollars and completely contrary to the terms of contracts and the bonus (compensation package) scheme.

The added advantage for contracted employees like me was the annual, sometimes bi-annual, bonus which could be as high as the limit of 25% of salary. Another reason for my decision to become contracted. But the GM was paying and was paid 100%.

I gave Bill the file to complete and then he returned home. I expected him to return two weeks later but there was delay after delay and I got flak from Tex when I was out on rotation as no one was there in my absence. The truth is nothing had really changed as I never had back up previously and was answering calls and emails daily at home and even on holiday in the Caribbean. Tex was piling on the pressure but I knew this was a ploy to make my position untenable. He just kept on chipping away with small things. I was contracted to work five and a half days a week with Saturday afternoon and Sundays off. I chose to work seven days as the job required that commitment. Once I was on top of the workload and requirements I took Sunday off. The first day I did this I got a call from Tex who asked where I was. I told him and he informed me that I should be in the office at work. If it was good enough for Jonathan his best mate then it was good enough for me, so I stuck to my guns and referred to my contract and told him I would see him Monday. It was still unsettling and I was sick of it, so I decided to act. I knew that I was virtually indispensable to Mark and Macca. If I left, Macca would have to take over and leave the comfort of Canada and one thing I knew for sure, he wasn't a fan of Tanzania.

It would take months to replace me even if they could find the right person and I was part way through building the new team. Margaret was close to Glen and Macca so I let slip over dinner that I was going on my next rotation in two weeks and not returning. She knew about the Tex situation but also that he had been openly briefing against Macca and had foolishly told people he thought he could trust that he would be replacing Macca in Toronto and Macca was living on borrowed time as Mark was tired of him messing up. He clearly hadn't read the script, this was never going to happen. Mark and Macca were blood brothers and their loyalty to one another unbreakable. Macca hated Tex and Mark had found out that Tex had been misleading him over a significant issue and then found out about him undermining Macca. From that point the die was cast and Tex's fate sealed.

So over dinner with Margaret that evening I told her my intentions. She was disappointed as we had become friends and had a mutual respect. But I knew that once Margaret was aware of the issues she would call either Glen or Macca immediately and so it proved. At 10pm that night in my hotel room and much sooner than I expected I got a call from Macca.

'Hey Nick, how's it going mate?'

'Yeah great Macca, how are you?'

'Nick, be honest with me mate, how are things really?'

'Well, Macca, I'm on rotation in a couple of weeks and I'm not coming back. I can't work with that prick anymore.'

Macca expressed his less than complementary feelings on Tex and asked me to trust him and to not make any decisions just yet. I agreed, I owed both he and Mark that much. Nicely done, Margaret I thought. I knew and hoped that she would call Toronto. My play was now in motion and couldn't be stopped by anyone other than Mark. It was a high-risk strategy but I really was that pissed off. The following evening was a Friday, barbecue night at the hotel in the gardens by the candle-lit pool. It would have been perfect if Jenny had been there but I was on my own as usual and sat at a table with a cold beer. My phone rang, it was Mark Wall.

Mark got straight to it, and explained that he had recruited me not solely for the investigations role but to be the next Security Director. I was flattered and said so. I explained what a massive arsehole Tex was being and that I genuinely could not stand another day longer than I needed to with him undermining me and laying traps around every corner. Mark tried to reassure me that within six months Tex would be gone. I told Mark that I didn't have six months and that I would be going home to enjoy retirement.

He asked me to give him some time to work through the problem, which I agreed to. I still had a couple of weeks till I rotated home. Truth be told, it wasn't purely Tex. I was missing my family and lifestyle and had been living in a hotel by myself for almost five months.

It sounds great I know, all meals catered for, swimming pool, gym, but reality is somewhat different. When you've eaten every choice on the menu twenty times over, it's not quite as appealing. I hardly used the pool as I worked 12–14-hour days, and usually seven days a week. Also the hotel was a transit point where guys rotating in and out form the various mines and oil rigs stayed so you would usually hear the scraping of furniture from the room above about 5am as they readied themselves for transport pick up to the airport. At weekends there were weddings and parties 'til the early hours making sleeping impossible and quite frankly, I didn't need the money. I knew the accommodation issue would be sorted as Margaret had found a new apartment block with all mod cons and we would move there shortly, but Tex was still a big problem.

I was incredibly busy and was all over the country in the following couple of weeks. I made myself scarce and flew to the mine site at Tulawaka.

En route we changed aircraft a Mwanza and I had a couple of hours to kill so got a taxi to a hotel on the shore of Lake Victoria. I had been once before with Arthur and loved the place. It was rustic and charming and I sat on the beach eating Tilapia and chips watching the enormous sea eagles coming in to land. These beautiful creatures would lie on the beach and spread their wings to cool down after a flight. It was one of those moments when I realised how fortunate I was to be there and to have such incredible experiences.

Tulawaka is in the middle of a rain forest having its own micro eco system. It was a beautiful location with monkeys, birds of prey, huge snakes passing by like they owned the place, but the accommodation and facilities were awful. One of the drills I learned very quickly was to check under the toilet bowl rim for snakes as it is a favourite hiding place of theirs. Even now I wince at the thought of what could happen. The mine itself was part underground and part open pit and trespassers would tunnel under the surface to steal the ore. Tunnel collapses resulting in fatalities and violent confrontations were common. One intruder was killed at night time when accidentally shot in the chest by a flare bang. Imagine the effect of a direct hit in the chest by a phosphorous explosive. I investigated and recommended to Mark the withdrawal of flare bang ammunition. After a second such incident they were withdrawn worldwide. The Police were satisfied with the investigation and no charges were brought against our security officers.

I was coming close to rotation when Mark called again. He asked me to fly home a couple of days early and to meet him and Macca at The Langham Hotel in London where we could discuss and agree a way forward.

I packed everything I owned in my cases prepared not to return and got the direct flight to Heathrow. I took a taxi from the airport and arrived at The Langham which is opposite the BBC at the top of Regent Street. The Langham is a magnificent hotel. Everywhere you look are swathes of pink and white fresh flowers. I checked in and my room was ready, I had a club room pre booked by Canada. In 2011 the room rate was £550 per night but there was an all-inclusive style club lounge serving high end snacks, champagne and pretty much any other booze you might require so it was really a bargain.

I called Macca to let him know I had arrived and he asked me to meet him in the boardroom. It was as you might imagine Olde English oak panelled walls with leather chairs and a huge conference table. You could have accommodated twenty people but there were just the three of us. Mark had to cancel due to yet another drama in Pascua Lama in Chile so it was Macca, his number two and Glen. It was their mission Macca said to make sure I stayed on board and in Tanzania. We discussed the issues surrounding Tex, which were also affecting Macca and timescales for when Tex might be moving on but I was adamant that I would not return to Dar. Glen said, 'Just go back for your next six week rotation and if we can't figure something out then pack all your stuff and come home.'

'Glen, seriously, I'm done, I have everything packed up and my cases are in my room, here.' Instantly, I felt the mood in the room alter, they now knew the reality of the situation.

Macca said, 'Nick whatever the outcome we will part as friends but I hope we can convince you to stay.' Tex was a deal breaker for me and they knew it. Macca wanted him gone but he said Mark had a plan for him which didn't involve major drama for the company. Tex was a company director when all said and done and sacking a director isn't a good look for the company and could even affect the share price.

We had talked for a couple of hours and once it was clear where I stood, Macca asked for some time with Glen and to call Mark. I went to the lounge for refreshments. I was completely at ease with the situation and was fairly convinced that I would be staying home this time. About half an hour had passed when I got the call to go back in. I really didn't know if I would have a job much longer but I was at the point where I didn't really care.

I sat down and Macca got straight into it. He said Mark planned to move Tex from Tanzania into a back office role in Toronto and that he would be gone from Tanzania within three months. I knew it would be impossible to expect better than that as recruitment for his replacement would take at least that long given my own experiences of Barrick human resource processes. Mark had already told me that he planned for me to take over as Security Director and I had total confidence he would follow through on his promise if I played my part. In reality taking rotations into account I would have a maximum of six weeks contact with Tex and I could make myself scarce if needs be. As I mulled this over Macca went on to say that Mark would offer me a retention bonus if I agreed to stay.

'Okay, Macca, I'm listening,' I replied.

'How does three months salary sound?'

Within a millisecond I replied, 'I tell you what Macca if you make it pounds you have a deal.'

Just as quickly Macca said, 'Done. Now let's go and get pissed.'

We shook hands and the meeting was closed. I had asked Bill to come to London to meet the guys as he would have stayed on with Barrick even if I had left. I called Bill into the conference room and we all had a good chat about the future for Security in Tanzania. I took the boys to a nearby Victorian pub and at Macca's request, googled the finest fish restaurant in London and whilst we were on our fifth or sixth beer booked a table. I had introduced Glen and Macca to pork scratchings in that east end pub which they loved and Macca reciprocated introducing me to a Sauvignon Blanc from the Marlborough estate in New Zealand, two bottles of which we consumed with three dozen rock oysters followed by sea bass. It had been a productive day and I was truly happy. I couldn't wait to tell Jenny. I took the train home the following day arriving home a day earlier than planned and told Jenny about the bonus. She was delighted and as supportive as always. Things could only get better and I knew that once I had like-minded people around me when my new team was in place life in Dar would become much more enjoyable. If I worked hard and beat off the competition for Tex's job I would be appointed Security Director, which was no bad thing and it would be a significant step up working at the executive level.

We had a two-week family holiday in the Dominican Republic only marred by Tex calling me on a regular basis just to keep the pressure on. He even told me to fire Bill as he wasn't in Dar. I told him that Bill was getting married and wasn't even contracted but that he soon would be and wasn't going anywhere. Little did Tex know of the plot surrounding him, I was going to enjoy his demise and him seeing my accession to his throne as he disappeared into obscurity in Toronto and then God knows what thereafter.

CHAPTER THIRTY-SIX

Another world

The thing that I quickly realised working for a globally successful company was that I was trusted to do the job I was paid for. I was supported when things didn't always go to plan and given the freedom to fail, to try new ideas, with budgets to reflect the faith and responsibility placed upon me.

How different this was from policing where senior officers were terrified of failure. In my own experience, risks wouldn't even be considered unless the Command Officer could keep their hands clean and could apportion blame elsewhere. Of course this breeds mistrust and germinates deceit. In such a climate people and in turn organisations do not flourish and grow as they should, they become inward looking. At Barrick we constantly invested in new risk-based approaches that had well reasoned business cases, whereas in Policing they were frequently ignored in favour of personal agendas. The critical fault with the policing system was that Senior Officers focussed primarily upon 'self interest' and not their staff or the public they served. In Barrick they focussed upon delivering for the organisation (people) and its shareholders (public). For those with ability personal success is therefore an inevitable consequence of this approach.

For the first time I felt liberated, trusted to deliver, given the support and resources to succeed and celebrated when we achieved success. And as a team, succeed we did.

I gave up on trying to recruit from Nottinghamshire and casting my net wider, placed an advert in the Police Review a British national magazine read by nearly every cop in the UK. I needed former experienced SIO's based at the mine sites to oversee investigations, train our ex-pats and Tanzanian nationals and become proactive prosecuting the target packages provided by the new source management and intelligence team.

It is important to mention at this point that outside of the Tanzanian Police and Military it is illegal to operate an intelligence function. We never mentioned the word intelligence in public. The Source Unit was headed by one of my new recruits, a former Detective Chief Inspector Andy Cumming. Andy was a former Europol Field Intelligence Officer (FIO) based in Rome and had recently retired. He was a maverick, and a seriously funny guy but didn't like being told what to do. I could manage that, he was a real asset to the team. Having had little interest from my old force I was pleasantly surprised by the response to the advert. I was inundated with applications for my unit from all over the UK and at all ranks, I even had Chief Superintendents applying for an Inspector SIO position. I scrutinised the CV's, short listing those I thought suitable and skype interviewed to find the best candidates. In the end I was delighted, I had a really talented pool of staff who would take us to the next level, it was a positive move forward but now I needed to deliver on my promises.

In total I brought in fourteen new people mainly from the UK and a couple from Australia on Macca's recommendation and of course I had Peter, Chacha and Tobias who would be invaluable. Tobias and Chacha were feral creatures, born and raised on the Serengeti. They were intelligent and disciplined and they had well established links with Mr Ngowi and the Intelligence Service. This was something I needed to strengthen and formalise. To that end I asked Mr Ngowi to meet with me and he agreed to come to my office. He arrived, minus the bodyguards on this occasion. We shook hands and exchanged greetings in the traditional Tanzanian way, 'Salaam Alaikum' (peace be unto you), he said to which I replied,

'Salamah.' (Peace) I threw in a habari azabui (good morning) for good measure and offered him a cup of Yorkshire tea which was served in my magnificent Huddersfield Town mug.

He sat down and immediately his phone rang. He pulled the device from his jacket pocket examined it and terminated the call placing it on the table and then another phone rang and he did the same. Mr Ngowi had four cell phones and he put them all on the table. I explained the plans I had and the construct of my team and how it could operate with his assistance and how we could both benefit from sharing information regarding the threats posed to both Barrick and Tanzanias shared interests.

Usefully he told me his four operational priorities handed down on tablets from the Tanzanian President himself. One of them was the protection of Tanzania's gold interests which of course included Barrick.

Barrick paid considerable taxes and provided jobs and community support across Tanzania. He was keen to engage, clearly seeing an opportunity and would use Tobias and Chacha as the conduit. They were tried and tested and he trusted them. This did however come at a cost. We would, in line with the Anti Bribery and Corruption Act (UK) and the (US) Foreign Corrupt Practices Act by which we were governed, agree to pay Mr Ngowi and any employees working in the direct interest of Barrick a per diem (day rate). This was already established informal practice with the Police and Security Service. But what did need to change was accountability. We had no records that would stand scrutiny. We didn't have a clue who had actually received the cash and frankly it could have gone anywhere. To remedy this situation I drew up Memoranda of Understanding (MoU) which was signed by Mr Ngowi and the Police Commissioner that spelled out the new practices and procedures. Every rank would have a scaled per diem and each officer would have to personally sign to say they had received their payment. There would be no more shady meetings in hotel lobbies.

Corruption was rife in Tanzania as it is pretty much everywhere in Africa. It was vitally important that I could account for every dollar spent and in particular in the engagement of the police and security service. To many not versed in the workings of foreign companies in Africa it may seem unbelievable that a private company should have access to the host countries Police Commissioner and Head of Intelligence but we did. Gold production was a significant part of Tanzania's Gross Domestic Product (GDP) and their growing economy, commercial and infrastructure development depended on it.

Sometimes the corruption became a complete pain. The Police were not well paid and as in many developing countries supplemented their income with extortion. One day I was travelling back to the office from a meeting with the Commissioner at Police HQ. I drove through a junction with the traffic signal on green but as I passed through a policeman in his white uniform stepped out into the road and signalled me to stop. I pulled the land cruiser to the kerb and he opened the passenger door climbing in. I asked him why he had stopped me and he said I had gone through the lights on red. He then asked me for fifty dollars. I refused but he was persistent and asked again several times before getting the message. As a last option and no doubt to really piss me off he gave me a ticket. It worked and I had to return to the police station where they were simply disinterested in my account of police corruption but told me to hand over my driving license. I was sent to another police station about five miles away to pay the fine which was a pain and by this time wished I'd just paid the cop his $50. The first station was in a pretty poor state but the second one looked more like a prison from a spaghetti western. There was a quadrangle which had cells all the way around the internal perimeter the fronts of which were vertical iron bar. It was full of people unfortunate enough not to be able to pay their fines or bribe their way out. I had been told unequivocally that under no circumstances were we to pay bribes to public officials as it would breach bribery legislation. I waited in the sweltering heat for an hour and eventually an officer took my paperwork and I paid the fine.

I returned to the first police station, collected my driving license and got back in my land cruiser. I drove back through the same lights again, on green and was stopped by the police once more. This must have been a well know spot for ripping off tourists and ex pats I thought. Just as the first one had, the cop got in the passenger seat and said, 'Give me money'. I refused, and then more aggressively 'Give me money for Kili' referring to the local beer Kilimanjaro. I refused yet again, and by this point I was not only pissed off but feeling rather uncomfortable with the situation. There's something quite sinister when this stuff happens to you and you simply can't control it. I'd had enough, I took out my wallet and a business card from the Chief Officer Simon Sirro. I showed it to my corrupt passenger and asked him to call him to explain the situation. He laughed and got out of the car. I was relieved to see him go and following this incident didn't leave the safety of the peninsula for a little while. I had heard stories circulating of ex-pats being locked up for similar things and I'm pretty sure the Chiefs business card saved me.

But we had similar problems with our own ex-pats in the company and I passed on my investigation into the GM to our General Counsel Katrina for her view and a decision on the next steps. The evidence was overwhelming and when I interviewed him and presented the evidence he resigned within 24-hours as did several of his implicated colleagues. I got a call from Glen and Coombsy to congratulate me on the outcome. They really didn't like that GM.

CHAPTER THIRTY-SEVEN

Julia who?

The peninsula was primarily an ex-pat enclave a section of coastline which the majority of the best hotels and foreign embassies occupied. There were supermarkets and bars even an air-conditioned gym. Its where most of the offices were located and upmarket accommodation. As soon as you left the enclave it was mayhem with terrible roads and gridlocked traffic.

However it wasn't all bad as whilst stuck in traffic or waiting at road junctions you would be entertained by street sellers. I have never seen people capable of carrying so much stuff which they would try to sell to the stranded motorists. Everything from mobile phone chargers to hat stands and some even had fish tanks... complete with water and tropical fish balanced precariously on their heads. And there were the beggars who you just could not turn away from. They were usually disabled and incapable of earning a living in Dar. I always put my loose change in the land cruisers cup holder for the traffic light stops. Once I was waiting for a taxi outside Mwanza airport where a young kid maybe eight or nine years old, wearing a grey suit five sizes too big for him tap danced for money at the entrance, a big smile on his face. One of the locals explained that his parents had died of Aids and he was sole carer for his grandmother. So no school for this boy just a life scratching a living to survive. I was with Arthur just on our way for lunch by the side of Lake Victoria. Arthur gave the kid $50. He might not have been the best manager I had but he had a heart as big as a lion. So many tragic stories across Africa, it's truly heart breaking.

Technically I was still in the employ of Nottinghamshire Police and out of the blue received an email from Chris Eyre my former boss and Deputy Chief. The Chief, Julia Hodson had raised concerns about whether I should be allowed to work for another company whilst still accountable for my conduct under Police Regulations. I couldn't believe it. Why would my success in Africa possibly be an issue of that much concern to her? How could it possibly negatively impact upon the reputation of the Nottinghamshire Police?

I asked Chris to speak with my old pal Malcolm Turner in Legal Services and take his view. Malcolm, pragmatic as ever said it was bullshit and was of no concern to Nottinghamshire Police. What did she think was going to happen anyway? That I would pack my bags and fly home because she demanded it.

'Dream on Julia,' I thought. It is events such as these that can make a person bitter about the past but I refuse to succumb to those pernicious individuals who would seek to do damage to others.

I cannot understand why people expend so much of their energy in negative behaviour when there is so much joy to be found in positivity.

Six months into my African adventure it was time to leave the Double Tree and I wasn't sad to depart and I was looking forward to an uninterrupted night's sleep. Barrick through Margaret had secured a number of apartments in a new tower block including the penthouse at $10k per month. I shared a two-bedroom apartment with Andy. It was extremely comfortable, I had a Jacuzzi bath and deluge shower, air con, double balcony and a well-equipped kitchen. We even had a big screen TV and satellite subscription to SA with all the SKY sports channels. I have no idea how they managed to construct such a building in Tanzania. The scaffolding was bamboo and as far as I could see the construction industry had yet to embrace the concept of health and safety. But it was built and was surprisingly well finished and equipped. There was a fully functional gym and even a squash court. There was an Olympic size pool to the front of the building and a smaller pool on the roof for the penthouse. This was currently occupied by Tex and his buddies... for now.

I was adjusting to life as an ex-pat. I had a new team around me and an actual social life when I wasn't out on site or out of the country. Things were going really well and the boys were making real progress developing sources and working closely with our new partners in the Security Service. Chacha and Tobias had embedded themselves both within the mine sites and with Mr Ngowi's team. They would visit the site and poke around speaking to employees, finding evidence of nefarious activity and provide actionable intelligence to the investigators to follow through. The investigators would work on the information at our base in Dar then fly to site and interview/investigate further. They uncovered numerous internal frauds within HR and finance and thefts from the numerous warehouses across the estate.

They discovered the creative ways that gold was being stolen from the processing plant and identified significant assets that were obtained illegally by employees which Mr Ngowi seized back for us. By way of example a member the HR Department was actually selling jobs to people in nearby villages and a worker in the process plant was taking gold ore from the smelting crucible and removing it in the recess of an aluminium ladder.

After six months I was comfortable that Jenny could come out and visit. I had good accommodation and personal security and life had settled down from its manic beginning and now with the team behind me and Bill now a permanent feature it was unlikely that I would have to respond to anything that required me to leave her in Dar alone.

Jenny flew out KLM and I met her at the airport. She met Margaret my life saver and they got on like a house on fire. They are both lovely, caring people who think of others before themselves. We had a really great week, I worked in the daytime popping home for lunch and then back for 5pm which was an early finish for me. I took Jenny to the best restaurants Dar had to offer and she loved it. We went to African street bars and as usual were well received. They were incredibly cheap. You could buy a bottle of local gin for four pounds but needed a strong stomach and some antacids to go with it. I had booked a couple of days off and surprised Jenny with a trip to Raskatani, a small beach resort on the Swahili coast. We took the land cruiser by ferry across the harbour in Dar. It only took 20 minutes but as is the way in Tanzania, the ferry which had a capacity to carry 400 passengers carried around 700. Space was at a premium so the locals climbed onto the roof of our car and even the running boards on the side. The ship was so unstable it was terrifying. When we had finished waddling across the sea we drove off at the other side only stopping to let our passengers alight. As we passed through the hustle and bustle of Dar es Salaam we soon left modern Africa behind and entered another ancient world. It really was like stepping back in time. The dwellings few and far between were the traditional wattle and mud construction small circular domed structures housing entire families who survive off the land and rear livestock. The tarmac road out of the City had given way to a graded red clay dirt track which followed the coastline.

After around forty minutes I saw a sign to the left for Raskatani. We drove slowly down an unmade track through sand dunes only passable in a 4 x 4. After five minutes of Jenny and I nodding like the Churchill dog at every bump, the rough terrain opened up into a large flat section of scrubland. In the near distance we could see the beautiful Indian Ocean and a little further on we entered the resort complex. It was quite beautiful. The main hotel and guest chalets were made from locally sourced wood, it was rustic and charming. We were greeted by a South African woman who was the manager. I had booked a sea view suite and she led us up a sharp inclined pathway to our accommodation. It was a desert island paradise, a large room with a king sized four poster bed with drapes that would act as mosquito nets. It had an inside and outside bathroom and a small pool. The view was incredible out over the roof of the hotel overlooking the ocean. There was a family of monkeys there to greet us which completed the island vibe, it was simply amazing. To this day it is Jenny's favourite place on earth. We had a wonderful few days being pampered and swimming in the crystal waters of the Indian Ocean. There were no beach beds but as soon as we set foot on the sand a young boy ran out and constructed one from bamboo and palm leaves.

CHAPTER THIRTY-EIGHT

Robbery in action

All chilled out when we arrived back at my apartment I got a call. It was Chacha and he sounded distressed. He had received information from Mr Ngowi of an armed robbery plot against the Bulyunhulu Mine. The specifics were that the armed group had a man inside our organisation who himself was armed with a hand gun. He would take the GM hostage forcing him to provide access to the Gold Room. Of course I needed to firm up the details and sent Chacha and Tobias to work in the field with Mr Ngowi's team. We knew that a gang of around eleven former Burundian soldiers and an unspecified number of Tanzanians were involved. This was source led and I was told that Mr Ngowi had infiltrated the group. The group were fluid and changed personnel frequently but the threat was real and immediate.

Over the coming hours I learned more specifics from Chacha who called me to ask for $100 to pay a Witch Doctor. Well this was a first for me.

Tanzanians are a superstitious people and they believe that remedies and potions concocted by a Witch Doctor can cure anything from HIV to cancer. African albinos live in fear for most of their lives as their body parts are considered to have magical properties which are regularly used by Witch Doctors. As I write this, the Tanzanian government have spent a fortune on an herbal remedy for Covid-19!

So the final plan was that the robbery group armed with RPG-7s, AK-47s and other firearms would visit the Witch Doctor to be blessed, as they believed it would render them invincible. At my behest, the Witch Doctor would tell the gang that they must leave their weapons with him overnight for the spell to take effect. The SIS would disable them by removing the firing pins. Everything went according to plan, until it didn't. The armed robbers would be tracked until they were ready to attack the mine but then the security forces would interdict nullifying the threat. Everything was kept on a need-to-know basis. The only person I took into my confidence was Arthur who in Tex's absence was acting security lead.

I swore him to secrecy and explicitly told him not to tell anyone on the mine site. So what did Arthur do? He called the GM, Denis Hoof and told him. He told him he was the target and that there was an inside man in the processing plant. But it was, 'OK,' Arthur said, Denis had been sworn to secrecy. Predictably, Denis called all his ex-pat managers into the Bulyanhulu briefing room and told them of the threat. They in turn told all of their trusted staff including the inside man. As soon as I found out I made clear to Arthur that he had put the lives of undercover sources and Chacha and Tobias at risk. I couldn't quite believe it.

I called Chacha. I knew if Mr Ngowi got wind of this debacle our shared understanding and SIS-Barrick relationship would be over, leaving us incredibly vulnerable. I told Chacha to tell his colleagues in the field there was a problem on site and that they needed to execute the interdiction immediately. I waited and waited with Jenny in my apartment for news.

First I heard that the incredibly brave Denis Hoof had flown out from site and had left his deputy in the hot seat… what a guy! Then I got the call from Mr Ngowi. He explained there had been twelve members of the robbery team, seven had been killed in an exchange of fire and five captured for interrogation, there were no other casualties. I congratulated him on a successful mission and we arranged to meet a few days later. Thankfully, he was none the wiser of our cock up and if he was he didn't let on.

I had trained for years as a Senior SIO to manage crimes in action from real-time robberies to acts of terrorism. But in reality these events happen rarely in Policing. During my time in Tanzania working with our partners we interdicted thirteen armed robbery threats to our mine sites. There was never a dull moment. Other Mining companies suffered also but weren't fortunate enough to have our intelligence assets and armed attacks were common. I was in the office in Dar one day when I was sent photographs of three armed robbers who had attacked a light aircraft on the airstrip carrying gold from the mine. They had got into a firefight with one of the mines security guards and he had killed all three of them. A brave guy, he had only a 9mm handgun and they had AK-47's. He was flown out of the country and back to SA immediately. To prevent such an attack at Barrick we used a twin-engine helicopter to ship the gold directly from the roof of the Gold Room which may have been more costly but avoided such risks of attack.

Chacha and Tobias were invaluable assets and were well rewarded. They were well paid and had excellent accommodation for their families. They were huge Manchester United fans and when I returned from rotation would bring them some Man Utd merchandise. We had built trust and had bonded, we were becoming a close-knit team and would have poolside barbecues at the weekend. But the elephant in the room remained… Tex.

He had started ramping up the pressure on me asking for various reports and tasks to be completed which were blatantly a distraction. He tried to write me up for poor performance and called me into his office. I tore his arguments to shreds and it went nowhere but it was clear he wanted rid of me before he left in order to protect Reece and Jonathan. I also found out he had put a close friend of his forward to Mark for the Director position and so he wanted me out of the picture. Tex had been given a leaving date and I was overjoyed. He thought he was being promoted to a new managerial role in Toronto but I knew different. It was disconcerting to be messed about and having to look over my shoulder whilst he ran down the clock but I had been well rewarded and had a loyalty to Mark and Macca.

CHAPTER THIRTY-NINE

Good times

Twice a year Mark held a security conference in Toronto for all the managers from Barrick's countries of operation, South America, Australia, PNG, Kenya and Zimbabwe and of course Tanzania. Mark invited me much to Tex's chagrin. Tex was the only Security Director in the company which reflected the nature of the Tanzanian challenge and of course it had four mining operations each with its own Security Manager.

It was a seven-day event during which time we would each present our performance achievements for the past six months and our plans for the year ahead. We would have outside facilitators and guest speakers focussing on teamwork and leadership and had loads of downtime for entertainment such as visiting Niagara Falls and watching the Maple Leafs play ice hockey.

Mark had arranged a different event each evening. I flew business from Dar to Amsterdam, a quick shower and breakfast and onto Toronto. For the first time in my life I was sat in the upper deck of a Boeing 747. I felt like a little boy, I was so excited and had to calm myself with a glass of Moet. I made the most of every second of the six-hour flight from Schiphol. Business had its own bar and the seats were luxurious. I had to pinch myself, it was absolutely fantastic. I rang the kids and sent them photographs. Me, flying business in a Jumbo jet. Another one ticked off the bucket list.

I got a limo, a Lincoln town car from the airport. The highways were spacious and uncongested, Toronto seemed very clean for a major city and had a feeling of space. The city centre was huge with wide roads and pavements but these are only used in warmer weather. It gets incredibly cold in winter down to -35 degrees, so Toronto has a subterranean layer, a parallel system of escalators shopping malls and walk ways. It's a bit like one city on top of another. I braved the cold one time at -35 and my denim jeans stuck to my legs.

I arrived at my hotel, Trump Tower. What a beautiful place and it had just opened. My room even had a TV in the bathroom mirror and I watched some of the 2012 Euros whilst taking a shower. Mark loved to put on a show and to reward his people for their hard work in some of the most challenging places. He awarded prizes for everything. I won best performance presentation and received an Apple iPad. And for my presentation on security problem solving through community engagement a Canon DSLR. When I returned home on rotation my kids stole them both.

In the evenings we ate in the CN Towers revolving restaurant, on another occasion whilst drinking a bucket load of exceptional red wine we made a three-course meal with a chef teaching from the front of the room and each person had their own cooking work station. Just like Master Chef only without the edible food at the end. We had seven course tasting menus that cost a fortune but left you wanting a KFC afterwards as you were still hungry. We were spoiled. Mark even hired out the entire dining room of a castle which had been moved brick by brick from Scotland and rebuilt in Toronto. We had an afternoon paint balling with unlimited ammo, it was brutal but tremendous fun.

It was great to get to know everyone and build relationships. To conclude the week Mark cleared everyone's bar tab and we returned home. I went on rotation back to the UK.

I had booked a week in Palma with the family but spent most of my time on a sun lounger swotting up for my interview for Security

Director. I was interviewed whilst on holiday via Skype and as usual I over prepared and stayed in the hotel room whilst the Olivia, Ben and Jenny went to the pool, leaving Savannah in bed pretending to be asleep. It started at 07.30 and lasted over an hour but I was confident it was mine as I had rehearsed all possible questions and answers a dozen times in my head. As expected, Tex had put forward his former Lieutenant Colonel, so I had some credible opposition. I didn't hear back for a couple of days but as I was at the bottom of the aircraft steps about to board the flight home my phone rang. I took the call, 'Nick, it's Macca.' I could barely make out what he was saying over the engine noise next to me and the ground crew shouting at me to get off my phone. 'You got the job mate, congratulations.'

'Cheers pal, talk later I've got to go, just getting on the plane home,' and with that, I boarded the plane a happy man. I was delighted and so were the family, it had been a great holiday all round. On the flight home we cracked open the bubbly and as I drank it dawned on me that I was now a Director of a FTSE 100 company I wasn't sure of the salary but it had to be pretty decent. Not bad for a daft lad from Brighouse. The self defeatism and notion that I was a loser was long behind me, I was now one of life's winners and I intended for it to remain that way.

CHAPTER FORTY

Another level

When I got back to Dar everyone had heard the news and when I saw her Margaret was beaming and we had the biggest hug. I made a promise to myself to repay her for her invaluable support. But others were clearly less enthusiastic. Tex was fuming by all accounts but I could care less and I just tried to stay out of his way. That said I did pick up on some information of a significant 'fuck up' by him and kept it in my back pocket for as and when I might need it.

Reece now worked for me in intelligence and not Tex and I instructed him to let me have the source files for review. I now had the authority as the next incumbent to have sight of these 'eyes only' protected documents. I was required to attend the next Barrick Board meeting to present the initial progress of the newly formed team, I guess they wanted to see what they were getting for $3 million dollars. I compiled an analytical report detailing the historic source, cost and productivity and also my new team's equivalent data. I sent it to Reece for comment as I wanted to be fair in my presentation of the facts and told him it was strictly embargoed until after the board meeting in London two weeks hence. I gave him clear instructions not to share this with Tex. Of course I knew he probably would and Tex would be at that meeting. He was still Security Director but had only a couple of weeks before leaving. The report was completely accurate and irrefutable highlighting the wasted resources and lack of productivity of the former intelligence capability set against the significant positive outcomes from newly developed sources and inter-governmental liaison of the new team. Before the London meeting I met Mark and Macca for a beer at the Langham bar. It was buzzing with luvvies from the BBC television centre across the street. With my seven quid bottle of Heineken in my hand I told them what was to come. I asked them to keep an eye on Tex to see if he revealed that he had prior sight of my report which they knew was strictly embargoed. Up to this point even they hadn't seen it. I informed them that Tex had previously asked for the report and I had made it clear it was embargoed until the meeting.

The following day I circulated copies of the report around the table and presented by PowerPoint. All started well and the facts spoke volumes but Tex couldn't help himself and within minutes attempted to discredit my work, referring to detail that had not yet been covered. Mark immediately turned on him, 'Tex, have you already seen this report?'

'Well yes, Reece sent it to me,' Tex replied sheepishly.

'But Tex, why did he do that? It was embargoed. Right, Nick?' I nodded. Instantly Tex knew he had fucked up, big time.

I explained what had been said to Reece and Tex looked crestfallen, he had just dropped himself and Reece well and truly in the shit. Perfect!

What followed was carnage. I could clearly show that under Tex's purview, Reece and Jonathan had spent tens of thousands of dollars on travelling, sometimes to other countries to meet sources and had produced very little of value to the company. I could also reveal what the new team in just a few weeks had achieved in mitigating threat and risk and the recovery of stolen property as well identifying areas of company fraud. Several new sources had been registered and vetted, one even by me in the middle of the rain forest near the Tulawaka gold mine. By way of example I spoke on this to the meeting. This guy had been paid a modest sum to provide information on illegal gold processing operations. The Tanzanians were very creative building their own crushing machines using truck engines and chemical processing apparatus using Nitric and Hydrochloric acid. Having passed this information on to the Police working on our behalf, two process plants were seized and destroyed. This was more like it, I could show tangible outcomes from minimal investment. It was a good day in London as I had clearly demonstrated the value of our enterprise. The added bonus was the professional humiliation of Tex and Reece. After the meeting we all grabbed a beer and stepped out onto the roof terrace which overlooks Regent Street. Everyone that is except Mark and Tex. As we sipped a cold one we could hear a furious Mark ripping Tex a new one. What goes around, comes around I suppose.

We ate and drank well that night on Marks company credit card as always and life felt great. I was working with some top people and revelled in the position of responsibility. Party over, when I got back to Dar, Tex asked to see me in his office to hand over the reins. It turned out to be more like the inquisition, Tex went off on one throwing accusations at me which were bizarre and largely unfounded. He was clearly feeling the pressure and his world was crumbling around him. He didn't really hand over so much as throw me the keys and walk away but not before I got him to show me the finances. I picked up on a deficit of a couple of thousand dollars and asked why that was. He said that one of our Tanzanian employees had been robbed in his car and some gold (seized as evidence) and fifteen hundred dollars had been stolen. I asked Tex for the Police report but he didn't have one. As far as I could see he had just let it slide when it seemed more than likely that our employee had stolen the gold and cash and made up a bullshit story which Tex had accepted without even seeing the police report or conducting his own investigation. Incredulously he then said I would have to find a way to make up the shortfall. I wondered what planet he was on and knew then I had another nail for his career coffin. Tex was gone on rotation and for good two weeks after my return from London and I was appointed Director of Security.

I moved office and made myself comfortable. I had a solid team in place with Arthur, a work in progress as my immediate security deputy, Bill running Investigations and Andy on Intelligence. We had our British SIO's at each mine site running investigations and hands on training the Tanzanians which proved invaluable later on. I had much more capacity on a personal and organisation level. I had free time for once so joined the ex-pat Yacht Club and bought a super charged Waver Runner. Sports motorcycles are not an option on Tanzanian roads so the next best thing was a jet ski that could do 70 mph across the water.

The Yacht Club was like a movie set from *White Mischief* the membership being mostly ex-pats, the majority of which were South African and wealthy Indian Tanzanian business people who owned impressive looking leisure cruisers. It was situated on the peninsula complete with a gorgeous beach and slipway. There were boats of every size and purpose.

One of my guys had a 30 metre sail boat and we would sail and jet ski out to the three small uninhabited islands offshore. The first was 3 km, the second 6 km and the last one which disappeared at high tide, 9 km from shore. We would take beer and food, barbecuing on the beach. It was incredibly beautiful with crystal clear water and fish of all sizes everywhere.

There were large breakers at the back of the first island and one day I was showing off jumping the three metre waves when I got thrown off into the ocean losing my precious Oakley's. However I was less concerned with them and more so on my ride which was being pushed by waves towards the rocks! I have never swum so fast, finally getting back on board gasping for air and averting a disaster by the skin of my teeth. I didn't do that again.

Jenny loved the islands and we would visit them when she came out. Her visits became more frequent now that I had settled down and she loved everything about Dar.

With Tex out of the picture I moved into the master suite of the penthouse. The penthouse itself had a sixteen-seater cinema complete with reclining leather chairs and a three metre drop down screen and theatre surround sound. There was a small gym with an exercise bike, a treadmill and a descent set of free weights. The open plan living room and kitchen was straight out of celebrity cribs and the bifold doors opened onto the large roof terrace complete with swimming pool and barbecue. The views were incredible and you could see the ocean from every angle. My room had remote controlled curtains, huge TV a King size bed and a jacuzzi bathroom, it was as good as it gets and this is in Africa!

Ali the owner had spared no expense and he ran the place with his family who were all incredibly friendly. Sadly, Ali was killed in car crash which unfortunately is all too common in Africa. Hardly a week seemed to pass without multiple fatalities in bus wrecks but having driven there for two years it's easy to see why. The roads are in a poor state of repair, there are no MOT's so cars can be seriously unsafe, the traffic light system is a lottery as no one abides by them and public transport is always massively over capacity. So when there is an incident there are usually significant numbers of fatalities.

Jonathan the spook had seen the writing on the wall and got himself redeployed working for Katrina the Company Legal Counsel doing God knows what, but it didn't interest me as it was one less problem to solve and one I didn't relish as I really liked Jonathan. Reece however was on notice after breaching confidentiality by leaking my report to Tex. I sat him down and made clear that there was still a place for him on the team but he needed to play by the rules. Within weeks he messed up on two occasions and I let him go with a three-month salary 're-settlement' bonus. He came to see me and explained he realised he had messed up and deeply regretted his actions. He was just stupid, blowing a great job with prospects and he had a Doctorate! I guess it wasn't in common sense.

It's difficult leading a team or group when you have individuals who are playing for a different team. It distracts attention away from the mission and creates negative energy. It's like an orchestra playing with a violin out of tune. Once the team was set it was a good place to be. We always had each other's backs and we even had a social life. I now had a corporate credit card and would find any excuse to take the team out when they were all or most of them in Dar. I would take them to the best restaurant in town The Great Wall which is the finest authentic Chinese I've ever eaten. Tex had us working seven days a week which I had no problem with when needs must and I had little else to do with my time. But after a couple of weeks in the chair I could see we had a bunch of grafters who needed minimal supervision. They went above and beyond when the job required it, as it often did and so I rewarded them with a 'work hard, play hard' common understanding. Our guys could be working long hours for up to two weeks at a time and without complaint so I made the decision to give them Saturday afternoon and Sundays off when in Dar.

Work was unpredictable, one day you could be in Dar and the next up to a site to investigate the deaths of intruders. Locals would tunnel under the security fencing into the mines and mine the rock. These tunnels were only a couple of metres below the surface and wherever you looked you could see the entry points like human sized fox holes. These guys would excavate at night in sweltering claustrophobic conditions and frequently light fires to make the rock more brittle and easier to break. As a consequence it was not uncommon for them to suffocate due to a lack of oxygen. When this happened we would get a call from relatives notifying us of the event. Our investigators would immediately fly to the site and utilise mining machinery to dig the bodies out, exposing the network of tunnels. It was dangerous work. Tunnels were not supported in anyway by timber or steel props and would collapse on the unfortunate miners without warning. Numerous illegal miners died this way but even though they were trespassers stealing from the company they were treated with dignity and respect and returned to their loved ones.

With our new found freedom, whoever was in Dar at the weekend would go and watch rugby or Premier League football which was shown everywhere.

Tanzania as in most of Africa is obsessed with English football. Seemingly every citizen has a replica premier league shirt and the local bars are packed when a game is on. It was a great experience sitting in an open-air bar drinking Kili with a couple of hundred locals watching Manchester United versus Liverpool, the two most popular teams. The African imagination was captured by the success of Didier Drogba and Yaya Toure who achieved great things in the Premier League and Africans who see themselves as one nation take great pride in that.

One of these bars the Choma Hut was my favourite, it had white plastic patio chairs and tables about a hundred of them and made the best barbecue chicken. You could get a whole chicken and chips and a Kili for four pounds. When your meal arrived it came accompanied by a kettle of warm water to wash your hands before and after. One of the staff, Ismail was my favourite, he was 19 years old and his parents had died from HIV. He had to support his sister through school and lived with his grandmother. He loved Liverpool and my Premier team was Man United so we always had football banter. I would tip him on the sly to make sure he could keep it and when I asked him what he would like me to bring him back from England he said, 'a pair of shoes for work'. Not a football shirt, but a pair of something most of us simply take for granted. On my next rotation home I got him some cross trainers. When I gave him them his eyes filled with tears, as did mine. I have never seen anyone so happy. As he walked away to hide them he kissed the box. Ismail was a great kid, he never asked me for anything.

Our productivity was increasing and after six months in the big chair I was required to present the security portfolios achievements and yearly plan to the African Barrick leadership team in country and in London to the Board of Directors. I was confident that they would be impressed and my experience as a Divisional Commander and in Corporate Development came for the fore. I could demonstrate and articulate the risks across each business area and mine site with a mitigation strategy. I presented a cost benefit analysis against outputs and could show real tangible outcomes such as robbery threats averted, stolen property including stolen gold recovered and numerous fraud interventions. Both meetings went as well as I could have hoped for and my position had been solidified. I took the opportunity whilst in London to bring Jenny and the girls down, we stayed at The Langham and they loved it. The club lounge was hammered, Haagen-Dazs, pastries and sweets for the kids and Jenny on the Moet. Whilst I met with the board in our companies offices across the street they went on a shopping spree down Oxford and Regent Street. It was a great day and one we all remember fondly.

I was still travelling a lot between London, Africa, South Africa and Toronto. I grew to love the travel which I'm sure isn't difficult to imagine when you're flying Business Class everywhere.

CHAPTER FORTY-ONE

China Gold the end of an era

It was just before Christmas 2011 when we heard that China Gold were carrying out due diligence on African Barrick as prospective buyers. As Security Director I was required to prepare several reports for their perusal. It was clear they were extremely risk averse and security was the number one issue for them in considering the deal. China Gold is a state-run company and its senior figures have ambitions, not to be business leaders but political leaders. Risk aversion is therefore understandable as failure in a state-owned business will almost certainly result in a removal from office.

I wondered how long I might have a job for if we were sold but took some comfort in the 20% salary bonus I would get if it actually happened.

I travelled to Johannesburg for a week of meetings and presentations with the Chinese. We stayed in a smart hotel on Mandela Square where my gastronomic baptism continued. I ate ostrich, springbok, kudu and impala. They love their meat down there. South Africans must be the most carnivorous people on earth. Not too many vegetables on offer though and if you order a salad you are treated like some kind of alien.

In between mealtimes the presentations continued. I was surprised on the number of people involved. Barrick sent about twenty senior people but the Chinese had around eighty. There was a formal dinner each evening which we all attended. The Chinese love a drink, particularly whiskey and lots of it. I noticed however that they operated as a tag team. They sent different people each night presumably to give their livers a rest. No matter what time we concluded the evening and it could be 1am, the Chinese would meet in a conference room to debrief. They were very thorough and well organised.

I'm pretty sure the final nail in the coffin for the deal was their visit to North Mara. Imagine if you are the Chief Operating Officer of a gold company from China, whose operations are all in China where compliance is expected and civil disobedience rare, to then stand overlooking an open pit mine in Africa only to witness a thousand illegal intruders invade to steal your ore. It was clearly a risk no one was prepared to consider and China Gold pulled out. So my bonus went up in smoke but I still had a job.

I was home at Christmas time and received an email from the Director of HR. It informed me that a 20% of my salary bonus would be payable should the deal be successful. But the deal had fallen through so that was the end of that. I had opened the email on my Blackberry and didn't see or read the second page which stated that regardless of the outcome if I was still employed by African Barrick Gold on 1 April 2012, I would still receive the bonus. So when I opened my bank account in April I got a very nice surprise.

It wasn't all penthouses and fine dining, though during my time in Tanzania I fell ill four times with infections, the cause of which no one could establish. This wasn't unusual in Africa. The grim reality was that some guys died on site and the cause of death would be unknown. We had access to private medical facilities and had a Doctor 24/7 at each of the mine sites and I was in need of their services on one occasion. I thought I was going deaf so saw the Doctor who examined my ears. He placed my head on the examination table and took out a pair of tweezers. The next thing I saw was a two-inch length of tissue paper held by the tweezers and a Doctor with a curious look on his face. I explained that I lived in the hotel in Dar and at night it could be very noisy so I had used toilet roll to plug my ears. We burst out laughing at the same time. What a plonker I'd been working for days with this squeaky noise in my head wondering what the hell it was.

One day I was in Dar and started to feel unwell around lunchtime. I got back to the penthouse around 6:30pm and thought that the air con must have been on freezing all day. I was shivering and put on a fleece. Andy was sat in a T-shirt, shorts and flip flops. I felt really weak and rang Jenny for advice. I was running a temperature with fever and she told me to go see a Doctor immediately. I made the short drive to the private hospital and checked in. I was seen quickly and told to lie on an examination table. The Doctor took various readings and a blood sample and put me on a saline drip. I fell asleep and when I woke a doctor with a concerned expression was looking down on me. I apologised for nodding off and he asked worriedly, 'Do you suffer from epilepsy?'

'No,' I replied, 'why?'

'Because you've just had a seizure.' Well, that wasn't good news.

The Doctor put a cocktail of fluids through the drip and the blood tests were done on site. Whilst I waited for the result I heard screams and wailing from the cubicle next to mine. The guy who had checked in shortly before me had died. I can't lie, I felt vulnerable and alone, I hated it. When I was younger I felt immortal but that had ebbed with the passing years. I was 52 and thinking, 'What am I doing here? Maybe it's a good time to call it a day and go home.' But then my results came in, I had been diagnosed with Typhoid.

Typhoid is contracted by ingesting human faeces. Charming, clearly someone wasn't big on washing their hands after going for a dump. I knew where I had eaten a couple of days previously and it had to be at the English Pub, the George and Dragon on the peninsula. Fillet steak with a side order of shit. Lovely.

I was told I had to be admitted for treatment and observations. I had the worlds worse case of diarrhoea and felt incredibly weak. My private medical cover meant I should have had a private room but the hospital was full so I had to share a room with a couple of guys from Peru who had been airlifted off an oil rig out at sea. They had Typhoid and had been there two weeks. I went to the bathroom and the toilet looked like a hand grenade had gone off in a slurry pit. Shit, everywhere.

It is amazing how quickly the human body can deteriorate. One minute I was on top of the world, and the next in hospital surrounded by the dying. Having drained my system of all nutrients I woke at 2am starving. I asked a nurse for some food and she asked me for twenty dollars. Wasn't this a private hospital? I handed over my cash and half an hour later was presented with a plastic take away box containing rice and chicken.

'Change?' I enquired of the nurse.

'Twenty dollar,' she replied.

Of course it was! It wasn't much and definitely not worth the twenty dollars but I devoured it.

The following morning desperate to get out of that place I checked out with the Doctors blessing. I figured I was safer in the penthouse than the hospital.

In the months that followed the team ran like clockwork and averted thirteen armed robbery threats working with our partners. I had inherited the ongoing Barrick security strategy which I had to implement across the sites. Primarily this meant building concrete walls around our open pits at a cost of tens of millions of dollars. Imagine building a sixteen feet high concrete wall around Central Park in New York and you get the scale and we had three to construct. The CCTV network and Forward Looking Infra Red (FLIR) camera system was excellent but the intruders either broke through the walls or found a way over the sixteen-foot barriers. It was an impossible problem to solve and in truth it only mitigated the threat to minimise harm to the company and its employees. Our security staff would frequently come under attack and I witnessed one intruder confront one of my security officers and then in the altercation that followed chop the foot off the guard with a panga (machete). The police reacted quickly and shot the assailant dead.

Ironically given my initial reaction to being on site I had grown to prefer being there more than Dar, away from the politics which had started to impact upon my part of the organisation. A new senior guy PG had been brought in primarily to support the GMs in developing more profitable mining plans but as his influence grew we began to cross swords. His main beef was the chain of command. I had two line managers, Marco the COO and Mark Wall, VP of Barrick. Marco trusted Mark and vice versa so I could get on with my job. I would have a monthly catch up with Marco to keep him across everything we were doing and to make sure he didn't get any nasty surprises when talking with others and he was happy and trusted me. I had line management of all the security managers and their staff on site as I had to hold them to account for delivering the security strategy. A couple of the GMs were unhappy that they could not control this part of their business and occasionally objected to being told how to spend their budgets. Everything had been manageable by building good working relationships with them, that was until PG arrived. We conflicted regularly but I always had the ace card to play. We were the same rank in the company but Mark always outgunned Marco with his seniority. PG was annoying but manageable but then the business fell into financial difficulty. I more than anyone given my experiences with austerity cuts to policing understand that once money gets tight budgets come under scrutiny and get squeezed. Production of gold was not meeting the set predicted targets and revenue was falling whilst costs were rising. So each Director had to justify their existence. I had been here before.

After lots of pontification it was decided to make blanket cuts of 20% across each business area. Not exactly scientific or business led but I guess it was a start and would provide some clarity on what might get cut and in order of priority. Now we were established in

Dar and in the field on site I knew where we could afford to save resources.

Cuts can create opportunity to modify working practices and move people who are not performing to the required standard. I had a huge team of 1,200 security staff on the payroll and scope to trim the fat. I submitted my plan first to Mark for approval and then to Marco. I had a plan 'B' in my back pocket for if deeper cuts were necessary.

I decided to accelerate my plan to nationalise some key roles undertaken by highly paid and skilled ex-pats. I had built a succession plan for every position in my organisation both in Dar and at site. Every position had a Tanzanian national pencilled in to take over along with a time frame and personal development plan. From the outset I had been keen to invest in our Tanzanian staff and had brought in trainers from the UK to teach them everything from crime investigation to foot and vehicle surveillance. The local staff who had minimal training felt more valued, became more productive and were now an integral part of the team.

So the budget squeeze allowed me to lose some ex-pats and promote nationals into their positions. For some time Barrick had been under pressure from the Tanzanian government. Their position on ex-pats had been made crystal clear, they simply didn't want any in their country and were clearly of the belief that there were Tanzanian nationals who were more than capable of doing any of the jobs currently occupied by an ex-pat. In part this pressure came in the form of visa blocking. Work visas were granted to run for twelve months but when they came up for renewal our applications would disappear into the ether of the immigration ministry.

This became problematic as when ex-pats on expired work visas returned to Tanzania from rotation they were blocked from entering the country. They then had to buy a tourist visa but could not work and had to stay in a hotel. This happened to me and I worked for a few days in my hotel until I got frustrated and went to work regardless. I called in a favour from my old friend Mr Ngowi and miraculously I was given a work visa. To try and resolve the issue we met with Business and Immigration Ministers. It was clear they wanted ex-pats out of Tanzania and the gold business to be run by Tanzanians. I couldn't argue with their philosophy but in reality they just didn't have the people with the necessary skills and experience.

The ministry for work and immigration were playing games and there were dozens of ex-pats waiting for visas. Eventually the problem was resolved but the company needed a nationalisation plan.

I was heading towards two years in Tanzania and had decided it was time to go home for good. I knew with cuts looming my time would be limited in any event. PG who had gained more influence had his sights set on moving all security staff to site and under the management of the GM's. I was leaving under my terms and at the right time. I didn't want to be responsible for messing people I recruited around or firing them. Thankfully, most of the guys managed to see out their contracts.

I had a clear out of my stuff in preparation to leave and put a bag of clothes in the dumpster outside the apartment block and by the time I got back to the room and looked out over the terrace balcony one of the Tanzanian chauffeurs for British Petroleum was foraging in the dumpster and took my clothes. Good for him I thought perhaps I should donate some of my other gear. I saw him the day after in my Stone Island chinos and Hugo Boss polo. Truth is they looked better on him than they ever did on me.

Jenny came out for one last visit and it was her birthday. We went to our favourite restaurant, Alexander's and had a fantastic time. We were all packed and took a taxi to have one last drink at our favourite bar. We said farewell to our friend Ismail and gave him some cash in an envelope. It was enough to set him up with his own Tuk-Tuk. I hope he is happy and prosperous.

The final trip to the airport was eventful, the roads were

gridlocked at 8pm as usual and we were running late. Our driver chose to go off-roading over the pavements to get us to the airport in time for our flight home. It was quite scary almost like Tanzania saying, 'farewell Nick, bet you're happy you're leaving'.

Tanzania was an amazing experience, I learned so much about myself. It's not easy stepping out from the comfort and security of a normal life in the UK into the unknowns of Africa and a completely new profession. It can be lonely and isolating, challenging your resolve and self-belief. But learning new skills, language and cultures makes the challenge more rewarding. It took all my mental strength and drew on my knowledge and experience in order to succeed. I got to work in the real world away from the constraints of the public sector. I was free to lead and to flourish, trusted to deliver and that is empowering. I am forever grateful for the opportunities I have had. The opportunity to work in complex environments and to be well rewarded for those efforts. This has provided a lifetime of financial security for my family and I will always be thankful.

CHAPTER FORTY-TWO

Pastures new

However, even after returning home to the UK, I continued to work for Barrick. I established my own security company 'Cerberus Security Services' and was fortunate enough to work for Barrick in Toronto, Saudi Arabia and the UK. It was always good to catch up with Mark, Glen and Macca over a beer.

One day I took a call from Ed Bolton, the former Director of Health and Safety for Barrick a man I worked with closely. He asked if I would be interested in some consultative work for El Dorado Gold at their newly prospected gold mine in northern Greece. It was a blank canvas. Each gold mine requires its own unique processes for extracting, crushing and processing gold ore. Some processes use toxic chemicals to separate the valuable metal from the rock in which it is held, others do not. When the rock is mined through blasting with high explosives it is taken by enormous 450-ton haul trucks to the stock pile. From there it enters a crusher to reduce the rock into a manageable size. Giant centrifuges smash the rock and remove some of the gold through gravity. The smaller pulverised rock can then be treated with chemicals as part of the leaching processes to extract more gold. Process plants are gargantuan structures which contain end to end gold production apparatus and need therefore to be secure. They usually contain smelting plants where gold ore is set in 'fine' 24-carat gold dore bars or as they are more commonly know bullion bars as you might imagine are housed in a gold reserve like Fort Knox. The bullion is stored on site prior to shipping in a secure gold room and with upwards of $30m of gold in the room security is paramount.

I agreed to meet with the Head of Security for the project Martin Derbyshire a Brit. We met in Amsterdam and over dinner structured a scope of works for my consultation. Martin had little mining security experience so it was relatively easy to impress him with my knowledge of things he needed to consider. He was in his early fifties like me and had landed a good number working under zero pressure for El Dorado in Halkidiki. He lived in Northern Cyprus with his wife but was based in Greece.

As requested I prepared a flexible implementation plan to cover all eventualities and a couple of weeks later flew to Greece via Istanbul.

Martin met me at the airport and we drove to site. We met with the COO and I caught up with my old buddy from Africa Ed Bolton and gave him decent bottle of scotch as a thank you for the introduction. He was living the dream in a beach front house with his wife in Halkidiki. I had a tour round the mine site which had already commenced construction. It was part of a densely forested mountain range which had produced gold for centuries dating back to the time of Alexander the Great who used the gold to fund his military conquests across Europe. The presentation to the senior team and COO went well and I returned home. The security plan was agreed and it was all systems go and I was due to return to Greece to help with its implementation.

Then El Dorado ran into some issues. Greece seems to have been in financial turmoil forever and its treasury decided to renege on the initial taxation arrangement's with El Dorado hiking up their slice. Not unsurprisingly El Dorado told them to do one and pulled out having already invested millions of dollars in the project. It is difficult to comprehend why Greece would do this. Ten percent of millions is far better than 15% of nothing and five years later not one ounce of gold has come out of the ground. I was disappointed not to have the work continue I enjoyed it immensely but a few weeks later I received another call from Martin. He told me that the top man, the

CEO of El Dorado had seen my work and wanted me to undertake a security review of all El Dorado's mines, worldwide. I was ecstatic but it was short lived as the news came of the Greek collapse. Martin was redeployed to fulfil the role that I had been offered. Well that's fate, sometimes you win and sometimes…

Thankfully Mark had another job lined up for me. To teach Saudi Arabian security staff the basics of investigation. It was a two-week gig and I was excited to see Saudi, a place I had never imagined visiting. It wasn't that high up on my must-see list but Mark was picking up the tab.

I put together a course lesson plan with scenarios to enable the students to learn the practicalities of investigation. It was bread and butter stuff to be honest but another experience and another culture to absorb. I enjoyed it, it was good to be involved. I flew to Saudi and walked out of the air-conditioned airport into a hundred degree oven. The air was dry and sucked the breath from your lungs, imagine working in this heat I thought. I was picked up by a Barrick driver and taken to my accommodation for the night prior to leaving early the following day for site.

We drove down the main highway in Jeddah and all I could see was exclusive car dealerships, Lamborghini, Ferrari, Aston Martin. Not a Hyundai or Skoda franchise in sight. Saudi is a country of extremes. I learned that the two thousand members of the Royal family share enormous wealth generated by oil production. Saudi is the largest oil producer on earth, but as one of my new Saudi friends said to me, 'when will they have enough that they might share that wealth with the people.' Everywhere I travelled I saw only poverty.

My overnight accommodation was an ex-pat enclave a complex of buildings and leisure facilities surrounded by an enormous perimeter wall with two guards on the entrance gate armed with light machine guns. Must be a good reason for those I thought. The following morning I set off on the six-hour drive to the mine site Jabal Sayid, which is a copper mine owned by Barrick. It was the time of the Hajj the annual Islamic pilgrimage to Mecca in Saudi Arabia. This is a mandatory religious duty for all Muslims that must be undertaken at least once in their lifetime. It was the end of July 2014 and if it was hot in England it was like a furnace in Saudi. We stopped en route a couple of times at the Saudi version of a service station. There was fuel and a small shop and the biggest open plan toilet block I have ever seen. There were no cubicle doors and as I walked in the stench made me retch, you could have cut it with a knife. It appeared the plumbing had either given up under the load or never existed in the first place. There were dozens of white ceramic standing plates either side of toilet shaped holes in the floor. Men in flowing white robes squatted and defecated. There were no washing facilities. It was disgusting. But I surprised even myself whilst in there, I realised I could hold my breath for around two minutes. It really is amazing what you can achieve when required. Walking around the service area we stood out like a sore thumb as the only westerners in a throng of a hundred or so Arabs. The atmosphere felt hostile and the looks we got were decidedly unfriendly.

As we drove along the highway there were abandoned car wrecks at the roadside, they were everywhere. We arrived at Jabal Sayed a huge facility which had yet to commence mining operations. I met my twenty student investigators and the mine Security Manager and was immediately impressed. They spoke English and were smartly dressed and both welcoming and courteous towards me. I fired up the PowerPoint and introduced myself to try and establish some credibility and we got on with the business of learning. On the second day I was invited to have lunch with them. I was their guest of honour and they had sacrificed a goat which had been slow cooked for sixteen hours in a covered fire pit. I was led into a traditional Saudi domed tent with extravagant rugs hanging from the sides and covering the floor with brightly embroidered cushions to sit on. Incense was burning and candles were lit. It was quite beautiful but also bit surreal as there was also a massive flatscreen TV showing Sky Sports. Really! It's everywhere!

We sat on cushions in a circle around a table cover on which were all manner of exotic fruits and spices. The centre piece was the entire goat, head, eyeballs and all. No doubt like me you will have seen Michael Palin or some other traveller experiencing this but it was a new one for me. I was flattered but really hoped that they didn't offer me any of the more unfamiliar parts of an animal such as those eyes or worse its genitalia. We ate traditionally with our hands scooping the meat from the carcass. Then just as I was relaxing a little it happened, one of the guys popped one of the goats eyes out of its socket and offered it to me. 'Mr Nick, it is an honour to have you feast with us. Please take this as a symbol of our respect.' I must have looked panic stricken because as one they burst into laughter. Thank God, it was a wind up.

The men and they were all men (there were 2,000 employees and all were men) were keen to learn and easy to instruct, we ran through investigative scenarios stage by stage and had everyone in role play. The week went well, we said our farewells and it was time to return to Jeddah. I wrote up performance reports for each student and produced a PowerPoint with accompanying lesson notes so they could teach 'in house'. After 10 alcohol-free days I was on my way home. Sat in the business lounge of Jeddah airport I saw several European women come in wearing full body coverings and headscarves, they would disappear into the bathroom reappearing in shorts and T-shirts. Saudi is a very strict Muslim country and at this time women were not even allowed to drive a car. It had been an almost surreal experience which was both interesting and slightly intimidating.

When I went out of the compound for a walk I always felt like there were a dozen set of eyes watching my every move. I was grateful for the experience but glad to leave. I wouldn't be leaving any positive comments on Trip Advisor that's for sure.

Shortly after returning from Saudi, Mark contacted me to tell me that Barrick was in financial difficulty. As a consequence Mark had to decimate his security team and as is always the case in these situations consultants like me were a luxury item. My three-year relationship with Barrick had come to a close. It had been enjoyable, most of the time and an incredible experience. I had met some great people along the way and faced the steepest of learning curves coming out with great personal satisfaction at the other side. I was so pleased that once again I had stepped outside my comfort zone and taken on new challenges.

CHAPTER FORTY-THREE

Retirement. The slow death?

Once home for good I decided to retire permanently at the age of 55. It may seem very young to most people but I remembered being told something a few years previously. 'You should only retire if you can afford to and you really want to.' And I ticked both of those boxes.

In retirement I took up golf like so many people do. I played for a couple of years, enjoying the social side and even managed to play reasonably well.

But I became bored and lost interest so stopped playing. I had ridden sports motorcycles all my life from the age of 15, selling my last one when I shipped out to Tanzania. So on impulse, which is me all over, I bought a classic Ducati 996 which needed restoring, a perfect retirement project. I discovered that I thoroughly enjoyed taking something that wasn't in the best of health and restoring it to its former glory. Once completed I rode it for a while before crashing and writing it off. I bought the bike back from the insurers, rebuilt it, even making a tidy profit when I sold it. It didn't put me off bikes though and I replaced the 996 with a Ducati 1199 Panigale an awesome machine and a thing of real beauty.

I traded a few cars as one of my friends had a car auction dealership card. Again it was a risky business as you didn't always know exactly what you were going to get. But more often than not I turned a profit. I enjoyed the excitement of researching which cars to buy and the live bidding process trying not to get carried away and over bidding. I probably sold about 18 cars and then as the market changed packed in.

Jenny and I decided to revisit Cornwall for a west coast road trip. We started at Bude and were stopping at Padstow and St Agnes, ending in St Ives. I had been looking for a holiday lodge for a little while and had contacted the sales guy at Ocean Cove where we had been previously whilst at Tintagel for Olivia's 21st birthday immediately before I departed for Africa. We decided to pop in as we were pretty much passing the door and called into the sales office. Incredibly a lodge had just come up for sale and it was front row with amazing ocean views. We were excited and took the keys to have a closer look. We couldn't believe it as we approached the lodge and saw it was the same one the deck of which we had stood on four years previously. It was perfect, as new and fully kitted out with the best views of the Cornish coastline I have ever seen. The site had a gym and swimming pool so it was ideal. But, there was just the small matter of paying for it. The lodge was sold as new five years previously for £185,000 and the owner was desperate to sell and had dropped the price twice already. We told the sales guy we were interested but needed to do some numbers. We drove to Padstow checked into our hotel and found a pub.

We sat outside in the sunshine and I got out my pen and paper. We had only just invested a significant sum of money in a holiday home in Cape Verde so things were tight. After we looked everywhere including behind the sofa we had £85,000 immediately available so I made the call. I put forward our offer as a 'first and only' explaining we had no further latitude to increase the offer and that also everything had to be left as was, hoover, TV's, everything. We didn't expect a reply other than 'F... off' so when we were called back within an hour with an acceptance we looked at one another with a mixture of excitement and fear. We really would be leaving ourselves with very little in savings although we had some investments and I had some work coming in, my pension and Jenny was working of course. So the risk was low and we did the deal. The kids loved it and

I spent a lot of time down there during the summer months.

In October 2015 my daughter Olivia married Ben West. About forty friends and family flew out to the Caribbean for two weeks and we had the best of times. The hotel was perfect. Jenny and I had visited a couple of times previously to make sure everything would go to plan. To make the marriage legally binding they were married by a Judge under a beautiful white domed gazebo. He exuded dignity and added to the sense of occasion. But the event wasn't without drama, whilst the boys all played golf in the morning a thunderstorm struck the resort leading to a power outage. The bridal party had to be whisked by SUV to another resort for hair and makeup. It rained and rained but we stuck with the plan for a 4pm-wedding with an outdoor reception. At 3.45pm the clouds parted and the sun reappeared for the remainder of the day. It was an emotional day and Olivia looked stunning. I walked her down the petal strewn aisle to the sound of a local violinist playing 'all of me' by John Legend. I admit I shed a tear but one of absolute happiness. We had a DJ, Cigar roller, a band and of course enough booze to sink a battleship. Olivia and I had a dance together and rapped to 'The Message' by Grand Master Flash and the Furious Five, which is 'our' song. At the end of the evening Olivia told me it was the best wedding imaginable and she felt like a celebrity. As a father all I ever wanted for my children was for them to succeed in life and realise their potential but most importantly of all, be happy. I feel very content that as a father I have done the best I could.

Then in December 2015 only two months later I woke up at 4am one Monday morning with severe abdominal pain. I made a cup of tea and 'googled' the symptoms. Google informed me that I probably had a gall bladder obstruction. Within a couple of hours the pain became intolerable so I woke Jenny and called an ambulance. I was offered morphine en route but declined which was a big mistake. I was fast tracked through triage and A&E and onto a ward where in mind numbing pain I finally got some intravenous morphine. The doctor sent me for an ultrasound and X-ray scans. I knew the radiographer from my gym and she showed me the images. My gall bladder looked like a bag full of marbles. Prior to this I'd had no symptoms whatsoever, maybe a little heartburn. I was told I also had a blood infection and was treated with broad spectrum antibiotics. The Consultant said I needed immediate surgery and would be going to theatre that day. He returned a while later and said theatre time had run out so I would be sent home and booked in for Sunday. It seemed strange that it was urgent and then it wasn't. He's the doctor I thought so I asked, 'why', he said he wanted the infection under control prior to operating. I was sceptical.

I left the hospital with a bag full of painkillers, got home, made a cup of tea and started doing some ironing. Jenny popped into work as everything seemed fine. As I steamed another shirt I could feel myself getting cold and shivery. Then the rigors hit me. I have never felt anything like it.

Uncontrollable tremors with every bit of my body shaking violently, I could barely speak, my teeth were chattering like a cartoon character. I didn't know the human body could convulse so violently.

I panicked, it was like a seizure but I was wide awake. I tried to pick up my phone dropping it several times and could just managed to hit one button, redial I called Jenny who was 25 minutes away, she called her sister, Maggie who came five minutes later. When she saw me she looked in shock bursting into tears. I asked her to call an ambulance. I had tried but the rigors meant I couldn't even hold my phone and hitting the correct keys would have been like trying to thread a needle wearing boxing gloves. The ambulance arrived as the rigours subsided, it had lasted twenty-five minutes. I was blue lighted back and re admitted to Kings Mill Hospital, Mansfield and was immediately put on Tazocin antibiotics which I knew were very expensive, meaning I must have been in pretty bad shape. On the ward I was assessed again and a blood test taken. I was told the infection was sepsis, not only that but it had now spread to my other organs. Another doctor came to see me after I had been admitted onto the ward. He told me it was too dangerous to operate and remove my gall bladder and they had to wait for the antibiotics to control the infection. I had a drip in each arm for saline and antibiotics and a catheter placed in one orifice that a gentleman never wants to see a plastic tube sticking from. That alone was horrible. If I wanted the bathroom it was a major operation, I had to disconnect wires and carry my catheter bag and wheeled drip stand. I had surgery on a shoulder fractured whilst mountain biking a couple of weeks previously and moving around with one arm was a pain, literally. I was a mess. The days passed with constant blood tests and monitoring. I was needle phobic before this experience but I had so many samples taken, drips and injections it no longer became an issue.

I was still having rigors two or three times a day. This was due to the infection causing a steep rise in my temperature which then caused my body to react defensively. The treatment was simple I just needed intravenous paracetamol to draw down my temperature which prevented the rigors. After a few episodes I could anticipate when they were about to happen. If the nurses were quick they could administer the paracetamol but it took two staff to unlock the controlled drugs store and usually they were too late and I would be well into my 25 minutes of bed rattling. I don't mean this as a criticism in any way, the nursing staff were exceptional, as a patient I found that when you really needed their care and support they are with you and when you no longer need it they are with someone who does. They would sit and hold my hand through the attacks. They were so violent sometimes I would black out. As each day passed I grew weaker and every day another consultant would review me and tell me I was too poorly and infected for them to operate as there was a strong possibility that I would not survive the procedure. On the sixth day I believed in my own mind I was dying and didn't have much longer to go. Having been in healthcare for over thirty years and now a Matron, Jenny knew the on-duty consultant Mr Richard

Hind and she asked for his opinion. Having reviewed my history and all the medical notes and data, he approached the foot of my bed, joined by his intensive care anaesthetist Gareth. Whilst Jenny and Olivia knew of my serious condition and visited every day, Savannah was at university completing her Broadcast Journalism degree. We had kept the gravity of my situation from her until now to ensure she focussed on her coursework. Ironically she arrived at the same time as Richard and Gareth. Richard held an iPad in his hands and asked me, 'How do you feel?'

I replied, 'If I'm being honest, I feel like I won't be here tomorrow.' And said, 'Look doctor, if it's about money and this can be done privately I am happy to pay no matter the cost.'

I was desperate and knew I was on my way out.

'Well,' he said, 'the good news is we are operating today because if we don't, you are right you probably won't be here tomorrow.'

Savannah looked in shock and she and Olivia burst into tears with Jenny hugging them both. I just felt an overwhelming sense of relief. At last I could move forward and I had every confidence I was in the best of hands. They told me it was still very high risk due to the level of infection in my organs but because I was otherwise a healthy and fit person they believed I could withstand the surgery. I was immediately prep'd for theatre and got to chat with Jenny and the girls before being wheeled to theatre. Gareth was a great guy, good looking, supremely confident, clearly a top anaesthetist and I liked him. I knew I was in the best place possible.

Gareth did his thing putting the catheter into the vein on the back of my hand through which he would administer the anaesthetic. He reassured me telling me that he only worked on critically ill patients and his experience had taught him who would make it off the table to recovery. He was confident I would be fine. Then whilst we talked about the impending England rugby game he put me to sleep.

I woke up in intensive care with my brain fogged by the drugs that had been administered and the morphine drip feeding pain relief through my catheter.

I spent three days in intensive care and can only recall one thing clearly. England were playing an international game of rugby and I was provided a radio to listen in. Obviously, Jenny and the girls came to visit but I can't recall much except seeing Savannah and calling her my guardian angel. I'm not usually given to emotion, it must have been the drugs. I left ICU and went back on the ward. I was on strong antibiotics to supplement the surgical clear out of my infected organs. They made me nauseous but I was still feeling better than I had. After a couple of days I felt ready to leave, that's when you know it's time. When you're really ill you don't want to be anywhere else but when you start to recover you just want to be at home. I had a 15 cm wound diagonally across my stomach which had been stapled together. Once the medical team were happy it was healing and my infection was under control I was ready for discharge.

Jenny brought in flowers and boxes of chocolates for the nursing team and I gave my consultants, Gareth and Richard bottles of Bollinger. A small price to pay someone for saving your life. I was and always will be eternally grateful for the tremendous care I received.

When I arrived home I was wearing a sweater which used to be a neat fit and when Savannah saw me she cried. The thing was hanging off me.

When I fell ill I was hammering the gym and was 14 stone 10 pounds with 14% body fat but when I came home after surgery I was 11 stone 7 pounds. That's how Sepsis can ravage your body in the space of just eight days and if you don't catch it in time or have the physical resilience to fight it you're in trouble. Sepsis is the biggest cause of death in the NHS and in 2015, 36,900 people died as a result of the infection and many, many more have been permanently disabled from it. I was lucky to get out from under it relatively unscathed. I had some medical issues as a consequence with poor circulation but that is easily treatable with blood thinners and dilators. I've had a few brushes with death in the past – diving in the North Sea and nearly drowning, several motorcycle accidents and in particular the one when I was just seventeen. I have broken numerous bones in accidents usually in the pursuit of adrenaline but nothing compares to the profound impact having Sepsis had upon me. Maybe it is my time of life and the feeling of mortality that I am not invincible as I once thought I was. Sepsis knocked me back and I had a period of feeling sadness and loss which I can't explain. It made me appreciate my family so much more and to value the time we have together. It made me determined to enjoy my financial freedom and to ensure my children had all the support they would ever need. They will never struggle as I did.

We had a great family Christmas and I soon built my body back up with my mind and soul soon following. I was back in the gym and back to fourteen and a half stone within a few months.

CHAPTER FORTY-FOUR

New tricks

Thankfully I managed to see Savannah graduate from university and qualify as a Teacher at a challenging inner city secondary school. She might be diminutive but is strong and determined. She is settled in her new home with her partner Rory a fellow Yorkshireman who has ironically just been accepted into the Police.

When younger I always wanted to race motorcycles on the track but didn't think I had the skills and definitely not the money. I had never tried it as I thought I wouldn't be very good and would embarrass myself. But at the age of 56 with my son-in-law Ben we booked the Ron Haslam race school experience at Donington Park, GP circuit. What a day, all equipment was provided including Honda CBR 600s. We had classroom instruction where we learned the layout of the circuit, how to identify breaking points, tipping in points and where to hit the gas on exiting the corners. Then it was time to suit up and hit the track. The first session was tentative led by an experienced racer with a ratio of one to four or five, we completed seven or eight laps following his body and track position. We came back in and were put into groups dependent upon ability and potential. I had one on one tuition with an Isle of Man TT racer and before we left the pits he used a static machine to perfect my body position and movement on the bike. Back on track I got my knee down within minutes and went from strength to strength lapping faster and smoother through the session. At the end of the day we were scored out of 100. I had the highest score for the day at 98% although I'm not sure where I lost the other 2%, Ben was told he had more guts than ability but it would come with time. In truth Ben hadn't even passed his road bike test so it was pretty good for a complete novice. It had been a great day and I now knew I really could ride a motorcycle on track. I couldn't help the feeling that I had missed out on years of doing something I loved and I wasn't getting any younger.

I had never felt adrenalin like it since my skiing days. I was addicted so did no more than buy a Yamaha R1, with near 175 horse power as my first track bike. After a couple of track days I needed more. I knew I could ride and was fortunate to be in the position to afford something decent so bought a BMW S1000RR, 197 horse power and a brilliant state of the art machine with loads of rider aids to make going fast, safer and all the Moto GP technology to make it ride and handle like a dream.

My mate Roger, who is a former competition racer has taught me much more, very quickly. After a few track days we would dog fight for the front. Of course Roger usually came out ahead. Ben has lived as part of our family for thirteen years and is like a son and I gave him the R1 for Christmas. It was great for us to spend time together doing something we both loved.

I was getting faster and closer to the 'limit' of my ability as I discovered at Anglesey International race track. It was a beautiful day at the coast as it always seems to be when we go there. There are usually eight, twenty-minute sessions in a day of around ten laps each. It was a hot day and by the seventh session I was knackered. I was flying, confident and passing everyone, although it does help to have an S1000. On the penultimate lap I came into a right-hand corner, feeling happy with my speed but perhaps due to fatigue didn't hang off the bike enough and tipped it too far over. I felt the back tyre lose grip and I was off. Rolling across the tarmac my bike just ahead of me a shower of plastic and sparks. We both ended up in the runoff grassed area. I was unhurt except for a sore middle finger. My bike though was really poorly and I saw flames coming from the belly pan which in the absence of an extinguisher I put out with my gloves, which melted. So helmet, leathers, gloves all ruined and the bike looked extremely sorry for itself. When the adrenaline started to subside I felt the pain in my hand. I was taken to the first aid area and it was established I had torn the tendons in my middle finger, I couldn't move it at all. I was told I should go to Bangor Hospital and waiting times were five hours. It was the World Cup quarter final England versus Sweden that evening so there was no chance I was going to A&E. I got strapped up and went to find Ben and Roger. My bike had been brought to them and it looked grim. Ah well, it was going to happen one day and I could repair it myself. We loaded up and returned to our accommodation sat in the sunshine with some medicinal beer and watched England thrash Sweden 3–0.

I fixed the bike and got back on the horse but it did take a while to get my confidence back. BMW launched their new generation superbike in 2020 and I bought one for the track. Ben now has my old one. I may be 60 years old but when I put that helmet on no one knows who you are or how old. I feel like a young man again and can keep up with most of the young 'uns round a track. There's really no feeling like it. If the government knew how much fun it was they'd tax it or make it illegal.

Back in April 2017 we moved house not far from where we were and in the same village. We had sold ours and I found the perfect project for retirement, a bungalow that had a great plot and location. It was perfect in my view for development into our dream home. We had recently sold our lodge in Cornwall which had lost its novelty and appeal. There really is a limit to the number of times you can visit Padstow before it loses its charm. We broke even on the sale which was a result.

The design and project management of the new home kept me busy for nine months and was really enjoyable. We were so fortunate to have the means to build and furnish it to our own requirements and I had lots of friends and contacts who helped out keeping costs down. It is a home for life capable of being adapted when necessary for our later years.

I was flattered to be asked by the local Secondary School to award the prizes to the schools high achievers. I was asked to give a motivational speech which I agreed to do. It was well received and I have now been asked to do the same with some of their more challenging pupils who are in danger of taking the wrong path. This excites me and I hope that my story resonates with them and shows what can be achieved with a little hard work.

I decided to occupy my spare time buying crashed super bikes and rebuilding them, mainly BMW's. There's no real money in it but I love the challenge of something new and turning a mongrel into a Crufts winner.

So I've made it to sixty years of age. I still feel fit and mentally agile and still looking for the next challenge. I play Call of Duty and am convinced it should be on prescription to help older people stay mentally fit.

As I reflect back at my life I realise that I was constantly seeking the next challenge, maybe trying to prove something to myself and just as importantly, others. The longest time I spent in the same role was three and a half years as a uniformed constable. After this 'rite of passage' I was constantly looking for the next learning curve to challenge me and once I'd reached the peak, the excitement and my interest diminished. The adrenaline rush of starting something new, daunting and challenging is not for everyone and many people are happy to stay in the same job for life and if that makes them happy then great, however it would have bored me to death.

To this point I have been driven by a need to succeed and to prove to myself and others that underneath the alpha male, intolerant exterior I am a good person. I have no religion but that doesn't mean I don't have values. I care for and support others in need, I protect those that cannot protect themselves and I will challenge anyone who tries to intimidate or bully another – I cannot sit by on the sidelines. I have faced and overcome many challenges and I am no longer the 'loser' from the bar in Londonderry.

Why? Because I have developed tenacity, resilience, self-belief and discipline, but more than all of these positive qualities, I care about people. This is in my view the greatest attribute anyone can possess, compassion.

I don't dwell on the past or on my achievements. The past has been and gone, the future is what I am focused upon. I have no medals on display or framed pictures of the military, police or my commendations, Oxford diplomas or Bachelors Degree. Quite simply they are a significant part of how I developed and succeeded in life but they do not define me.

That said, I do have pictures of my family including my grandson Marley and also some racing the bike. That is the here and now and what really matters to me, and long may that continue.

If anyone actually reads this I would implore you to do just one thing in your future. Step outside your comfort zone, it's a great place to be and you will never, ever regret it.

15. As a Superintendent at Nottingham City Police –
Press conference after the murder of Danielle Beccan.

16. As Chief Super having just left Homicide and being presented by Chief Constable
Steve Green a Judges Commendation for the Daniel Williams Murder Investigation.

17. My wife Jenny and me all dressed up for the Senior Officers mess Christmas party.

18. An example of my weekly newsletter as Divisional Commander.

19. Divisional Commanders Commendation awards for my Division.

20. The All Star line up of the Oxford SLP. Some serious high flyers in the group not least my good friends Mark Wall (second row centre black shirt) now Senior Vice President at Barrick Gold and Jennifer Nero (far right front row) now retired from the Caribbean Bank but on the cricket board for the West Indies.

21. Ariel shot of one of the three vast open pits at North Mara gold mine.

22. The walls surrounding mining operations and costing millions of dollars were only a deterrent and Security Officers close in on them in Rovers.

23. A small incursion of trespassers seeking the gold bearing rocks. Sometimes up to 1000 would enter the mines.

24. A typical wattle and daub Masai village near to the mines on the serangett.

25. Part of the miles of concrete wall being erected at North Mara to deter trespassers.

26. Post firefight 2012. Three armed robbers lay dead on the airstrip having attempted to steal $30 million in gold bullion.

27. *A prime example of the ugliest bird alive a Carabou/Marabou stalk which woke me every morning at North Mara tap dancing on the tin roof.*

28. *Post retirement. Riding at Cadwell Park getting 'lift off' on 'The Mountain'.*

29. *Donnington Park, one of my favourite tracks and close to home. Number '60' for my time of life.*

ABOUT THE AUTHOR

Nick Holmes is a former Marine, Soldier, Senior Police Officer and African Gold miner. He has a Bachelor of Science Degree in Policing and Criminology and is an alumni of the Oxford University Business School.

Printed in Great Britain
by Amazon

59526142R00165